The Dual Reality of Salvation and the Church in Nigeria

This book is part of the Peter Lang Humanities list.
Every volume is peer reviewed and meets
the highest quality standards for content and production.

PETER LANG
New York • Bern • Frankfurt • Berlin
Brussels • Vienna • Oxford • Warsaw

Gabriel T. Wankar

The Dual Reality of Salvation and the Church in Nigeria

PETER LANG
New York • Bern • Frankfurt • Berlin
Brussels • Vienna • Oxford • Warsaw

Library of Congress Cataloging-in-Publication Data

Names: Wankar, Gabriel T., author.
Title: The dual reality of salvation and the church in Nigeria /
Gabriel T. Wankar.
Description: New York: Peter Lang Publishing, 2017.
Includes bibliographical references.
Identifiers: LCCN 2017026093 | ISBN 978-1-4331-4560-5 (hardback: alk. paper)
ISBN 978-1-4331-4561-2 (epdf) | ISBN 978-1-4331-4562-9 (epub)
ISBN 978-1-4331-4563-6 (mobi)
Subjects: LCSH: Catholic Church—Nigeria. | Salvation—Catholic Church.
Theology, Doctrinal—Nigeria. | Pastoral theology—Nigeria.
Catholic Church—Doctrines.
Classification: LCC BX1682.N5 W36 2017 | DDC 282/.669—dc23
LC record available at https://lccn.loc.gov/2017026093
DOI 10.3726/b12038

Bibliographic information published by **Die Deutsche Nationalbibliothek**.
Die Deutsche Nationalbibliothek lists this publication in the "Deutsche
Nationalbibliografie"; detailed bibliographic data are available
on the Internet at http://dnb.d-nb.de/.

The paper in this book meets the guidelines for permanence and durability
of the Committee on Production Guidelines for Book Longevity
of the Council of Library Resources.

Printed in Germany

This work is dedicated to my parents, through whom I came to life:

Late Francis Wankar Ameladu (my father)

Judith Mdewaren Wankar (my mother)

and

To the memories of late Martha Kwaghkule (my grandmother)

Late Demvihin (my immediate sister whom I lost in childhood)

Late Bishop Athanasius Atule Usuh (a father, for his guidance and trust)

Late Frs. Edward Igbokoh & Emmanuel Ikyo.

TABLE OF CONTENTS

ACKNOWLEDGMENTS

The initial impulse for this study is to explore how the Catholic Church in Nigeria, in the spirit of the African Synods I and II, can overcome the tendency that confines Christianity to its personal and familial dimensions, and rediscover its sense of mission in service of God's kingdom here "on earth as it is in heaven." First of all, my gratitude to Most. Revd. William A. Avenya, the Catholic Bishop of the Diocese of Gboko, Nigeria for his encouragement and support. I remain indebted to all who have supported me in any way on this quest, especially the loving kindness of late Bishop Athanasius A. Usuh, of the Catholic Diocese of Makurdi, Nigeria for every opportunity he accorded me. Thank you to Most Revd. Peter I. Adoboh, Frs Simeon Iber, Daniel Ude Asue, Moses I. Iorapuu, Stephen Beba, Godwin Udaa, and Titus Imojime for being there for me all the way.

Professors Bill O'Neil, SJ, Paul G. Crowley, SJ, Eduardo Fernandez, SJ, Iheanyi M. Enwerem, OP, Kevin Burke, SJ, and Alison Banders, have been inspiring mentors, excellent teachers and caring friends. Their critical insights, invaluable advice, and encouragement have made this research possible, and I am eternally grateful to them. The scholars whose works I have built upon in writing this book, I duly and most humbly acknowledge their ideas and thoughts as listed in the bibliography. Father Stephen Saawuan introduced me to caring friends who have become family away from family. Thank you to parishioners of Holy Spirit's Community, Rock Springs, Wyoming. Lori J. Hasterd, Madeline Sessa, Pat Greenlee, Stan & Judy Mckee, Marilou Granthom, Rod & Carmen Wittkop, Fathers Carl Beavers, Andrew Duncan, and George Quickly SJ.

I owe a special debt of gratitude to Melba Marin who has been a mother away from home, the parish community of St. John the Baptist, El Cerrito in California, for hosting me during my studies. I am deeply grateful for the personal sacrifices of John Wilmes, Chris Devcich, Fr Thuong Nguyen, Dr. and Mrs Gabriel Patino, Sister Angela Egbikuadje, and Larry Mundi. This same gratitude goes to Governor Samuel Ortom, Dr. And Mrs George Akume, KSJ., Dr. Gabriel Suswam, Gen. T. T. Waya, Joe Waya, Chia Waya, the Ugbah family, David and Charity Unongo, Kay and Thalia Cayetano. John Huber, Magdalen Yum, and Dr. Son Gyoh deserve a special mention for their time, selfless sacrifices, and helpful comments.

To my mum, Judith Mdewaren Wankar and the rest of my siblings, I say thank you for the moral and personal support. Thanks to Fathers Kenneth Agede, Dan Melaba, Clement Iorliam, Paul Utser, Donald Komboh, Sebastine Bula, Martin Njoalu, Stephen Injoalu, John Paul Otanwa, Thomas Dekaa, Nathaniel Mma, Paulinus Nweke, Peter Atsewe, Chris Bologo, Moses Ate, Thaddeaus Auve, Robert Waya, Thomas Orpin, and Kieran Danfulani for their inspiration and encouragement. To Sister Benedicta, Fr Paschal Kumaga, and many other friends who have been companions on this journey, I deeply cherish your friendship and support as well as colleagues at the Jesuit School of Theology, Berkeley.

INTRODUCTION

Theology of Historical Reality?

The greatest drama in contemporary Africa is the rupture between the good news of the kingdom of God and integral human development.[1] This study makes the claim that, although the Catholic Church in Nigeria has always eloquently affirmed an inseparable link between the two, the tangible signs of the actuality of the kingdom of God proclaimed by the Church remain largely invisible for most Nigerians. What is clear to many,[2] however, is that the Church's participation in social transformation does not go far enough in unmasking and working to eliminate evil. Among other things, poverty of leadership has been identified as a major factor standing in the way of the Church's witness as a credible agent for social change in Nigeria.[3] Iheanyi M. Enwerem chronicles concrete instances illustrating poverty of leadership by Nigerian Church leaders, noting that a growing number of the Catholic clergy in Nigeria are beset with "weaknesses that border on the poverty of transparency, accountability, credibility, and ethical dealings."[4] Most of the senior clergy would seem to share the joint benefits of the standards and the status symbols of the affluent in the society, just as they share in many of its possibilities of power.[5]

The considerable access to the political elite translates to sharing some of the privileges of power, which creates a tension between the traditional role of the Church as an arbiter of conscience, and guardian of the social responsibility of those in authority. The need to maintain a state of tranquility in this relationship results to ambivalent social teaching, making the Church in Nigeria appear to succumb to the temptation of evading her historical identity and mission by allowing for a scandalous silence, so long as the privileges of the leadership of the Church are not jeopardized. Moreover, since faith formation within most of the Roman Catholic Church, is effected through structured catechesis, theological formation, and deference to traditional transmission accepted from generation to generation, the formation of pastoral agents especially in the seminaries is done in such a way that perpetuates the status quo. Thus, many Catholics in Nigeria have not begun to appreciate some of the most basic teachings of Vatican II, fifty years after the Council, not mentioning the rich corpus of Catholic social teaching, including the Apostolic Exhortations of two African Synods.[6]

This study proposes ways in which the Catholic Church in Nigeria can embrace and practically mediate a salvation that is longed for and desperately needed in daily events of life. Drawing on the insights from African Synods I and II as well as from long tradition of Catholic social thought, this work will argue for a historical understanding of salvation and the Kingdom of God that requires believers to confront exploitation and address the social conditions that perpetuate the inhuman suffering of most Nigerians. The specific contribution of this book will be a retrieval of Jesus' dedication to the inauguration of the reign of God on earth in the spirit of African Synods I and II to define clear imperatives of ecclesial renewal and social witness for the Church in Nigeria. The goal will be a rediscovery of the Church's identity and mission as a "sacrament of liberation,"[7] that works for liberation from unjust structures and the creation of new structures that foster dignity and freedom as constitutive of the Church's mission of reconciliation, justice, and peace. Enabling people to fulfill themselves is much in accord with God's will and carries with it eternal consequences as does freeing them from sinfulness. At present, structures of exploitation persist in Nigeria and grow when people who benefit from them (and even those who are negatively affected by such systems) fail to recognize and resist them. It is precisely here that the Church needs to be present and active in the world.

The response of the Catholic Church in Nigeria to the tragedy of the kidnapping of the schoolgirls by Boko Haram in 2014 illustrates the separation of transcendence from history as a tendency of that Church. Since the abduction of over 200 girls, which took place in Northeastern Nigeria on April 14, 2014, social activists, women across Nigeria, and civil society organizations stood firm in their commitment to bring attention to the matter until it went viral. The international community, world leaders, artists, and musicians joined the call for the girl's release; *#Bringbackourgirls#* circled the world with supporters from Pope Francis to Michelle Obama. However, in a response that seems entirely too typical of the Nigerian Church's position on social concerns, the President of the Catholic Bishops Conference of Nigeria (CBCN), Archbishop Ignatius Kaigama, issued a letter calling for a "Holy Hour of Eucharistic Adoration" by all the Catholic faithful in the country, praying for God's intervention in the release of the abducted school girls. Addressed to all Catholic Bishops in the country, it stated among other things:

> As bishops, we lead our people in prayer, and so, I wish to humbly suggest that in addition to the Masses and prayers already being offered, we lead our people in a Holy Hour of Eucharistic Adoration to invoke God's mercy for the release of the innocent school girls kidnapped some weeks ago. I understand that some more girls have been kidnapped again. This is very worrisome.[8]

The Holy Hour was scheduled on Sunday, May 11 2014, from 6 to 7 pm across all dioceses in the country, at which the Archbishop hoped that his fellow bishops would "kindly encourage people to pray for the liberation of all these young girls, conversion of heart of those who do such evil by maiming, killing, destroying, and abusing human dignity and for God's mercy for the victims either dead, injured or traumatized."[9] Without minimizing the importance of prayer, the Christian maxim *labore et orare* insists that prayer should be accompanied by actions. If one may ask, where was the voice of the Church when the Nigerian police banned all protests over the kidnapped Chibok schoolgirls in the Federal Capital Territory (FCT) on Monday June 2, 2014?[10] The Commissioner of Police in the FCT at the time, Mr. Joseph Mbu, announced the ban at a news conference in Abuja, claiming that the protests were posing a serious security threat. While such call for prayers has become a consistent response of the Church in the face of social challenges, there seem to be an unfortunate spillover of this attitude into the political space, where government functionaries in Nigeria, from the president to state governors call for weeks/months of fasting and prayers in confronting challenges that deflect their responsibility/accountability.

Nevertheless, whatever else may be said about the Church, theologians and historians agree that it is a human group, a social reality.[11] This, for example, was the essence of what Pope John XXIII was attempting to communicate when he spoke of *aggiornamento* in convoking the Second Vatican Council, which became one of the Council's principal slogans. This is the sense, too, in which Sanks said:

> Some [fifty-three] years ago, Karl Rahner, writing during the Second Vatican Council, said, '[Furthermore], the constantly changing external historical situation of the Church demands a constant renewal of the concrete expressions of her permanent, essential structure, corresponding to the conditions of the particular time, because in fact also the *real essence of the Church (which is something more than the idea of her essence) always exists in man [sic] as contingent and historical and in the Church's historically conditioned action.*'[12]

In other words, the Church is constructed and conditioned socially; hence, it is possible to speak of a theology of historical reality as a theology that takes its own historical context seriously.[13]

The Second Vatican Council, offered new contours for all devotional, theological as well as institutional dynamics of the Roman Catholic Church. It affected not only the Roman Catholic Church but also all Christians and non-Christians. The Council involved the Church in matters of war and peace, of social justice and poverty, in the economic and political orders, and recognized the growing interdependence and cultural diversity in the world. It introduced and enabled changes within the Church in terms of liturgy, prayer, spirituality, ministry, and religious life. It proposed a positive engagement with the world outside the Church, a reversal of the Church's defensive and sometimes condemnatory stance in the 19th and early 20th centuries. Most importantly, the Council "required and allowed the Roman Church to find innovative ways to articulate its self-understanding and mission."[14] Among other things, it aided in articulating a new self-understanding and mission of the Church that has profoundly affected its conception and understanding of salvation. As the founder of political theology in Europe, Johannes Baptist Metz reminds his readers, it becomes incumbent on any theological reflection on the Church to take the historical background and situation of the people into consideration if it is to deal responsibly with prevailing challenges of and possibilities within contemporary society.

This manner of theologizing, which over the past few decades, has been taking roots among Christians in parts of the third world, especially in Latin

America, has increasingly brought Christians face to face with the challenges posed to their faith by the injustices and the privileges of a few against the masses of people. Indeed, historical and scientific consciousness has led to a critical discovery of the world of the oppressed through radical questioning of the prevailing way of living where a few have too much while a vast majority have nothing.[15] This line of questioning asks how people are to live out their faith as Christians in the face of exploitation and dependency, in which many are subjected perpetually to violence on the part of the established structures of society and how living the Gospel can inspire the creation and restoration of a just society for all.[16] Conceiving of faith and doing theology in this manner modifies necessarily traditional understandings of theology. Above all, when theology is done considering faith not only as an interpretation of the content of revelation, but also as a critical reflection on historical faith practice, it asks the question, "What is to be done?"[17]

The small Latin American nation of El Salvador serves as an icon of a historical understanding of theology. Salvadoran theologian, Jesuit, Ignacio Ellacuría, for example, bases his theology in a philosophy of historical reality and interprets the suffering of "the crucified peoples" (the poor of El Salvador) in light of Jesus' crucifixion.[18] Although Ellacuría lived in El Salvador, a place and a context far removed from that of Nigeria, I argue that his thoughts and approach to theology are strikingly applicable to the social reality of Nigeria, even though Nigeria is a larger and far more complex reality than El Salvador. In Nigeria, as is the case in most of Africa, most those to whom the message of salvation—"the good news"—is being preached are today, in the words of the Catholic Bishops' Conference of Nigeria, "not only distressed, but traumatized!"[19] The historical experience of most Nigerians is indeed of human-made poverty, large-scale corruption, structural injustice, political repression, widespread abuse of human rights, disease, unemployment, violence, and even death. People live for the most part in situations of want and squalor.

In Nigeria, the missionary zeal of Vatican II impacted the Church in the areas of education and school apostolate by establishing many mission schools by the missionaries, promoting local clergy/religious, attempting an initial translation of prayer books and simple prayers into local languages, setting up healthcare facilities for basic health needs of the people and opening numerous parish communities. However, unlike the kind of response that greeted the Second Vatican Council in Latin America, translating into a ferment of incarnational dimensions of faith lived out in pursuit of the common good, the emergent ecclesiological model of church as the People of God from Vatican II can hardly be said to have effected any meaningful changes in the faith practice of the Nigerian Church.[20] A few Catholic clergy in Nigeria, like Matthew Hassan Kukah, and most recently, Ejike Mbaka, who have been inclined to bridge this gap, have rather attracted the wrath of the Church hierarchy at times.

Among other reasons, Vatican II coincided with a very difficult period in the life of the nation that led eventually to the 1967–970 Nigerian civil war. This probably affected the implementation of the Council's initiatives, forcing the Church to pay greater attention to the immediate need of healing from the ravages of the war. Additionally, important, is the fact that the colonization of Nigeria, like other African nations, followed the invariable pattern of trade relations, followed by the arrival of the missionaries and then the colonial administrators. Consequently, the new political and administrative leaders of postindependent Nigeria were educated largely in mission schools; in most cases, they came from the same class and the same families as the church leaders. The missions were so important as an innovating force in Nigerian society that it was inevitable that the people who linked themselves most closely with them, benefiting from this new and elitist network of education and employment, should constitute a sizable part of the current establishment of oppressive neo-colonialism.[21] Hence, leaders of the major churches in Nigeria, including the Catholic Church, are almost as integral a part of the governing minority in independent Nigeria as they were in Colonial times.

Confronted with the challenge of defending or of giving an account of their hope (1 Peter 3:15)[22] in the midst of a people held under siege by an abusive, exploitative, fraudulent, insensitive, callous and greedy elite, the Church in Nigeria tends sometimes to spiritualize evil and suffering by emphasizing the eternal and the other-worldly nature of salvation of the individual in heaven, thereby neglecting the social dimension of historical sins, which condition politically the behavior of individuals and the transcendent import of their actions.[23] Often, individual bishops and the Catholic Bishops' Conference of Nigeria as a body issue statements condemning various situations as they arise, but they go no further. The salvation, which the Christian Church proclaims, should be much more than mere rhetoric.

In order to advance my argument for the Church as a sacrament of liberation, I will employ the praxis method to call for a historical understanding of salvation that entails a creative and mutually transformative engagement with historical reality as articulated by Ignacio Ellacuría, using the interpretations of scholars, to propose an African theology of historical reality, manifested especially in the context of Nigeria.[24] This praxis method presupposes, although not exclusively, coming face to face with reality and elevating it to a theological concept. I will emphasize Ellacuría's liberative praxis of Christian salvation to link a critical understanding of salvation to an efficacious understanding and practice of Church that can overcome the tendency to evade the social dimensions of its mission as well as to ignore the problems of the modern world. The goal will be to invite the Church to rediscover its sense of mission in service of God's kingdom here *on earth as it is in heaven*.[25] I intend to reveal that the Second Vatican Council, especially in *Gaudium et Spes*, insists that the Church is in the world, sharing its hopes and fears,[26] and to explore the implications of that presence in the light of the African Synods I and II. This consciousness has allowed theology to discover new avenues and aims for its reflection. It enables us to live out our Christian faith today in view of the ultimate liberation and freedom of the children of God in the kingdom, which also includes historical liberation as an anticipation and concretization of that ultimate liberation.[27] And since liberation always occurs in a concrete and a historical context, the public character of faith arises as it relates to the economic, political and cultural dimensions of life.

In Nigeria, today any account of historical reality can only be fully understood within the larger context of the nature and the causes of poverty and neglect of the masses and regions of the nation, which is corruption. Thus, in Chapter 1, I will present a general diagnosis and appraisal of the historical evolution of the Nigerian State, with a view to unveil areas in the social lives of people, which should be the target of the Church's message of salvation. The diagnosis I offer will outline the specific historical evolution of the Nigerian State with an emphasis on current political and economic realities that affect the people, and will review the life of the Church in Nigeria, paying attention to how the Church in its limited way approaches the needs of the people.

In Chapters 2 and 3, I review the literature pertinent to this study. I will begin in Chapter 2 by drawing selectively from Biblical sources and the writings of the early church Fathers, as well as from papal encyclicals, to illustrate the historical reality of the Church at various times in her history. In doing this, I yield to other historical accounts and interpretations that may better account for different epochs in church history.[28] The bible relates the ordering of right relationships by Christians and, by extension, the Church, and creating a dwelling place for the word of God in human history as constitutive of the essence of Church. Basing their teaching on this foundation, the Fathers of the Church taught that love and generosity born of Christian faith are necessary ingredients to make the Church a new people through transformed values and purified desires. The values of Christianity are meant to make the Church a leaven in society where all are to live as children of God who care for one another. Equally, the magisterial teaching of the Church from the time of Pope Leo XIII to Pope Francis, has emphasized that the unity of the whole human race can only be achieved by establishing a just society that upholds the dignity of all, and that the Church is called to be a sign in the world of what a truly just society can be, as the essential thrust of the social teaching of the Church.

The review in Chapter 3 will reveal an interpretation of the Christian Gospel that occasioned a new understanding of the role and mission of the Church in society and inspired action toward the liberation of the Children of God in Latin America, especially and beyond, including Europe and Africa. It will begin by examining this significant new social orientation of the Church in Latin America toward the historical reality of the continent in the past few decades, specifically as an active interpretation of the mission of the Church as the body of Christ present and active in history. This new orientation in Latin America caught my attention and encourages me to enquire in this book how the Church in Nigeria can apply such an understanding of Church spirituality to the historical reality of the nation. My focus will be narrowed to the reality of liberation theology in El Salvador as a mirror for the entirety of the impact of that theology in Latin America, drawing on the life and the witness of Archbishop Oscar Romero and two out of his many collaborators, Theologians Ignacio Ellacuría and Jon Sobrino, who shared and upheld Romero's view of Church.

In Chapter 4, I propose to develop an approach to the connection between salvation theory and ecclesial spirituality in Nigeria, indicating how the factors of economic, political, and religious coexistence are related, with implications for a deeper understanding of salvation. Considering African Synods I and II, I will propose a paradigm shift toward a new pastoral option for the Church in Nigeria in the program for seminary formation, in which the priority should be to strengthen of ecumenical/interreligious structures of dialogue and collaboration as a process of rapprochement to enable an emancipatory praxis to come to existence for the Church's ministry and witnessing to "become flesh" in the reality of people's lives. This will entail articulating and living out a deeper spiritual and practical understanding of religion by Muslims and Christians, couched in terms of dialogue that translates into alliances and cooperation for the common good based on ties common to both religions. These alliances will not just be intra/interreligious, but most importantly, the possibility of forming synergies with civil society organizations in pursuit of the common good.

In Chapter 5, I provide a summary of the implications for following Christ in contemporary Nigeria, and with the benefit of the analysis of historicization from the work of Ellacuría, I will propose the way forward by connecting historical praxis and the Reign of God theology which enables Nigerians to experience the Reign of God here on earth as it is in heaven. In conclusion, my analysis will render an articulation of an integrated African theology of Church and of salvation as a theology which accounts systematically for the coherence that exists between the social context of the Nigerian Christian and the goals Nigerians have set for themselves in relation to their faith which should include issues relating to poverty, sickness, hunger, corruption and bad governance, since no account of faith cannot be offered independently of the way it is mediated historically.

Notes

1. Nathanael Yaovi Soede, "The Enduring Scourge of Poverty in Africa," in *Reconciliation, Justice, and Peace: The Second African Synod*, ed. Agbonkhianmeghe E. Orobator (Maryknoll, New York: Orbis Books, 2011), 186.
2. Several Nigerian theologians agree on this point. For a detailed sampling of their views on this issue, see, Agbonkhianmeghe E. Orobator, S. J. *From Crisis to Kairos: The Mission of the Church in the Time of Hiv/Aids, Refugees and Poverty*, Nairobi: Pauline Publications Africa; Peter Schineller, S. J. ed. *The Church Teaches: Stand of the Catholic Bishops of Nigeria on Issues of Faith and Life*. Abuja: The Catholic Secretariat of Nigeria, 2003; George Omaku Ehusani, *A Prophetic Church* (Ibadan, Nigeria: Provincial Pastoral Institute, 1996). Ehusani was a one-time Secretary General of the Catholic Secretariat of Nigeria, in the late 1990s to early 2000s; Ernest Munachi Ezeogu, Cssp. *Bible and Politics: Can Nigerian Catholics Baptize the "dirty game" of Politics?* (Enugu, Nigeria: Snaap Press Ltd, 2007); John O. Onaiyekan, *Thy Kingdom Come: Democracy and Politics in Nigeria Today- A Catholic Perspective*. (Faith and Life Series Vol 13) (Abuja: Gaudium et Spes Institute, 2003) Onaiyekan is the Cardinal Archbishop of Abuja; Matthew Hassan Kukah, *The Church and the Politics of Social Responsibility* (Lagos: Sovereign Prints Nig. Ltd. 2007) Kukah is the Catholic Bishop of Sokoto in Nigeria, and was a long-serving Secretary General of the Catholic Secretariat of Nigeria from the 1980s to the 90s; Moses Aondover Iorapuu, *Patriarchal Ideologies and Media Access: How to Overcome Discrimination Against Tiv Women for Sustainable Rural Development Promoting People Controlled and Participatory Communities* (Doctoral Thesis No. 819 Salesian Pontifical University, Rome, 2012).

3. Iheanyi M. Enwerem, *Crossing the Rubicon: a Socio-Political Analysis of Political Catholicism in Nigeria* (Ibadan: BookBuilders, 2010), 254.

4. Enwerem, *Crossing the Rubicon*, 253–334. Such failures on the part of leadership make it hardly realizable for the Church to effect any meaningful changes in the order of things beyond mere pronouncements.

5. *Ibid.* 153–199. Enwerem makes the case pointedly that the Catholic Bishops are religious "Big Men" in Nigeria. *Cf.* Agbonkhianmeghe E. Orobator, *The Church as Family: African Ecclesiology in its Social Context* (Nairobi: Paulines Publications Africa, 2000), 78–87.

6. Ehusani, "Memorandum on The Decline of Church Attendance and Anti-Clericalism in Ireland: Lessons and Challenges for Nigeria," 14.

7. In his essay "Church of the Poor: Historical Sacrament of Liberation" in the collection *Essays on History, Liberation, and Salvation* Edited by Michael E. Lee (Maryknoll, New York: Orbis Books, 2013) Ignacio Ellacuría insists that "Salvation is always the salvation of someone – and in that person, of something," 229.

8. Archbishop Ignatius A. Kaigama, "A plea for Holy Hour in supplication for the release of the Chibok School girls," an appeal letter to fellow bishops by the President of the Catholic Bishops' Conference of Nigeria, May 6, 2014.

9. *Ibid.*

10. Nigerian President at the time, Jonathan Goodluck said through his aids that the protests were mischievously directed at the government and security forces when they should be protesting the rebels.

11. T. Howland Sanks, *Salt, Leaven, and Light: The Community Called Church* (New York: The Crossroad Publishing Company, 2003), 23.

12. Sanks, "Globalization, Postmodernity and Governance in the Church," *Louvain Studies* 28, 2003. 194.

13. Sanks, "Globalization, Postmodernity and Governance in the Church," 194.

14. Kevin Burke, *The Ground Beneath the Cross: The Theology of Ignacio Ellacuría* (Washington D. C.: Georgetown University Press, 2000), 2.

15. Claude Geffre, editorial to *The Mystical and Political Dimensions of the Christian Faith, Concilium: 1974/6*, eds.Claude Geffre and Gustavo Gutiérrez (New York: Herder and Herder), 7–14.

16. *Ibid.*

17. *Ibid.*

18. Michael E. Lee's interpretation of Ellacuría's philosophical monograph *Filosofía de la realidad historica* (San Salvador: UCA Editories, 1999) in the introduction to, *Essays on History, Liberation, and Salvation*, by Ignacio Ellacuría, ed. Michael E. Lee (Maryknoll, New York: Orbis Books, 2013), 1–23. *Cf.* Michael E. Lee, *Bearing the Weight of Salvation: The Soteriology of Ignacio Ellacuría*, (New York: Herder & Herder, The Crossroad Publishing Company, 2009), Burke, *The Ground Beneath the Cross*, 43–97.

19. *Cf.* Peter Schineller, ed. *The Church Teaches: Stand of the Catholic Bishops of Nigeria on Issues of Faith and Life*. Abuja: The Catholic Secretariat of Nigeria, 2003.

20. Orobator, *The Church as Family*, 78–87.

21. Ehusani, *A Prophetic Church* (Ibadan: Provincial Pastoral Institute, 1996), 47–74. *Cf.* George Ehusani, "Memorandum on The Decline of Church Attendance and Anti-

Clericalism in Ireland: Lessons and Challenges for Nigeria" in *Challenges for the Church in the 21st Century: A Memorandum*, 2nd Edition, ed. George Ehusani, (Lagos: Catholic Secretariat of Nigeria, 2003).

22. Johannes Baptist Metz, "Between Evolution and Dialectics: On the Point of Departure for a Contemporary Fundamental Theology," *Faith in History and Society: Toward a Practical Fundamental Theology*, 23. Metz categorically asserts that "the intention and task of any Christian theology may be defined as an apology for hope."

23. Ellacuría, *Freedom Made Flesh*, 156.

24. Ellacuría uses the term "Praxis" in reference to a consciously reflected human action aimed at changing or transforming reality. This research adopts his usage of the term. I will rely on the interpretations of Burke, Lee and Lassalle-Klein. Burke, has written extensively about Ignacio Ellacuría, especially in his major work, *The Ground Beneath the Cross*. Other important works on Ellacuría include, Michael E. Lee, *Bearing the Weight of Salvation: The Soteriology of Ignacio Ellacuría*, (New York: Herder & Herder, The Crossroad Publishing Company, 2009); Robert Lassalle-Klein, *Blood and Ink: Ignacio Ellacuría, Jon Sobrino, and the Jesuit Martyrs of the University of Central America* (Maryknoll, New York: Orbis Books, 2014); Teresa Whitfield, *Paying the Price: Ignacio Ellacuría and the Murdered Jesuits of El Salvador* (Philadelphia: Temple University Press, 1995).

25. Dorothy Soelle, *On Earth as in Heaven: A Liberation Spirituality of Sharing*, trans. Marc Batco (Louisville, Kentucky: Westminster/John Knox Press, 1993).

26. Per Vatican Council II, "The joys and the hopes, the griefs and the anxieties of the men of this age, especially those who are poor or in any way afflicted, these too are the joys and hopes, the griefs and anxieties of the followers of Christ. . .. To carry out such a task, the Church has always had the duty of scrutinizing the signs of the times and of interpreting them in the light of the gospel. . .. We must therefore recognize and understand the world in which we live, its expectations, its longings, and its often-dramatic characteristics. (*Gaudium et Spes* #1–4). The above is the purpose of the Christian community per Vatican II. (Quotations from Vatican II are from W. M. Abbot [ed.], *The Documents of VaticanII*, New York: Guild Press, 1966).

27. Joseph Ogbonnaya, *African Catholocism and Hermeneutics of Culture: Essays in the Light of African Synod II* (Eugene, Oregon: Wipf and Stock Publishers, 2014); Agbonkhianmeghe E. Orobator, "The Synod as Ecclesial Conversation" in *Reconciliation, Justice, and Peace: The Second African Synod*. ed. Agbonkhianmeghe E. Orobator (New York: Orbis Books, 2011). This is a consistent position of most Latin American Liberation Theologians, including Leornardo Boff, *Church, Charism and Power: Liberation Theology and the Institutional Church* (London: SCM, 1985), 8–9. Gustavo Gutierréz, Ignacio Ellacuría, Jon Sobrino, Archbishop Oscar Romero, José Comblin, Dom Helder Camara, and many others. We shall focus more on the works of Ellacuría and Sobrino in this research.

28. Roger Haight, S. J., *Christian Community in History: Historical Ecclesiology* Vol. 1 (New York: Continuum, 2004), 2.

· 1 ·

STATE OF THE QUESTION

The Historical Reality of Nigeria and the Need for Salvation

This chapter, which serves as the basis of this investigation, presents a general diagnosis and appraisal of the historical evolution of the Nigerian State, with a view to unveil aspects of the social lives of those people which should be the target of the Church's message of salvation. My diagnosis will, first, provide an outline of the specific historical evolution of the Nigerian State from the time of its colonization to contemporary independent Nigeria, emphasizing current political and economic realities that affect the Nigerian people. Second, it will review the life of the Church in Nigeria, paying attention to the concept of salvation as it relates to the situation of the people, and how in its limited way, the Church approaches social issues of economic and political exclusion of a dysfunctional democracy.

It is important to state from the outset that the Nigerian Church does not exist in a vacuum, but that it is always conditioned by historical factors of both time and place. The Church in Nigeria, therefore, cannot be treated in isolation from the conditions of social life, which are prevalent in that country. Hence, any assessment made regarding the Church's actions or inactions towards prevalent social conditions of poverty, death, corruption, and disregard for the rule of law by a small corrupt clique should be viewed against the background of its existence in a society that suffers from these vices. This review will indicate what the Nigerian Catholic Church needs to put into practice, in a dual ontology of liberation, to mediate salvation here and now for the people, not only to pray and to talk, but to pray and to perform actions prayerfully.

An Overview of Nigerian Historical Reality

Some historians believe that the name "Nigeria" is derived from one of the most remarkable geographical features of the country, the river Niger,[1] while others believe that the name was adopted arbitrarily by the British adventurer, George Dashwood Taubman Goldie, who dreamed of establishing a British controlled commercial empire from the Niger River delta to the Nile. Seasoned journalist Karl Maier reports:

> Goldie's influence on the course of events was so powerful that when it came time to name the new colony, Goldesia, reminiscent of Cecil Rhodes's Rhodesia, was considered along with Niger Sudan and *Negretia*. London finally settled on Nigeria, a name coined sixteen years before Lugard's future wife, Flora Shaw, [Lugard was later Governor General of British colonial Nigeria] in an article she wrote for the British establishment newspaper, *The Times*.[2]

Nigerian theologian Simeon Tsetim Iber[3] has proven that the historical reality of Nigeria originated in the colonial era, starting in 1914, and among other things, revolves around four major areas: the social context of the Nigerian State; the State and Citizenship in Nigeria; the political and Administrative Structures in Nigeria, and the State and Capital in Nigeria.[4] Quoting Nigerian professor Eghosa E. Osaghae, Iber asserts:

> The year 1914 is significant in Nigeria because it is the official birthday of the nation. January 1, 1914, the day when Lord Lugard effected the amalgamation of the Protectorate of Northern Nigeria Colony and Protectorate of Southern Nigeria which were previously administered as separate though related territories, is generally regarded as the birth date of the Nigerian State. Before it – indeed, before the advent of colonial rule – there was no Nigeria and the likelihood that a State like it could have evolved was quite remote. What existed in the period before the establishment of colonial rule was a motley [collection] of diverse groups whose histories and interactions, interlaced as they were by external influences – principally trade with Europeans and with the Arab world – had nevertheless crystallized in three clearly discernible regional formations by the end of the nineteenth century.[5]

This stance agrees with other important accounts such as Sir Henry William's report[6] as well as those of Professors Rotimi T. Suberu[7] and Paul E. Lovejoy,[8] who all agree on the structural classifications that shaped historical developments in Nigeria, which form the basis for current Nigerian politics. In order to understand the current historical circumstances of Nigerian reality, it is important to highlight the structural organization of the major regional groupings prior to the amalgamation, when the different regions in the country were united to form what is today called Nigeria, and how the effects of this amalgamation manifested themselves in postindependent Nigeria's history, which indicates that colonial effects on Nigeria have persisted to this day.

Specific Traditional and Social Factors

Northern Nigeria is one of the three main regions of the country. Prior to Nigeria's political "independence"[9] from Britain in 1960, prolonged trade relations, which were established along the trans-Saharan route and migrations brought about the Hausa States; the Kanem Bornu Empire in Northern Nigeria. In 1804, the Fulani people of Northern Nigeria launched a jihad to incorporate the North central region known as the Middle Belt region of Nigeria, under the Islamic theocratic and central rule of the Sokoto Caliphate.[10] This move met with fierce opposition around the Benue and Plateau regions, where groups, such as the Tiv, Idoma, the Ngas and the Berom refused to embrace the religion of Islam, despite its having had successes in the far north.

Per Osaghae, this Islamization agenda provoked two major consequences, both of which were reinforced under the practices and the legal system of colonial rule and shaped ethnic relations in Nigeria even after the country's independence in 1960.[11] On the one hand, Osaghae states, the colonial administration perceived and, in fact, accepted Muslim groups and their followers as the group having the most authority over the ethnic groups in the North. Consequently, non-Islamic minorities were rendered as inconsequential and powerless, overshadowed by the numerical strength of the Muslims. Furthermore, the Indirect Rule policy developed by the British colonial government through which they utilized the base and network of pre-existing local power structures to control all regions of their colonial empire, instituted that "appointees of the Caliphate and Emirates were imposed as rulers on non-Muslim groups,"[12] to consolidate the political agenda of the colonial rulers. The second consequence of the process of Islamization in the north was the adaption by the British colonial government of the political and the social organization of the Sokoto Caliphate as the ideal model to enforce its policies in the whole of what was to emerge as independent Nigeria.

In the second major region of Nigeria, the Western part of the country before the time of British colonization, the political, social, and religious structures of the ancient Oyo and Benin kingdoms provided solid ground for the future of this region. The major tribal groups of the old Oyo kingdom included the Yorubas, a collective of several subgroups, linked to a common ancestry that traces their origin to the legendary *Oduduwa* "the creator of the earth and ancestor of the Yoruba kings." The Benin kingdom consisted of different ethnic communities such as the Edo-speaking people comprising the Urhobo, Isoko, and some Igbos who had no common ancestry as part of the kingdom. These kingdoms of the Oyo and the Benin witnessed several tribal and clannish wars in the late nineteenth century that led gradually to their decline and, consequently, helped as new regional powers and political arrangements emerged. Osaghae believes that the reorganization of political arrangements in the Western region was orchestrated by the Northern political figures in alliance with the Colonial powers for their own economic and religious interests:

> The wars and crises in the West were instigated and fuelled by the meddling of the Fulani jihadists whose sphere of influence spread to Oyo and other northernmost parts of the West, and European traders and colonialists who, particularly since the era of the slave trade, pursued manipulative and divisionist strategies to gain trade advantages and retain political-cum-military control in the region.[13]

Accusations against the north of regional hegemony have become an enduring rhetoric in Nigerian political discourse, often pitting one region's elite and ethnic groups conveniently against another.

In the third major region of Nigeria, the Eastern region, there existed diverse ethnic groups, the Igbo people were the largest; but other smaller ethnic minorities such as the Ijaw, the Efik, the Annang, the Kalabari, and many others, for their part, managed to maintain some individual tribal autonomy and organized their village settlements in a noncentralized fashion. The Igbo-speaking ethnic group occupied most of the territory in that region. While upholding the identity of its sub-group, the Igbos were united by the Arochukwu, an Igbo clan of mixed Igbo and Ibibio origins which had entered various alliances and treaties with other Igbo clans. These groups exercised political and religious power in many of the areas of their jurisdiction. Iber argues that, although these groups organized around local tribal rule autonomously, they maintained some degree of independence and held on to a degree of limited power within the larger ethnic group, so it is wrong to suggest that they were stateless as some scholars have argued.[14]

The relative independent structures of the social organization of the ethnic groups living in the Eastern region of Nigeria seems to be responsible for the unsuccessful effort by the British to unite all of those regions under the Islamic rule of the Caliphate. This explains in part how the Eastern as well as the Western regions of Nigeria became more accessible to Christian missionaries, and therefore, embraced Western European models of education before the Northern region. One effect is that, despite the dominance of the north in political issues and through its leadership due to the skewed arrangements of the British colonial rulers, the Eastern and the Western regions of Nigeria were more developed and educated. It is possible to argue that colonialism by itself was not the defining factor in ascertaining the direction, the speed, and the scope of change for any colonized country. The nature and the ideology of the succeeding elite, Nigerian geography, traditions, patriotism, and ethnic tribal cultures are fundamental to explain any people's reaction to events, which occurred throughout their history. This explains why the reaction of the Yoruba Muslims in the Western region of the country to religious and political issues may have been different from those of the Hausa/Fulani Muslims of the Northern region, although the religion they profess is considered by outsiders to be the same.

Political scientist Ali Mazrui[15] illustrates that generally, at the core of Africa's political maladjustments in countries such as Nigeria, is the concept of arbitrary amalgamation of diverse regions and ethnic groups into single nation states by the various European colonial powers. Indeed, the emergence of the Nigerian State was a creation of the British colonial power that brought their political might as an empire to bear on the developing independent city-states in West-Africa. As a consequence, every clan, tribe and ethnic group in Nigeria carries its own bag of particularities and idiosyncrasies, turning its reality of multiethnicity into a site of cultural, religious and social struggles with tragic repercussions both in the past and in the present.[16] Thus, Nigeria is home to 380 linguistic forms of communication, as many as 20 distinct geographical regions with varying forms of political organization such as clans, communities, villages, republics, city-states, chiefdoms, kingdoms, and a Caliphate.[17]

The arbitrary fusion of this geographical entity with diverse ethnic groups manifests itself in Nigeria today in the form of politicized religion, birthing radical violent groups such as The Movement for the Emancipation of the

Niger Delta (MEND, or Niger Delta militants)[18] in the eastern geographical region, while the radical Islamic group *Boko Haram*[19] continues to command sympathy in the north and threatens the unity of the country. The frequency and the ferocity of the activities of these groups threatens Nigeria with becoming a more insecure country, rife with conflicts occurring between national citizens, various ethnic communities and stirring up general sentiment of communal intolerance and distrust. On a whole, it is legitimate to argue that "The rise in ethnic tensions in postindependence Nigeria is a direct consequence of the failure to recognize the identity of minority groups and the important role that these groups of people will play in the Nigerian federation."[20] This was championed by the British policy of colonial administration.

Nevertheless, it would be simplistic to attribute the conception and evolution of the Nigerian federation exclusively to the British colonial interest. Clearly, the ranks of Nigeria's nationalist leaders also supported and collaborated with the British and helped to fashion the form of constitutional self-governance that emerged in Nigeria. Scholars argue that Nigerian nationalist leaders were each promoting their regional bases and were interested in the national question only to the extent that their being placed in leadership roles at the federal level would better enhance their regional causes. Suberu supports this side of the argument as well, stating:

> As Ladipo Adamolekun and Bamindele Ayo have argued, Nigerian federalism "resulted from a consensus decision reached between Nigeria's nationalist leaders and the British colonial authorities." Beginning with the landmark Ibadan General Constitutional Conference of 1950, the Nigerian political class collaborated with the British to fashion the basic outlines of a constitution for a self-governing Nigeria. At the conference, and in subsequent constitutional deliberations, the majority of Nigeria's leaders increasingly and persistently emphasized the need to grant the fullest autonomy to the country's component groups or regions. Indeed, as Eme Awa has shown, these leaders behaved as if "original sovereignty" lay with the regions, which could, therefore, appropriately allocate functions to the center and reserve the residue to themselves.[21]

The creation of Nigerian federalism, therefore, emerged because of a combination of factors, traceable both to the British colonial administration and to the collaboration of Nigerian nationalist leaders, who were concerned only with securing their regional interests. Hence, loyalty to regional issues became the yardstick for aspiring leaders in their political campaigns and party coalitions that brought about the first republic at the time of Nigeria's independence from Britain on October 1, 1960. Having reviewed Nigerian historical transition from the period of colonialism to independence, I will turn now to explore the consequences these historical developments had on social conditions, from the first republic to the present day, with the intention to determine how the Church in Nigeria has been able to correlate its self-understanding and theology to these experiences.

Corruption, Injustice, and Unrest

Nigeria has witnessed four political transition eras in its 55 years, but has produced only three successful governments, with others either failing or being truncated due to military interventions. Since a feeling of gloom gradually succeeded the emotion of the populace soon after post-independence euphoria, Nigeria has observed no less than eight rounds of military dictatorships (in1966, 1966, 1975, 1976, 1983, 1985, 1993, and 1998), four failed or misdirected civilian governments (1963–1966, 1979–1983, 1999–2007, 2007–2010, 2011–2015, 2015 to date), an aborted republic and three attempted constitutional conventions. In the sections that follow, for the purposes of analytical clarity, I shall review the social conditions of Nigerian historical reality throughout the different republics.

The First Republic: 1960–1966

This period in Nigeria's history, referred to as the first republic, covers a span of five years and three months from October 1, 1960, to January, 1966. The major features of the 1954 colonial Constitution merged into the 1960 Independence Constitution to form the first Nigerian postindependence civilian administration. Sir Abubakar Tafawa Balewa, leader of the Northern region, emerged as the Prime Minister, and Nnamdi Azikiwe, leader of the Eastern region, emerged as President in 1963 when Nigeria became a formal Republic.[22] This era, which was immediately following independence, gave much power to the federal government and was celebrated as positive and competitive for regional autonomy. However, the country, as a federation, never moved out of this divisiveness, and continued to exacerbate ethnic and regional divisions. There were instances when regional and federal autonomy conflicted in matters of statecraft, particularly in the areas of revenue allocations and development loans. Moreover, the large size of the Northern region in comparison to the other regions was used as a tool to maintain dominance in political and economic activities. Thus, with political power having to shift to the center, the North became a determining regional power in the federation, a situation that naturally, over time, met with the displeasure of the other regions.[23]

Thus, Iber suggests, "the major challenge before the first Nigerian administration was how to balance power between the central federal government and the regions. The government favored centralization without making adequate provision for the regions."[24] Ensuing perceptions of neglect, domination, and control by one region over the others led to the first military coup of 1966 that ended the first republic. In the chaos, Major General J. T. U. Aguyi-Ironsi, an Igbo who became the first military head of State, lasted for only six months and was toppled in another bloody coup in July 1966, headed by officers mostly from the North. Next on August 1, 1966, Lt. Col. Yakubu Gowon, a Christian consensus candidate, emerged from the Ngas minority tribe in the Middle Belt region of Nigeria as the second military head of State, with steadily growing opposition from the Eastern and Western parts of Nigeria that resulted in the Nigerian civil war[25] from July 1967 to January 1970. As it turned out, the war propaganda was colored by rhetoric of a genocide waged by the Muslims of Northern Nigeria to exterminate the Catholic Igbos of Eastern Nigeria from the face of the earth.

However, in Nigeria, class, ethnic and religious consciousness is often intertwined. The quest for political power, economic security, and social status is all tied up with one's ethnic affiliation or geographical location. Hence, Moses A. Iorapuu[26] and Pade Badru[27] both argue that the economic class distinction that existed between the regions was a major factor in the civil war. Since the British colonial powers supported the Northern class, it was inevitable that they formed the core of the emerging elite in the first republic, supported by their numbers. Their dominance, coupled with irresponsible stewardship, occasioned this bloody civil war from 1967 to 1970.

In 1975 after the civil war, the Gowon regime was ousted by the Murtala Muhammed/Olusegun Obasanjo military regime. Murtala's rule lasted only six months, when he was assassinated in an abortive coup, and Obasanjo, his deputy, became head of State from February, 1976, to October, 1979, maintaining key officers of the Murtala administration and retaining its structural makeup and policies.[28] Both regimes are taken as one, since one was simply a continuation of the other. An enduring legacy of this administration in Nigerian history is the fact that Murtala set in motion a four-year time table for a transition to a civilian government, which was adhered to despite his death, and which resulted in a smooth handover to the civilian administration of Alhaji Shehu Shagari on October 1, 1979.

In summary, although political independence brought about some changes to the composition of the state managers in Nigeria, the character of the state remained much as it had been during the colonial era.[29] Rampant corruption continued. In 1956, Nnamdi Azikiwe, who later became Nigeria's first president (1963–1966), was accused of corruption for depositing illicit money into the African Continental Bank to save it from bankruptcy. It was a public liability company, but he had an interest in it.[30] Likewise in 1962, the premier of western Nigeria, Obafemi Awolowo was accused of corruption for misapplying public funds.[31] Although Tafawa Balewa, Nigeria's first Prime Minister was thought to be above the fray, his government faced constant allegations of corruption and high-handedness.[32]

The Second Republic: 1979–1983

The 1979 elections under the Obasanjo military regime ushered in Nigeria's Second Republic on October 1, 1979, with Alhaji Shehu Shagari, a northerner, as president after a much-disputed election by the Nigerian Federal Electoral Commission. Following the recommendation of the Constitution Drafting Committee (CDC), which the Murtala/Obansanjo military regime established before Murtala's assassination—as part of the time table for transition to civilian administration, the new Shagari government upheld the promotion of the "Federal Character Principle," in a well-intentioned but failed attempt to balance political and economic power between "Northern" and "Southern" Nigeria.[33] Eghosae defines this principle:

> The federal character principle is a variant of the consociational principle of proportional representation or quota system where the main objective was to ensure that the kaleidoscope of the country's diversity was reflected in composition of government at all levels.[34]

Despite reconciliatory measures by the government to heal wounds of mistrust and domination to form national unity and integration, it was difficult to strike a balance between ethnic groups, which overlapped several states or which were the majority population in the same state. Furthermore, the desire for equal representation in executive bodies to serve as a mechanism for power sharing failed because it sacrificed competence to satisfy representation, and extremely inept people became leaders of the most important arms of government simply because they represented their ethnic group. Thus, per Iber, "The administration became very corrupt, substituting state power sharing with personal power sharing, and state representation for patronage representation."[35]

In retrospect, this period appears to mark the beginning of entrenched corruption in the official corridors of power as the norm for doing business. This corruption continued from the military government General Olesegun Obasanjo handed over to President Shehu Shagari in 1979.[36] Obasanjo secured the first IMF/World Bank loan in 1976 and Shagari secured another loan in 1980 to help the failing economy due to corruption. Worse still, Umaru Dikko, the chairman of a presidential task force on the importation of rice to ease the impending famine, diverted allegedly 4 million naira (USD$60 million), into his personal account, and fled into exile for protection to England on December 31, 1983, when Major General Muhammed Buhari (1983–1985) staged a coup that terminated Nigeria's second republic.

When the government of General Buhari arose to power in 1983, his government launched a War against Indiscipline, including an attack on corrupt practices. There was some momentary restraint; Buhari's government was overthrown in 1985 through a coup making General Ibrahim Babangida (1985–1993) the next president, a dictator who steered the affairs of Nigeria for eight years while he built himself a multibillion dollar business empire. "An early glimpse into his involvement in shady business became possible in what is internationally now known as the BCCI affair."[37] Besides attaining the reputation of world-class plutocrats such as the late Ferdinand Marcos of the Philippines and the late Mobuto Sese Seko of Zaire,[38] the Babangida administration reached an apex of deceit and unreliability with the cancellation of June 12, 1993 elections that would have ushered in M. K. O. Abiola as president of Nigeria's Third Republic. Between December 1991 and November 1993, civilian governors elected in elections conducted by the Babangida administration ruled states under the military whose power was held at the central government. They looked forward to the presidential elections, which were held but then were cancelled, thereby aborting the Third Republic. The corruption, however, continued uninterrupted.

When the late General Sani Abacha (1993–1998) came to power after a set of politically confusing events led to Babangida's leaving office unceremoniously, Abacha waged a war against corruption with the slogan, "War against Indiscipline and Corruption." He also inaugurated the Failed Banks Tribunal to check illegal monetary activities, especially money laundering. While praising his desire for bank reforms, he, himself, flaunted the rules so much that he became one of the most corrupt presidents. Roughly 3000 Nigerian officials at the time were said to have Swiss Bank accounts totaling USD $33 billion."[39] The sudden death of Abacha in June, 1998, which many viewed as divine intervention, ushered in the regime of General Abdulsalami Abubakar, who revised Abacha's transition program within a year and ushered in the Fourth Republic in May, 1999.

The Fourth Republic: 1999–2007

Former military head of State, Olusegun Obasanjo, won the presidential elections conducted by the Abdusalami administration, and was sworn in on May 29, 1999 as president. He was the first Nigerian leader to be "recycled" in the crisis of leadership with another retired General, Muhammadu Buhari winning the April 2015 presidential elections. Key among the accusations the Obasanjo-led government confronted was cries of marginalization and ethnic tension coming from different parts of the country. Upon assuming office, Obasanjo dismissed or retired several military officers from the North, creating an imbalance in key ministerial appointments between the North and the Southwest, Obasanjo's home region. Also, his tenure saw the invasion of federal troops in oil-rich Odi communities of Bayelsa State, and the Tiv of the Middle Belt area, killing hundreds of people and destroying much property, using the excuse that these communities had killed soldiers.[40]

Despite Obasanjo's posture as an anticorruption crusader, not only did he attempt to make himself a president-for-life, but also to address the stiff opposition of Nigerians, since his administration was also very corrupt. In fact, Iber notes, "in 2003, Nigeria was voted by Transparency International the second most corrupt country in the world, a position it has maintained for several years."[41] Key members of his administration were indicted by several panels at different times, most especially by the Independent Corrupt Practices and Other Related Offences Commission (ICPC), which appeared to show that there was a commitment on the part of his administration to fight corruption. Yet they went unpunished. To be sure, some analysts identified positive marks in his administration, such as instituting budgeting practices, reform of the banking system, and a massive reduction of foreign debt.[42] However, most Nigerians still believe that high levels of corruption characterized the Obasanjo administration.

The Fourth Republic: 2007–2010

The Obasanjo administration (1999–2007) ended in a disaster as could be measured by Nigeria's development indices. After failing in his desperate attempt to amend the Constitution to run for a Third Term, Obasanjo imposed on the nation a physically sick loyalist, Musa Yar' Adua, as president. At his inauguration on May 29, 2007, Yar'Adua gave an inspiring speech acknowledging the failures in the elections that brought him to power and promised to enact electoral reform. Although the declaration of assets by Yar'Adua as president was a novelty in the Nigerian political scene, his short stint as president brought the EFCC, the agency constituted to fight corruption to total collapse. Hopes for lasting reform as he promised at his inauguration were dashed when he died in office in 2009, two years into his tenure.

Per Iber, the best assessor of the Yar'Adua administration was Nasiru El Rufai, former minister of the Federal Capital Territory under the Obasanjo administration:

> It was the reversal of the war against corruption that the Yar'Adua administration did the most damage to its credibility with Nigerians and the international community. The systemic destruction of the EFCC by the Yar'Adua administration began as soon as James Ibori- former governor of Delta State was charged for money laundering and corruption at the Federal High Court in December 2007.[43]

Yar'Adua's anticorruption fight having lost the steam, the rest of his seven-point agenda[44] was equally lost. His laudable actions to create an amnesty and peace pact with militant groups in the Niger Delta to achieve regional development there ended as a source of enrichment to individual community leaders and leaders of militant groups without the much-needed development to the area. Above all, his greatest challenge, which turned out to be his ill health, claimed his life eventually two years into his tenure in 2009. Yar'Adua's vice president, Jonathan Goodluck, found himself in the saddle, after the National assembly of Nigeria adopted a resolution on February 9, 210, to empower the vice-president to act as President and Commander-in-Chief of the Nigerian Armed Forces following the protracted illness (78 days out of office) of the president who was incapacitated, as required by the constitution. The death of President Yar'Adua on May 5, 2010, put an end to his presidency and ushered in Jonathan Goodluck as president.

The Fourth Republic: 2010–2015

On May 6, 2010, Jonathan Goodluck was sworn in as President and Commander-in-Chief of the armed forces of the Federal Republic of Nigeria. He completed the term of the late Yar' Adua's presidency he inherited in 2011, since Nigeria has a four-year term, and was re-elected as president. A distinctive feature of his administration was a relative and steady supply of petrol and gas in filling stations throughout Nigeria. Indeed, his emergence as president from the Ijaw, a minority tribal group of Bayelsa State, an oil producing state, was considered a breakthrough in Nigerian politics, working toward promising unity and integration of the entire nation. However, events in his administration proved contrary, since, besides witnessing the worse economic conditions, Nigerians faced the most horrible security challenges in its history since the civil war of 1967. Consequently, Goodluck contested and lost the presidential election held March 28, 2015, paving the way for former military leader General Muhammadu Buhari, to become the first opposition candidate to win presidential elections in Nigeria. Buhari was sworn in on May 29, 2015, and is believed to have won the elections due largely to the gross non-performance of Goodluck's People's Democratic Party (PDP), which led the administration that many Nigerians estimate today to be the worst period in the political history of Nigeria.

Unrestrained corruption has made politics the most lucrative and attractive economic trade in Nigeria. Despite high levels of poverty among the populace, Nigerian senators earn a salary of about USD $1.7 million and members of congress earn USD $1.45 million per annum, considerably more than their counterparts in the United States and the United Kingdom. Meanwhile, Nigeria has a very low standard of living, a low per capita income with growing rates of poverty. In 2009, Nigeria dropped nine places to 130th position out of 180 countries ranked on the global Corruption Perceptions Index (CPI) by Transparency International (TI), a global anticorruption campaign organization based in Berlin, Germany.[45]

Officials observing Nigeria from the outside describe the sorry state of the nation with alarming detail. According to the 2012 Transparency International CPI index, Nigeria was ranked 139th out of 176 countries globally. The "US Country Reports on Human Rights Practices for 2012" on Nigeria states that the country lost about USD $6.8 billion to "endemic corruption and entrenched inefficiency."[46] The Nigerian In-Country Director of the World Bank, Marie- Francoise Marie- Nelly, said that out of a population of just under 170 million in 2013, Nigeria has 100 million people living in abject poverty.[47] Despite all this, the ability of Nigerian leaders to travel freely around the world and to conduct business in the United States and Europe with various multinational corporations highlights the gaps in international accountability and justice mechanisms. Nigeria has a well-earned reputation for corruption, yet its leaders and politicians engage freely with the international community in business and are continually given loans by world financial institutions.

This history provides the context for the kind of salvation that will be most meaningful to Nigerians. Since the Church, lives and operates within the same society, what has been the place of the Church in Nigeria within the twists and turns of Nigeria's historical experiences over time? The failure of leadership is the most disturbing political challenge threatening the Nigerian State. The absolute premium on political power in the name of democracy without the institutional support to moderate political competition has pushed the Nigeria political scene to the point of total warfare. State power is used to control the economy and to appropriate wealth, thereby creating an unproductive version of state capitalism that spawns administrative controls and regulations using enforcement corruptly. Without doubt, the political situation has conditioned the presence and witness of the Church. My question then is: How has the Church's message of salvation impacted on this reality?

The Nigerian Church

The analysis of the historical reality of Nigeria demonstrates that all is not well, and there is a need for the Church to propose ways to salvage the decaying structural and moral fabric of Nigerian society. Living in the same reality, the Church's prophetic role challenges its members to participate in liberating humanity and in bringing hope to suffering people on earth. It is, thus, incumbent on the Church in Nigeria to work towards realizing this much-needed goal in the life of Nigeria. In this section, I will address the history of the Church's efforts to fulfill that that prophetic role in Nigeria and how it can be better envisioned and practiced today.

In 1996, Father George Ehusani's[48] book, A Prophetic Church, stirred much debate about the self-understanding and the mission of the Church in Nigeria. He raises the question about the right of the Church to exist as he explores aspects relating to the imminence and the transcendence of the Church. Twenty years after Ehusani wrote, the problems of the Church remain and his concerns face the Nigerian Church still. This study assumes that the Church in Nigeria exists is in a twofold relationship: (1) the Church is spiritual, related to the transcendent God, and (2) the Church serves as the expression of God's love for the world and the human race. It is related equally to the world, because it is part of this world and undeniably, part of the world's secular history.[49] These two relationships are interdependent recipro-cally and mutually. If, in a bid to be relevant to the world, the Church capitu-lates completely to society and culture, especially in ways of life that are sinful, it loses its transcendence. On the other hand, if the Church claims a priority for transcendence that leads to it isolating itself from the world and becoming disinterested in "this sinful world," then it loses its hold on its immanent role. Put simply, the credibility and truth claims of the Church depend entirely on its actual ability to exercise transcendence in this world, embodied concretely in the daily lives of the people.[50] What might this mean, then, for the Church in Nigeria? I will employ the word "Church" in this study mostly about the administrative structure of the Catholic Church organized and institution-alized to varying degrees and at various levels in Nigeria, since the Church's official voice on social justice issues in Nigeria originates most often from its hierarchy, most especially the bishops. In a similar manner to the previous review of Nigerian politics, a review of the Nigerian Church must also begin with the colonial era.

Colonial Antecedents and the Origins of the Catholic Church in Nigeria

One of the major events in European history of the nineteenth century was mass European emigration to North America, Australia, Africa, and Latin America, which had implications bearing not only on economic and political realms, but religious as well. Sylvanus Ifeanyichukwu Nnoruka,[51] like most Af-rican historians, reports that Christianity was first introduced to West Africa in 1482. A Portuguese expedition of about six hundred men landed in Elmina, near Cape Coast, Ghana on January 20, 1482, under command of Don Diogo d' Azambuja.[52] Upon securing an audience with the king in Elmina, and meet-ing his approval, initial missionary work began with the local population. The king's approval was tied mostly to understanding, "the king of Portugal would make alliances with the African king and profitable trade relationships would be established between them."[53] On the strength of this understanding, the missionaries secured land from the king and erected a chapel and a fort, both dedicated to Saint George.

In Nigeria, around 1485, the king of the ancient Benin kingdom invit-ed the Portuguese to send missionaries to his kingdom.[54] Like his Ghanian counterpart, the real intent behind the request of the Benin chief was to seek alliances with Portugal for military assistance, since it was a time when such kingdoms waged war to conquer their neighbors. Six years later, a king of Benin was baptized into the Christian faith because of this contact. About a century later, in 1591, Jesuit Father Barrerius baptized another king of Benin.[55] About 1655, Spanish Friars visited Benin and baptized yet another king. These initial successes were short-lived, owing to bitter conflict between Portugal and Spain about this time. Basically, difficulties of a harsh environment for missionaries, language barriers, and conflict between early missionaries for territory were the major set-backs to the attempts to evangelize this region.

Generally, the Catholic Church missionized West Africa, for the most, until the end of 1617. Soon however, in 1618, the English "Company of Adventure of London to Africa," built two forts along the coast, one in Gambia, and the other at Cormantine along the Gold Coast, signaling the start of Protestant missionary activity in the subregion. The Dutch arrived in 1637, with France, Denmark, and Sweden all following a little later, setting up forts along the Coasts. The Danes built a fort at Christinasbury near Accra, which would later serve as the Government House of the Accra region in Ghana.[56] These forts served primarily for commercial purposes, but chaplains were appointed for each denomination to serve the spiritual needs of their specific European inhabitants. However, those chaplains, who enjoyed elevated social status, second only to the Director General, took initiative to minister independently to the needs of the African natives as well. Clergy from European Protestant colonizers performed most of these missionary activities.

Catholic Missionary efforts in the West Africa reopened only about the mid-nineteenth century when Bishop Melchior de Marion Bresillac, founded the *Societas Missionum ad Afros* (Society of African Missions-SMA), on December 8, 1856 in Lyon, France, "to organize a society of young European missionaries, who would devote their lives to the conversion of Africans. They were to spend their whole life among their converts in the mission field, instruct them in the Catholic faith, administer the Holy Sacraments, and work as Parish Priests."[57] The first team of missionaries from this group arrived in Sierra Leone on June 12, 1859, including Fathers Baptiste Bresson, Louis Raymond, and Brother Eugene Raynoud. Bishop de Bresillac himself, Father Louis Riocreux and Brother Gratian Monnoyeur, who joined them later, all died after a few months of illness caused by harsh weather.[58] The mission was taken over by the Holy Ghost Fathers in later years.

In Nigeria, the SMA Vicariate Apostolic of Dahomey, erected on August 29, 1860, opened the page for the next round of missionary activity. The Italian Father Francesco Borghero, of the diocese of Genoa, headed the first team of missionaries, who arrived in January 1861. He made an exploratory tour of the Guinea Coast in 1862, with Lagos one of the first places he visited. There at Ouidah, he met a community of repatriated slaves from Brazil who had converted to Catholicism while enslaved, whose priest was Padre Antonio. They learned trades such as: carpentry, tailoring and masonry while they were still slaves, and settled around Campus Square in Lagos.[59] Father Borghero opened a new station there in 1868, and two years later, Father Courdioux replaced him as the new superior of Dahomey Vicariate Apostolic. The latter appointed Father Cloud to oversee Lagos, with his major objective to establish an agricultural settlement for the converts. The Governor of Lagos granted Father Cloud's application for a nine-mile piece of land on July 26, 1876 to set up a new mission at Topo. Sir James Marshal was instrumental in persuading the governor to grant this request, and first group of missionaries to Topo were comprised of Father Baudin, Brother Elie, four African boys, a cook and his wife.

Per Modupe Odudoye, the negative experience of the society in Sierra Leone was responsible for their opening up the Topo mission. They now preferred to reach out to "the untouched native in his paganism to the sophisticated colonial in coastal seaports."[60] Hence, they opted to create a separate Christian community where they taught monogamy and discouraged local tribal rituals to encourage people to embrace the practices of Christianity. Many Nigerian families settled in Topo and by 1892, the Catholic Church opened a convent for girls. Sadly, agriculture, which served as a driving force for Father Cloud's missionary strategy, did not appeal to the children of those early settlers. Many young adults left to go to Lagos or Porto Novo in search of a better life. Todd makes a striking comparison between the Topo missionary experience and that of the Benedictine monasteries in the Middle Ages throughout Europe. There was not much direct religious impact in either situation. The Benedictine experience for example, rather, "stuffed the whole of society with a tangible ideal of industry and prayer, so that gradually without any striking conversions society was changed."[61] Many African historians, however, believe that a deliberate colonial policy used the missions as a direct source for raw materials for European industries, such as the California mission experiment where the natives served as cheap labor for colonial wealth generation from local products and the missionaries collaborated with this practice, sometimes to receive colonial protection. This model of colonial function characterized missionary activity in Nigeria throughout most its history.

The *Societas Missionum ad Afros* (Society of African Missions-SMA) recorded steady progress in their mission in Lagos, so much so that by 1877, they recorded the first administration of the Sacrament of Confirmation among the people. Construction work on the Holy Cross Cathedral in Lagos started in 1878, and in 1891, Monsignor Chausse was consecrated as Bishop of Lagos in Lyons, France. In 1889 and 1895, Father Hooley extended the mission work to Abeokuta and Ibadan respectively, and by 1905, the Society founded its first Seminary in Africa, the Saints Peter and Paul Seminary in Ibadan, which produced most of the first generation of Nigerian Catholic priests. Four nuns of the Franciscan Sisters of the Propagation of the Faith were the first order to join the SMA priests in Lagos in 1874.[62] Outstanding among this group was Sister Colette, who devoted her energies to developing the educational apostolate, through to the time when she died in 1916. Augustine Planque opened the first community of the Sisters of Our Lady of the Apostles in Lyons, France in 1876, which later sent a group of nuns to the Lagos mission. This congregation of sisters has continued to work there through to present day with indigenous sisters.

Despite its very small and difficult beginnings, the Catholic Church in Nigeria experienced phenomenal growth and expansion soon and Nigeria, like the rest of Africa, imbibed the trend of sending missionaries to Europe and around the world. On a whole, the Nigerian mission had challenges, including the language barrier, since the missionaries spoke mainly French with a few Italian priests, whereas Nigeria had been a British colony. To meet this challenge, an Apostolic School opened in Ireland in 1878 to train English-speaking missionaries and to aid with the eventual transfer of the greater part of the mission in Yoruba-land to the Irish Province. Most significantly, on June 4, 1883, Rome divided the Dahomey Mission into two sections: the English-speaking region, known as the Vicariate Apostolic of the Bight of Benin, stretched from Oueme to East of the Niger, with Father John Baptiste Chausse as the Provicar.[63] On May 12, 1891, he was nominated to be the Vicar Apostolic of the Bight of Benin, and he continued to spread the mission to parts of the Yoruba-land. Soon after, Joseph Lang was consecrated as bishop at the Holy Cross Cathedral, Lagos in 1902, and opened up stations in the Ijebu area, stretching to the eastern region in places such as Issele-Uku, Igbuzo, Ogwashi-Uku, Onitsha, and Olona. Lang's missionary activity also extended northeast of the Benue valley, and by 1911, he founded a station in Shendam, before his death on January 2, 1912. From Shendam, Monsignor Waller and his colleagues extended their mission to the northeastern Province of Nigeria.

Thus, for the most part, the Nigerian mission became staffed with English-speaking missionaries, mostly from Ireland and England.

Between 1889 and 1920, the area around the Benue valley was part of the newly formed Prefecture Apostolic of the lower Niger,[64] stretching east of the Niger River to south of the Benue River. In 1880, as had occurred in the Western and the Eastern regions of the country, the French Holy Ghost Fathers were the missionaries who first evangelized this area. Later, the Holy Ghost priests and brothers from Ireland joined them, and it was the latter who from 1911, began to make contacts with the people living in the Benue valley. In February 1917, the Vatican appointed Pere Dourvry Apostolic Administrator for the whole of Cameroon, but he resigned from the role and returned to Paris in August 1920.[65] Father Eugene Groetz succeeded Father Douvry in this mission, and by 1929 Father Joseph Soul, one of the General Councilors, arrived the Vicariate for an official visitation, taking time to visit Obudu, and travelled from there to Tivland.

His accidental visit resulted in the German Spiritans finally deciding to attempt to evangelize the people of the lower Benue, the Tiv, Idoma, the Igala and other smaller tribal groups, and by 1930, the first contingent of four priests and two brothers from their order arrived, exactly 45 years after Joseph Lutz and his companies established the mission at Onitsha. Their Apostolic zeal and energy were so great that by 1934 areas of the civil territory of Benue province, Northern Nigeria became the Prefecture Apostolic of Benue with first center of activity at Makurdi, and later, at Oturkpo.[66] The German priests and brothers made tremendous efforts and spread throughout the whole region from Idah on the River Niger to Wukari near the boundary of Benue and Adamawa provinces. Unfortunately, a major setback arose following the outbreak of World War II in 1939, when the British authorities required all German priests and brothers, to leave Nigeria.[67] Today this area covers the present dioceses of Oturkpo, Makurdi, Gboko, Katsina-Ala, along with Lafia and Jalingo to the north. Today, there is a diocese in almost each of the 36 States of Nigeria, including the Federal Capital territory, with some States accommodating two or three dioceses.

Despite the difficulties of diverse languages, harsh weather, and accessibility constraints, structures of the institutional and hierarchical Church became well established in Nigeria. Even as in succeeding years the Church has witnessed phenomenal growth, the emergence of Christianity within the context of pagan kingdoms in most of Africa has produced a curios trajectory as worshippers tend to be attracted to some exuberant theatrics of fighting and chasing demons. This fear of the powers of darkness is part of the social setting in which Christianity was introduced in most of Africa, and continues to linger on the perception of "evil," "salvation," and "deliverance," as almost exclusively relating to forces of witchcraft and wizards. The political leadership in Nigeria has tapped into these fears that have become the core narrative of many protestant denominations, glossing over the heinous evil of failed leadership and corruption, and so the failure of government is attributed to the devil.

Numerical Growth of the Catholic Church in Nigeria and the Need for Salvation

From its very humble beginnings as a mission church, today the Catholic Church in Nigeria has 54 ecclesiastical jurisdictions, all headed by indigenous bishops. These are divided into nine Provinces, parallel to the nine archdioceses in the country, with proximate dioceses serving as suffragans to each archdiocese. There are 16 Seminary training colleges located in different parts of the country, which are owned jointly by dioceses within different provinces, and missionary congregations, besides the *Veritas* University, owned by the Catholic Bishops' Conference of Nigeria (CBCN) in Abuja.[68] The CBCN, brings together the Bishops and Archbishops of the 54 ecclesiastical jurisdictions as shepherds to pray and to speak, with one voice as they spearhead teaching, prophetic and pastoral ministries of the Catholic Church in Nigeria.[69]

The executive body of the Nigerian Catholic Bishops' Conference includes the President, the Vice President, the Secretary, and the Assistant Secretary, who are all bishops. The plenary session of the conference is held twice a year. The Catholic Secretariat of Nigeria (CSN), the administrative coordinating unit of the Catholic Bishops' Conference, is the most visible symbol of the unity of the Catholic Church in Nigeria.[70] Headed by the Secretary General, the Secretariat has five Directorates: Pastoral Affairs, Pastoral Agents, Church and Society, Mission and Dialogue, and Social Communications, with several committees under each directorate, which serve to implement the decisions of the Conference and to facilitate the missionary, educational and human development work of the Bishops, priests, male and female religious and lay people involved with the Catholic Church in Nigeria. However, the Church's official voice on social justice issues in Nigeria emerges from the bishops themselves, through the means of communiqués, pastoral statements, and messages, released under the auspices of the aegis of the CBCN. Often, individual Bishops and the Catholic Bishops' Conference of Nigeria as a body issue statements and communiqués,[71] condemning various situations as they arise. Unfortunately, these statements are not usually followed with action by the CBCN. For purpose of this investigation, I will explore source documents from that organization, dating from the time of Nigeria's independence.

Despite a seemingly robust presence of the Catholic Church in Nigeria, the historical experience of most Nigerians is one of human-made poverty, large-scale corruption, structural injustice, and political repression. Nigerian theologian Agbonkhianmeghe E. Orobator explains that this situation is "an example of a Church whose self-understanding and social mission hinges on the exercise of ecclesiastical authority, especially manifested in the issuance of public declarations."[72] Indeed, the Church in Nigeria views itself as a locus of salvation, as it must. Yet, Orobator notes,

> In Nigeria, the dominant understanding of the prophetic mission of the church collapses this mission into the function of issuing statements by "church leaders" on the country's socioeconomic and political condition. How this function becomes the collective and mobilizing self-understanding of the ecclesial community remains unclear. . . . the claim the church in Nigeria makes on the self-designation 'prophetic church' appears more like the privilege of hierarchical leadership than a shared mission of the church as the people of God, much less as family of God.[73]

Thus, after analyzing statements and communiqués of the CBCN from 1993 through 1997, Orobator concludes that the Church in Nigeria focuses its self-understanding at the level of ecclesiastical hierarchy, to the complete neglect of the major constituents of the ecclesial community, namely the laity and the theologians.[74] This approach by the Catholic Church in Nigeria shows that in praxis it faces a major drawback "in the obvious chasm between its declared prophetic mission and the means it adopts for translating it into effective action at the service of society."[75] Orobator's position on the self-understanding of the Church in Nigeria illustrates the backdrop for this research, that despite the bishops recognizing the underlying structural factors responsible for Nigeria's ills, they are still prone to rely on praying, calming the masses and rejecting violent means of effecting change as the most popular means they advocate to relieving these problems. He says, in fact "Nowhere in its official declarations do the bishops outline an effective program of action or identify means for realizing this goal . . . besides prayer programs and crusades."[76] Thus, the notion of salvation that colors the teachings of the Nigerian Catholic

Church is priority for individual eternal salvation, which is guaranteed and to a certain extent effected by the ecclesiastical organization. For the most part, there is an almost exclusive emphasis on internal, interpersonal, and individual sins, with an almost complete neglect of the social dimension of historical, economic, social, and political sins, which perpetually condition the behavior of the individuals and more specifically the elite and justify the transcendent import of their actions on a societal level.

Indeed, as earlier noted, the average Nigerian Christian faithful is typically deferential, perhaps even dependent, on the priests and bishops, especially when compared to most American faithful. The authentic following of Christ's teaching on communal ethics is devalued when the leadership stresses exclusively the primacy of individual sacramental grace. Thus, people are in danger of losing sight of the historical visibility of societal grace and the visible configuration of one's life in community in accordance with the historical life of Jesus of Nazareth as he lived with his disciples and other followers. The Christian dimension of activity in this world, in this place, now, is, therefore, often overlooked. Instead, there is a greater concern for maintaining the organization setup of the Church in its institutional and sociological form, than for reaching out to vulnerable people and restoring them to the richness and grace of interpersonal community.

Admittedly, one of the missions of the Church is to share Jesus' role in taking away the sins of the world. But it is not enough for the Church to content itself with preaching taking away the sins of the world. Christian salvation does not consist in the absence of sin alone, but, rather, in restoring people and creation into the fullness of life in community. Therefore, the Nigerian Catholic Church must work to promote the creation of a new human on a new earth as the clear eschatological sign of that which is yet to come but is already present and operative in the world. The Church must not rest in its laurels, content that its prophetic and apocalyptic denunciation is enough; a task, which it allowed the Bishop's Conference and other bodies to perform over the years through communiqués and statements. Indeed, it can and should never give up this work of denouncing individual sin.

Yet, fundamentally, the most urgent task of the Church is to proclaim the social restoration of justice, the destruction of communal structures of sin. It may not necessarily be the specific task of the Church to create the actual technical models to fulfill the proclamation. Its task is rather to work out the true meaning and the import of their creation and utilization. Of course, the Church must provide earthly relief for the oppressed, and at the same time interrogate the influence of governance and the use of divinity to cascade accountability, and detract from earthly interrogation or concretization. It must not let the oppressors go free to continue their exploits. However, it is one thing to diagnose a disease, yet another to heal it, and yet another to prevent it. Church life in Nigeria today needs courage to envision social action as the place and the way of Christian witness.

The questions, then, that the Church must ask itself are: What might this task imply in terms of the reality of Nigeria? How are the Church leaders prepared to answer this question? How are the future priests of the Church being formed in this regard? These should be the fundamental concerns of the Catholic Church in Nigeria today. In the next section, I will look approach the content of the formation program for agents of evangelization in the Catholic Church in Nigeria, most especially the role of the seminaries, since the Church considers seminary formation to be one of the most demanding and important tasks for the future of the evangelization agenda of humanity,[77] and the approach to evangelization is often largely the result of the quality of faith formation found in the seminaries.

An Overview of Seminary Formation in Nigeria

In a major study reviewing seminary formation program in Nigeria, renowned Nigerian theologian and social analyst, George Ehusani, establishes "the history of the Catholic Church of Nigeria in the first one hundred years of its existence (1865–1965) is in large measure a chronicle of the heroism of the many Irish men and women who traversed this vast country, implanting the Catholic faith, opening schools and vocational centers and founding hospitals and orphanages."[78] Thus, Ehusani contends, "since we operate along the same models of Church," the Nigerian Church needs to learn from the experience of Ireland at the dawn of the twenty-first century. He notes specifically regarding seminary formation:

> The present method of formation at all levels appears to place too much emphasis on the cognitive and too little accent on the affective and intuitive dimensions of human development in general and the Christian enterprise in particular. Training in love, mercy and compassion, which are a function of the affective faculty of the human personality, have often been neglected in favor of an all too intellectual approach to catechesis and theology. The result is that we often have more professionals, scholars, and scrupulous functionaries among the clergy and religious than transformed men and women whose hearts have been won over by the love of God in Christ.[79]

In an earlier study, Ehusani notes emphatically:

> The form, organization and structure of our seminaries. . . [is] essentially European and often superfluous. These structures not only make an elite group out of the clergy and religious, often alienating them from the concrete socio-economic conditions of their people, but they also need continued financial input from foreign agencies.[80]

Therefore, his vision is to call for a paradigm shift in the formation of priests and agents of evangelization, that recognize fully "our traditional religious genius, our unique historical experience, our peculiar cultural patterns, and our contemporary socio-economic and political exigencies, for as they say 'God meets people where they are at.'"[81] Several respondents to the memorandum share the same views concerning the outdated Western European methodology of formation. Nigerian Professor Chris Ejizu recounts:

> One of the greatest challenges which the prevailing situation poses to the Nigerian Church is the need to constantly review the curriculum of training priests, religious and the laity. More often than not, candidates who pass out of our seminaries and religious institutes graduate without having been seriously exposed to the realities that are of immediate concern to people in the world they are going to minister. The curriculum of training the candidates does not sufficiently embody the realities of their society. The candidates graduate and get into the ministry only to begin to tinker with so many novel ideas and methods. I recommend that our seminaries and houses of formation borrow a leaf from what happens in secular institutions, in terms of curriculum development.[82]

Indeed, the call for a reappraisal of methodology of formation seems to be a common position of respondents. Nigerian political economist and social analyst, Pat Utomi, sharing this position asserts: "The reality is that orthodoxy, which the Church represents, tends to dispose institutions towards tradition. Tradition generally tends to be closely aligned to inertia. There is value here in that it helps unchanging truth to be preserved with the desired fidelity. The flip side is that inertia in a changing world means disequilibrium which brings about a crisis of relevance."[83] Overall therefore, it is possible to identify from these reactions the claim that the kind of formation obtained in Nigerian seminaries is largely responsible for the creation of a vast dichotomy between the vertical and the horizontal dimensions of faith, elevating the former over the latter. The human person as the subject of the social teachings of the Church integrates the body and the soul, so, any authentic witness of the gospel needs to address issues, which impact both the body and the soul.

Despite the CBCN having issued an updated version of *Ratio Fundamentalis Institutionis Sacerdotalis*[84] in 2005 as a guide for seminary formation in Nigeria, it is difficult to discuss any one specific model of seminary formation in Nigeria since there appears to be more than one. After surveying the historical development of seminary formation in the Roman Catholic Church in Europe—from the Tridentine model to the new model of Diocesan seminary of Paris—Nigerian educationist and theologian, Paul Uche Nwobi concludes, "a multifaceted seminary model in Nigeria has a strong tendency toward a highly institutionalized, academic system of the Tridentine model."[85]

Founded on the teaching of St Charles Borrmeo (1538–1584), seminary training is geared towards forming a priest as a dispenser of sacraments with the foundation of ascetical spirituality, during which time he is educated to obey rules of the institutional hierarchy.[86] Furthermore, Nwobi states that another model found in Nigerian seminaries is that of the French School through which the priest is trained to become a member of the "spiritual elite," as Christ's vicar and earthly representative. "Its' spirituality is divinization and participation in the incarnated Christ; its mission is denial of self and Eucharistic adoration; its education is relational (deeply confessor-penitent kind) like a novitiate training school."[87] This model, per Nwobi fosters a distinct gap between the priest and the people as well as undergirds various forms of clericalism, which separate the clergy and laity even further.

Moreover, he identifies the Vatican II model of ecclesiastical leadership formation as the one that is most operative in Nigerian seminaries. Drawing from Vatican II Council documents: *Optatam Totius, Presbyterorum Ordinis, Gaudium et Spes, Lumen Genitum*, as well as other Synodal documents: 1970 Synod of Bishops on Priestly Identity, 1990 Synod of Bishops on Priestly Formation, John Paul II Apostolic Exhortation *Pastores Dabo Vobis* of 1992, and the Post Synodal Apostolic Exhortation[s] of 1995, *Ecclesia in Africa* and *Africae Munus* of 2009, Nwobi illustrates that although these developed no new defined educational structure, a particular characteristic of the Vatican II model is "a strong tendency to program-solutions to all problems. If the seminarians are not doing well in liturgy, add more classes of liturgy. If a greater number of seminarians are misbehaving, add more rules. There is a belief that more is better and a belief in big numbers."[88]

A representative sample of the curricula for six select seminaries in Nigeria in appendix I, reveals a bewildering array of courses and subjects which a candidate for the priesthood is expected to master. Looking at the Curriculum for St Augustine Major Seminary Jos, for example, where this researcher trained for the priesthood, whereas several courses on Western Philosophy and Theology abound, there are no courses offered on African Theology, nor practical courses relating to leadership and service as well as poverty reduction in answer to the troubling issue of leadership, both in Church and in government. Neither is there a course relating in some way to the theology of accountability to respond to economic distress in Nigeria. As at 2003 when I graduated, there was no course on the First African Synod which had taken place close to ten years ago, neither is there any indication of a focus in the courses listed for a concerted training in critical analysis of contemporary issues affecting society.

A curious detail in the curricula sampled in Appendix I generally is the fact that some seminaries do not include a course on the vast corpus of Catholic social teachings, nor do they teach a comprehensive socio-political history of Nigeria. Except for the seminaries at Bigard, Bodija and Gwagwalada, most of the seminaries do not even have a single course on Catholic social teachings, neither any on African Theology or contemporary Nigerian or African history. Seminary formation somewhat follows a similar pattern of education the colonialists were willing to offer to Nigerians in colonial times; people were trained basically to serve colonial needs, to serve as clerks, interpreters and attendants. It would appear like the training of pastoral agents is done in such a way that calculatedly keeps them uninformed about the public character and demands of faith. This accounts in large measure for the poverty of leadership that has hindered a praxis-oriented witness of the faith in the Nigerian Church. This fact makes the claim of Edward P. DeBerri et al in *Catholic Social Teaching: Our Best Kept Secret*, ever more plausible when they underscore: "The Church has a developed body of teaching on social, economic, political, and cultural matters and what that body says seem to have been forgotten—or have never been known—by most of the Roman Catholic community."[89]

James Downey, writing over 30 years ago about seminary training in Nigeria where he served as seminary rector, decries the situation where "future ministry is mapped out for the candidate and reduced to a series of convergent problems which admit of mathematical and logical conclusions."[90] Rote memorization of Western theological concepts and Western Philosophical theories that are often removed from lived challenges of daily life, typically, is the characteristic form of the training seminarians currently receive. Apart from the so many courses offered in a wide array of subjects, the length of training and the seclusion of the seminarians during the period of formation only widens the gap between the training they receive and the unfolding experiences of the communities to which they minister. This obtains even as "common sense suggests that life, and especially the life of a priest, is a matter of divergent problems which have to be lived through and to which there is no mathematical answer."[91] Undoubtedly, this affects the pastoral efficiency of the priest as he embraces his ministry, since most of the issues he encounters are far from those already mapped out for him in the seminary. As a leader of the Christian community, it ultimately affects his leadership and the community too.

Indeed, contemporary theological discourse indicates that revelation is always to a community, and is mediated through finite, historical reality, which specifies the object of religious experience.[92] Faith is thus understood to be correlative to revelation, and they mutually define one another. Just as faith is always expressed in a community, revelation is always to a community in history. And given the peculiarities of the historical conditions of each faith community, it is only right that the Church in Nigeria evolves a training program that is specifically suited to respond to the pastoral needs of the people in the current circumstances.

The task of seminary training in Nigeria and the training of all agents of evangelization is not one of learning and reproducing "universal" philosophical and theological principles and applying them to the Nigerian reality. Conversely, philosophical and theological education should be geared to exploring in depth the Nigerian situation and applying to the said situation in Nigeria a creative and integrated response in the light of faith. Such faith, informed by a context driven philosophical and theological training will better respond to the problems that Nigerians face.[93] Indeed, if priests, as leaders of the Christian community, are not educated adequately about, and interested in a more holistic education, their ministry may suffer from serious deficiencies. The listing in Appendix I reveals an emphasis on spiritual life morality, and theoretical Western Philosophical thought to the neglect of active commitments of faith of the local community, lending weight to Downey's assertion that "the most important questions and problems of our time are not in the curriculum."[94]

To avoid the illusion of institutionalization where the solutions to the many challenges that priests and pastoral agents face in their day-to-day ministry are presumed to be provided by the seminary, the curriculum as Downey suggests should be pruned and rationalized to cope with diversified needs. Indeed, as he says, "in any field there is a limit to the areas in which one is proficient."[95] To be able to present salvation as true liberation to the people of Nigeria, evangelization ought to be seen as a necessary part of the educational formation to promotion of life in abundance. It must be viewed as an educational priority for the promotion of human development in its most comprehensive and elevated form. This can be achieved, not with many courses on different subjects, but a carefully designed program of formation that responds to the question "for what type of ministry is the candidate being trained?" The African Synods I and II provide answers to this question, spelling out the specific needs of the Church in contemporary Africa—to make the Gospel real in the daily lives of people.

What makes the Christian message Good News for the whole community is that Christ makes abundant life possible not only in the hereafter, but also, more importantly, in the here and now. For Latin American theologian, Jon Sobrino, "religion essentially has to liberate and bring joy and salvation in the lives of those to whom it is proclaimed and those who proclaim it."[96] For those who proclaim religion as well as those who receive it, for the proclamation to rise to the level of truly being Good News, it must be joyful, "something frequently forgotten in the mission of the Catholic church, which is often more concerned with communicating a 'truth' that has to be given and received in an orthodox manner, without bothering to present it with joy and to check whether or not it has produced joy."[97] The next chapter is, therefore, a portrait of what the Scriptures say of the body of Christ in history. In that chapter, I will offer a practical, historical perspective pertaining to more in depth developments in the life of the people of God over the centuries, how Jesus lived out and illustrated the nature of salvation and called the Church to continue his mission of liberation in the world.

Notes

1. Central Intelligence Agency, "The World Factbook," Webpage last updated on June 24, 2014, https://www.cia.gov/library/publications/the-world-factbook/goes/ni.html, accessed on December 10, 2014. Nigeria has an area of 923, 768 Square kilometers. It lies east of Benin Republic, south of Niger and Chad Republic, West of the Republic of Cameroon, and north of the Gulf of Guinea.

2. Karl Maier, *This House has Fallen* (London: Penguin Books, 2001), 10. Palm oil had replaced slave trade and Nigeria was a big market. Goldie had enlisted Lord Fredrick Lugard who was fresh in the routing of the French in Uganda.

3. Simeon Tsetim Iber, *The Principle of Subsidiarity in Catholic Social Thought: Implications for Social Justice and Civil Society in Nigeria*, American University Studies, Series VII, Vol 308,

(New York: Peter Lang, 2011), 143–196. This chapter will be informed largely by this important work that draws heavily on the analysis of Eghosa E. Osaghae, *Crippled Giant: Nigeria Since Independence* (Indianapolis: Indiana University Press, 1998), and other related sources.

4. Iber, *The Principle of Subsidiarity in Catholic Social Thought*, 143.

5. Eghosa E. Osaghae, as quoted by Iber, *The Principle of Subsidiarity in Catholic Social Thought*, 143–144.

6. *Sir Henry William's Report of the Commission Appointed to Enquire the Fears of Minorities and Means of Allaying them*, London, Her Majesty's Stationary Office, 1958, is a publication of the Commission established by the British colonial authorities that ruled Nigeria until independence in 1960. The intention of the Commission was to explore the concerns of the multiple ethnic minority groups in Nigeria and the fears these groups expressed in belonging to a newly independent country in anticipation of Nigerian independence. The Commission submitted its findings to Her Majesty in 1958; these findings are found in the "League of Human Rights."

7. Rotimi T. Suberu, *Federalism and Ethnic Conflict in Nigeria* (Washington, DC: United States Institute of Peace Press, 2001).

8. Paul E. Lovejoy, "Historical Setting," in *Nigeria: A Country Study*, ed. Helen Chapin Metz (Washington, DC: Library of Congress, 1992).

9. There are clear indications and some historians have argued that colonial rule left a legacy whereby the colonizers orchestrated a handover of government to their chosen Nigerian elite familial successors who could be entrusted to share their values and would be attentive to their economic, political, and social interests, among others. Hence, Nigeria has been unable to establish a viable self-perpetuating political foundation for governance, a fact that makes it even more difficult to consider Nigeria as being truly independent from outside colonizers by some observers.

10. Iber, *The Principle of Subsidiarity in Catholic Social Thought*, 144.

11. Osaghae, *Crippled Giant*, 2.

12. *Ibid.*

13. Lovejoy, *Nigeria: A Country Study*, 6–9.

14. Iber, *The Principle of Subsidiarity in Catholic Social Thought*, 145.

15. Ali Mazrui is one of Africa's leading intellectuals and commentator on the continent's character. *Cf.* Ali Mazrui, *Africa and other Civilazations: Conquest and Counter-Conquest*, eds. Ricardo Rene Laremont, Fouad Kalouche (New Jersey: Africa Word Press, 2002).

16. Moses Aondover Iorapuu, *Patriarchal Ideologies and Media Access: How to Overcome Discrimination Against Tiv Women for Sustainable Rural Development Promoting People Controlled and Participatory Communities* (Doctoral Thesis No. 819 Salesian Pontifical University, Rome, 2012), 25. *Cf.* John P. Mackintosh, "Federalism in Nigeria," in *Political Studies*, 10/3 (1962): 223–224; and Eghosa E. Osaghae, "The Status of State Governments in Nigeria's Federalism," in *Publius: The Journal of Federalism*, 22/3 (1992): 181–200.

17. Suberu, *Federalism and Ethnic Conflict in Nigeria*, 20.

18. The Movement for the Emancipation of the Niger Delta, or MEND, (Niger Delta's militant umbrella group) launched itself onto the international stage in January 2006 by claiming responsibility for the capture of four foreign oil workers. These militants like the

Niger Delta's population at large, object to environmental degradation, underdevelopment of the region and lack of benefits the community has received from its extensive oil resources. The group has been relatively calm since the Yar Adua administration granted them amnesty in 2009, offering them job opportunities and scholarships. Above all, with the death of President Yar Adua, and his consequent succession by Goodluck Jonathan, from one of the minority tribes in the Niger Delta, the region saw itself at the center of power and remained calm until the emergence of the Buhari led administration on May 29, 2015. Militancy has since resumed in the region.

19. *Boko Haram* (Western Education is Forbidden) officially called *Jama'atu Ahlis Sunna Lidda'Awati Wal-Jihad* (Group of the people of Sunna for Preaching Jihad) is a terrorist Islamist movement based in northern Nigeria. The group received training and funds from Al-Qaeda in the Islamic Maghreb, and was designated by the United States as a terrorist organization in November 2013. Membership has been estimated to number between a few hundred and a few thousand. The group has murdered close to 10,000 people between 2009 and present.

20. Iber, *The Principle of Subsidiarity in Catholic Social Thought*, 149.

21. Suberu, *Federalism and Ethnic Conflict in Nigeria*, 24.

22. Iber, *The Principle of Subsidiarity in Catholic Social Thought*, 150.

23. *Ibid.* 151.

24. *Ibid.*

25. The Eastern region of Nigeria, headed by Col. Chukwuemaka Odumegwu Ojukwu the military governor of the region, was bitter about the number of Igbo officers, which were killed, in the second coup. They considered it to be a counter coup targeted directly at the Igbos and, therefore, declared the State of Biafra independent from Nigeria on May 27, 1967.

26. Iorapuu, *Patriarchal Ideologies and Media Access*, 26–32.

27. Pade Badru, *Imperialism and Ethnic Politics in Nigeria* (Trenton: Africa World Press, 1998), 79–90, as quoted by Daniel Ude Asue, "Nigerian Catholic Bishops and Political Involvement." Unpublished Manuscript, 2015. The following section follows closely Asue's account of the history.

28. Iber, *The Principle of Subsidiarity in Catholic Social Thought*, 158.

29. Claude Ake, *Democracy and Development in Africa* (Ibadan, Nigeria: Spectrum Books, 2003), 3.

30. Maher J. et al. *The Europa World Year Book 2004, Vol. II* 45th Edition (London: Europa Publications, 2004), 3189.

31. Oyelaran O. O. "Awolowo's Planning Strategies," in *Obafemi Awolowo: The End of an Era?* eds. O. O. Oyelaran, *et al.* (Ile-Ife: Obafemi Awolowo University Press, 1988), 379.

32. K. Shillington, ed. "Balewa, Alhaji Sir Abu-Bakr (1912–1966) Prime Minister of Nigeria."*Encyclopedia of African History*. (New York: Fitzroy Dearborn, 2005), 121.

33. Iber, *The Principle of Subsidiarity in Catholic Social Thought*, 159.

34. Osaghae, *Crippled Giant*, 115.

35. Iber, *The Principle of Subsidiarity in Catholic Social Thought*, 160.

36. Asue, "Nigerian Catholic Bishops and Political Involvement." Unpublished Manuscript, 2015.

37. *TELL Magazine*, no. 41, October 1994, 8.
38. A. Apter, "IBB= 419: Nigerian Democracy and the Politics of Illusion." in *Civil Society and the Political Imagination in Africa*, eds. Jean L. John and Jean Comaroff (Chicago: The Chicago University Press, 2000), 279.
39. *TELL Magazine*, no. 41, October 1994, 10
40. See Iyorwuese Hagher, *Beyond Hate and Violence: Understanding the Tiv Struggle for Citizenship Rights and Social Justice in Nigeria* (Ibadan: Caltop Publications, 2002) 93–169 for details.
41. Iber, *The Principle of Subsidiarity in Catholic Social Thought*, 164.
42. Robert I. Rotberg, *Nigeria: Elections and Continuing Challenges* (New York: Council on Foreign Relations, April 2007), 5 ff. for details.
43. Nasiru El Rufai, as quoted by Iber, *The Principle of Subsidiarity in Catholic Social Thought* 167.
44. Yar'Adua's seven-point agenda included: (1) Infrastructure particularly electricity and transportation, (2) Niger Delta regional development, (3) Food Security, (4) Human Capital-investments in health, education and training, (5) Land Reforms and home ownership, (6) National Security, and (7) Wealth Creation.
45. *International Reporter 2009*. "The survey measures domestic public sector corruption in selected countries ... Nigeria, which had moved up 27 places to rank 121 out of 180 countries in 2008, placed 10th out of the 16 West African countries" that were surveyed in that study. Nigeria, a leading producer of oil, now imports nearly 70 percent of its petroleum because oil revenues were mismanaged and stolen.
46. Hanatu Musawa, "Underdeveloping a country," *Vanguard* (November 13, 2013). http://www.vanguardlink.com (accessed December 3, 2013).
47. Ali Adoyi, "100 Million Nigerians live in abject poverty- World Bank." *Vanguard* (November 13, 2013). http://www.vanguardlink.com (accessed December 3, 2013).
48. George Omaku Ehusani, was a one- time Secretary General of the Catholic Secretariat of Nigeria, in the late 1990s to early 2000s. His book, *A Prophetic Church* made a critical analysis of the Catholic Church's role in the Nigerian society and made proposals for a better engagement.
49. Roger Haight, "Mission: The Symbol for Understanding the Church Today." *Theological Studies* 37, (1976):620–649.
50. *Ibid*.
51. Sylvanus Ifeanyichukwu Nnoruka, a native of Anambra State in eastern Nigeria, studied at the Universite Catholique de Louvain, Belgium, is a Professor of Philosophy at the Seminary College of St Joseph, Ikot-Ekpene in Eastern Nigeria. His book *"Thy Kingdom Come": The Advent, Growth and Role of the Catholic Church in Umudioka- Dunukofia, Nigeria, 1913–2007* (London: IKO-Verlag fur Interkulturelle Communikation, 2007), offers a major insight on the history of the Catholic Church in Nigeria. For details of this history, see also Martin James Bane, *Catholic Pioneers in West Africa* (Dublin: Clonmore & Reynolds, 1956); C. P. Groves, *The Planting of Christianity in Africa,* (CPCK, London: 1948, Vol. 1); J. Kofi Agbeti, *West African Church History, Christian Missions and Church Foundations:1482–1919* (Leiden: E. J. Brill, 1986).
52. Nnoruka, *Thy Kingdom Come* 101.

53. J. Kofi Agbeti, *West African Church History, Christian Missions and Church Foundations:1482–1919* (Leiden: E. J. Brill, 1986), 3.
54. Nnoruka, *Thy Kingdom Come* 101.
55. *Ibid.*
56. *Ibid.* 102.
57. John M. Todd, *African Missions: A Historical Study of the Society of African Missions* (London: Burns & Oates, 1962), 38.
58. *Ibid.*
59. Modupe Odudoye, *The Planting of Christianity in Yoruba land* (Ibadan: Day Star Press, 1996), 61.
60. *Ibid.* 63.
61. Todd, *African Missions*, 201.
62. Nnoruka, *Thy Kingdom Come*, 107.
63. Martin James Bane, *Catholic Pioneers in West Africa* (Dublin: Claymore & Reynolds, 1956) 151.
64. This section relies on information found on the Official Site of the Catholic Diocese of Makurdi, Nigeria http://www.makurdidiocese.com (accessed April 15, 2015).
65. *Ibid.*
66. *Ibid.*
67. *Ibid.*
68. Bishop Felix A. Job, forward to *Catholic Church in Nigeria: Official Directory* (Abuja: Catholic Secretariat of Nigeria, 2009), v.
69. Official Site of the Catholic Secretariat of Nigeria http://www.csnigeria.org/ (accessed April 15, 2015).
70. *Ibid.*
71. For a detailed collection of the bishops' letters, see Peter Schineller, ed. *The Church Teaches: Stand of the Catholic Bishops of Nigeria on Issues of Faith and Life* (Abuja: The Catholic Secretariat of Nigeria, 2003).
72. Orobator, The Church as Family, 82.
73. *Ibid.*
74. *Ibid.* 86.
75. *Ibid.*
76. *Ibid.* 87.
77. John Paul II, Post-Synodal Apostolic Exhortation, *Pastores Dabo Vobis* # 2 (March 25, 1992), available from http://www.vatican.va (accessed April 4, 2015).
78. Ehusani, "Memorandum on The Decline of Church Attendance and Anti-Clericalism in Ireland: Lessons and Challenges for Nigeria," 6.
79. *Ibid.* 12.
80. Ehusani, *A Prophetic Church*, 71.
81. Ehusani, "Memorandum on The Decline of Church Attendance and Anti-Clericalism in Ireland: Lessons and Challenges for Nigeria," 13.
82. Rev. Fr. Chris Ejizu, "A Reaction" in *Challenges for the Church in the 21ˢᵗ Century: A Memorandum*, 36.

83. Dr Pat Utomi, "A Reaction" in *Challenges for the Church in the 21ˢᵗ Century: A Memorandum*, 6.

84. Here it is instructive that the bishops chose to update a document issued in January 1970, when other documents have developed on the provisions of this question. Indeed, this CBCN document states among other things "the priestly ministry is chiefly put into practice in the ministry of the word and in the work of sanctification." See Catholic Bishops Conference of Nigeria, *Ratio Fundamentalis Institutionis Sacerdotalis* (Abuja: Catholic Secretariat of Nigeria, 2005), 44.

85. Paul Uche Nwobi, *Poor Formation as a Principal Factor to the Crisis in Priesthood Today* (San Bernardino: Authorhouse, 2012), 61.

86. *Ibid.* 62.

87. *Ibid.*

88. *Ibid.* 63.

89. Edward P. DeBerri, James E. Hug, Peter J. Henriot, & Michael J. Schultheis *Catholic Social Teaching: Our Best Kept Secret*. Fourth Revised and Expanded Edition (Maryknoll: Orbis Books, 2003), 3.

90. James Downey, "The Creeping Curriculum," *African Ecclesiastical Review*, 24/6 (1982): 327.

91. *Ibid.*

92. See Haight, *Dynamics of Theology*, David Tracy, *Blessed Rage for Order*, The Seabury Press, New York, 1978.

93. In my 10 years of training for the priesthood in Nigeria, I took one seminar class as an elective, titled "Justice and Peace." The course revolved almost exclusively around John XXIII's *Pacem in Terris*. As shown in Appendix I, some seminaries in Nigeria still do not offer a course on the Catholic social teachings, and it is doubtful if these two synods have been studied in most of them.

94. Downey, "The Creeping Curriculum," 333.

95. *Ibid.*

96. Jon Sobrino, *Jesus the Liberator: A Historico-Theological View.* (Maryknoll: Orbis Books, 1993), 78.

97. *Ibid.*

· 2 ·

THE CHURCH IN THE WORLD AS REVEALED IN RECENT MAGISTERIAL DOCUMENTS

The document emerging from the Vatican Council II *Gaudium et Spes*, "the Pastoral Constitution on the Church in the Modern world" is considered among all the Council documents to be the crowning achievement of the Council because it corresponded most closely to Pope John XXIII's original vision of a pastoral council[1] Apart from its originating directly from a suggestion made on the floor of the council hall, it marks the first time in its 2000 year history when the Catholic Church, in an ecumenical council, attempted to respond to the question posed by the world: *"Church of Christ, what do you say of yourself?"* This, in turn, led the Catholic Church to reflect internally on how it conceived its relation to the contemporary world.

Over the centuries, especially after the Age of Reason and the French Revolution, the Catholic Church has often been "uneasy" about its relationship with "the world" and has too often resorted to using "other-worldly" or "abstract" language when it speaks about the relationship of Christians to the world, especially when it addresses theological themes such as "salvation." This uneasiness has not served Catholic theology or the Church well at all. Drawing from the Church's positive disposition to the world, which is evident in *Gaudium et Spes*, the review in this second chapter, will reflect on how the Catholic Church understands itself in relationship to the world as this theme emerges from recent magisterial teachings. The underlying framework for this review will be to answer the question: "What does the Church need to be and to do to fulfill its mission?"

Per William T. Cavanaugh, the early Church used the word *ekklesia* to describe itself. This, is the same word used in the Septuagint for Israel's public acts involving the people of God, such as covenant making (Deut. 4: 10), dedication of the temple (1 Kings 8: 14) and dedication of the city (Neh. 8).[2] Thus, Cavanaugh argues that in calling itself *ekklesia*, the Church was identifying itself as the "new Israel" and "the assembly that bears the public presence of God in history."[3] Historically, the Church has been described as the continuing presence in the world of the incarnate Word of God.[4] The church is where the people look to find a clear manifestation that to work for the good of others is a participation in what God communicates most fully through the incarnation of Christ.[5]

Catholic theologians in the twentieth century employed the concept of "sacrament" to refer to the reality of the body of Christ, the Church present in history. Four centuries earlier, the Council of Trent defined sacrament as "the visible form of an invisible grace."[6] As a full sign that manifests what it represents, a sacrament intensifies the reality it signifies existentially. In other words, sacraments contain the grace they signify and confer the grace they contain.[7] The sacraments establish contact between human beings and the Word of God in the person and in the actions of Jesus to redeem us. Through sacraments, Christ Jesus is made fully accessible to humankind. Per Avery Dulles, the conferral of a sacrament is regarded as an important and significant event as the self-accomplishment of a grace-filled dynamism seeking an appropriate bodily expression.[8] The Church as the body of Christ in history also finds itself as the most fitting expression as the sacrament of Christ in the world. As a sacrament of God's presence in the world, the Church, following the example of Jesus, is to be the place where humanity encounters the saving actions of God in Jesus.

J. G. Gager includes Cyprian, Augustine, and Aquinas among those early church fathers who describe the Church in Sacramental terms.[9] Augustine, for example, taught that the City of God addresses the importance of ordering matters that are considered public, because the City of God makes use of the same temporal goods as does the earthly city, though for different purposes.[10] This line of thought has matured in more recent times. One contemporary exponent of this understanding of Church is something Henri de Lubac reports, "If Christ is the sacrament of God, the Church is for us the sacrament of Christ, she represents him, in the full and ancient meaning of the term, and she really makes him present."[11] Karl Rahner dwells extensively on this understanding of Church in his *Theological Investigations* and other essays. According to Rahner, "The historical continuation of Christ in and through the community of those who believe in him, and who recognize him explicitly as the mediator of salvation in a profession of faith, is what we call the Church."[12] This perspective of Church is developed and treated further by theologians such as Yves Congar, Edward Schillebeeckx[13] and others.

Drawing from the insight of the "Church as sacrament," as an important theological theme, Ignacio Ellacuría takes a step further, establishing that the Church is in fact "a historical sacrament of liberation."[14] It must, therefore, commit itself in history to bring about what Jesus perfected through his life in service to be a sign of the presence of God among humanity. Following Ellacuría's image of the Church as a sacrament of liberation, which draws from the biblical background of the relationship between the children of God and "the world," and thinking about this issue in the light of Church teaching, the review in this chapter will enable this study to propose a form of engagement by the Church in the world that enables church leaders to address some of the fears that have diminished the Church's mission. The use of liberation in this work hinges on a dual ontology that connects both the spiritual and bodily realities of the human person, and how they are mutually obsessed. Our bodily experiences have exponential implications for realities in our spiritual journey.

In three major sections, I will draw selectively from Biblical sources, the writings of the early Fathers, as well as papal encyclicals toward this goal. This will enable me to reveal the historical reality of the Church as it has developed at various times throughout her history, although, yielding to other historical accounts and interpretations that may better account for the lived experience during different epochs in Church history.[15] The first section concentrates on the biblical and patristic background with the intent of prodding to discover first from the scriptures, how the ordering of right relationships by individual Christians and, by extension, the Church, creates a dwelling place for the word of God in human history. In the second part of the same section, I will explore how the Fathers of the Church, basing their teachings on the same biblical foundations, taught that the values of Christianity are meant to make the Church leaven in the society where all people are meant to live as children of God and to care for one another.

In the second section of the chapter, I will identify how the rationalistic movements in the Age of Reason in seeking answers to the question posed by scientific discoveries moved the Church to withdraw from engaging with the world. The Church instead, became self-complacent and thus has chosen over the years to avoid facing the world in its theology. The last major section concerning the magisterial teaching of the Church from Leo XIII to Francis will serve to emphasize how the social teaching of the Church over time has upheld that the unity of the whole human race can only be achieved by establishing a just society that upholds the dignity of all despite the contradictions in its practices when its chooses to avoid the world. The implication of this overview will be to invite the Church to assume a new posture in which it will be able to more directly address the lived challenges in the lives of the children of God who are situated throughout the world. I will begin by identifying the biblical and the patristic backgrounds.

Biblical and Patristic Background to the Relationship Between the Church and the World

The Second Vatican Council document on divine revelation, *Dei Verbum* professes:

> Sacred theology rests on the written word of God . . . as its primary and perpetual foundation. By scrutinizing in the light of faith all truth stored up in the mystery of Christ, theology is most powerfully strengthened and constantly rejuvenated by that word . . . The study of the sacred page is, as it were, the soul of theology.[16]

The promise of life-giving, deliverance, and rescue is at the core of the Christian faith and the life of God's instrument in this mission, Jesus, our savior. The Bible points to the essence of the role of the Church to consist not only to prepare people to hope for a better life to come. Rather, God formed a people to experience God's help in their lives as well. What is more, God's people exist only by virtue of having been saved.[17] Although the New Testament word "church" (*ecclesia*) may not have direct Old Testament precedents, the concept of the people of God in need of salvation has its roots in the Old Testament, and writers of the New Testament were steeped in the traditions and texts of the Old Testament.[18] The Revelation of John in the last canonical book of the Bible, for example, shows clearly an intimate connection between his New Testament vision of the redeemed and the Old Testament record of salvation history.[19] In Revelation 21, John's illustrating a direct link between the tribes of Old Testament Israel and the leaders of the New Testament Church is a striking reminder of the desire for continuity in God's dealings with God's people throughout the ages.[20] Surely, one can find discontinuities between the Old and New Testaments, yet there is still a strong sense of continuity and anticipation of the New in the Old, and so I will begin my investigation in the Old Testament.

God's Relationship to the People of God in the Old Testament

In the Old Testament, God reveals Godself to humanity as liberator of the oppressed and defender of the poor, demanding from humanity faith in Him and acts of justice toward their neighbors.[21] In fact, the word for "salvation" in Hebrew, *Yeshu*, is the same root word for the names Joshua and Jesus— which both translate roughly as "the savior."[22] Salvation, liberation, or rescue not only represent ideas about God's relationship with humanity, but also, in fact, provide the proper terms for those who mediate between God and humanity, making clear what God does for His people, namely, provide salvation.

Ignacio Ellacuría, in analogous manner to other scholars, interprets the Old Testament departure of the children of Israel from Egypt squarely as an instance of historical transcendence, where the liberating action of Yahweh creates a people.[23] Per him, the Exodus was the original precedent of salvation as liberation: "The cry of the Israelites has come to me, and I have seen how the Egyptians oppress them" (*Exodus 3:9*). In their job runway of oppression-liberation, Israel encounters God the liberator, and this revelation is contained in a concrete historical experience, their departure from Egypt as slaves and eventual composition as a unique people in history. Their oppression at the hands of the Egyptians serving as a major event, which launches their existence, makes their deliverance by Yahweh a defining mark of their continued existence as a people.[24] Henceforth, the Israelites would perceive God as God the liberator, who delivered them from the socioeconomic oppression of the Egyptians, and starting from this period of historical liberation, the Israelites would continue to discover the always-greater richness of God and the always-greater fullness of salvation-liberation.[25]

Agreeing with Ellacuría, T. D. Hanks maintains that in the Exodus event, Yahweh's unique relationship with the children of Israel as their liberator, defender, and sustainer, became so deeply embedded in Israel-ite psyche that everything in their life as a people would henceforth be seen and interpreted from that point on. Indeed, the Exodus experience became for Israel a perpetual "paradigm for the interpretation of all space and all time."[26] Thus, Israel is God's people, salvation/liberation is the characterizing factor in this relationship; and the "Church" is an extension of this relationship. This understanding of Church is vitally relevant in developing an understanding of salvation in the Nigerian Church today. The Church as a sacrament of liberation should offer healing, rescue, and deliverance to the people in the very ways and practicality that character-izes their lives.

God as liberator of God's people also finds expression in the Song of Miriam (Exodus 15:21), attributed to Moses' sister and sung after the deliv-erance at the Red Sea.[27] The song provides a compact summary of the most defining event in Israel's history: "Sing to the Lord, for he has triumphed gloriously; horse and rider he has thrown into the sea." The Book of Exodus also contains the so-called Song of Moses (Exodus 15: 2), which expands Miriam's short song, and then professes, "The Lord is my strength and my might, and he has become my *Yeshu* [salvation]." Here may be contained one of the oldest explicit references in scripture to the word salvation, with obvious reference to an important event in the life of the community: The people of Israel have been rescued from a pursuing army by means so mar-velous that they can only explain it as being linked to Yahweh's interven-tion.[28] This rescue story itself is given the name "salvation," providing the reader with the earliest clear biblical understanding of salvation (what God does for God's people). Simply put, it the story of God's people receiving God's help in a time of great need.

Additional evidence from prophetic literature indicates that the problems of unjust social relations seem to have been perennial throughout the history of Israel, the prophets for their part would constantly call Israel back to its obligations as a people of God who were supposed to be just and humane to all.[29] Time and time again, the prophets proclaimed vigorously that Yahweh is the defender of the little ones, the most vulnerable and so any injustice di-rected at them was considered to be indeed an assault on the character of God that would not escape divine judgment. This was at the heart of the prophecy of Amos, who insisted that Israel's special status as God's chosen people also implied that God could make more demands of it: "You alone have I favored, more than all the families of the earth; Therefore, I will punish you for all your crimes." Amos 3:2 [NAB]. The prophet Jeremiah offers an even more poignant denunciation against Israel for its violation of the standards of justice, specifically indicting its leadership:

> Woe to him who builds his house on wrong, his terraces on injustice; Who works his neighbor without pay, and gives him no wages. Who says, "I will build myself a spacious house, with airy rooms," Who cuts out windows for it, panels it with cedar, and paints it with vermillion. Must you prove your rank among kings by competing with them in cedar? Did not your father eat and drink? He did what was right and just, and it went well with him. Because he dispensed justice to the weak and the poor, it went well with him. Is this not true knowledge of me? Says the Lord. But your eyes and heart are set on nothing except on your own gain, On shedding innocent blood, on practicing oppression and extortion. Therefore, thus says the Lord concerning Jehoiakim, son of Josiah, king of Judah. They shall not lament him, "Alas, my brother"; "Alas! sister." They shall not lament him, "Alas, Lord! Alas, Majesty!" The burial of an ass shall he be given, dragged forth and cast out beyond the gates of Jerusalem. Jeremaiah 22: 13–19 [NAB].

Most significantly, the prophet Isaiah shifts away from the "prophetic pessimism of the present social order toward a more hopeful view of Yahweh's action in the future."[30] The writings of Isaiah, which appear to have been written over the years spanning the pre-exilic and early postexilic periods in the history of the people of Israel, all portray God encountering people in their sufferings and oppression, assuring them of hope in the midst of hopelessness.[31] Both functions of denunciation that are personified in the prophetic ministry Jeremiah, and those of encouragement and hope in Isaiah, have a meeting point in the core idea of liberation as central to the prophets as it is to my understanding of the Church. The Church is not only called to denounce evil for what it is, but also to encourage and to work for the liberation of the children of God as Isaiah counsels.

On a whole, in the Old Testament, God reveals God self to God's people as the liberator of the oppressed and the defender of the poor personified in actions such as: freeing slaves, cancelling debts, delivering from the forces of darkness and death, and effecting just relationships. This concern for the vulnerable in society is absolutely rooted Yahweh who is defender of the oppressed.[32] The Hebrew Bible, therefore, uses metaphors that have clear implications for the Church today as it continues to manifest in history the presence of Christ, who saves and frees from constraints. "To live" in the Old Testament sense, means to be healed, to be saved and to be restored to relationships.

The Church as the "Continuation of the Mission of Jesus" in the New Testament

The Second Vatican Council document, *Dei Verbum*, emphasizes the inter-relatedness of the Old and New Testaments of the Christian Bible, stating, "God the inspirer and author of the books of both testaments . . . has brought it about that the New should be hidden in the Old and the Old should be made manifest in the New."[33] Cavanaugh establishes rightly that in Christian theological tradition, the fulfillment of Israel is not any nation-state, but spe-cifically the Church. In his words, "the New Testament Church understood itself as the eschatological fulfillment of the gathering of Israel, consummated in the atoning death and resurrection of Jesus Christ."[34]

Scholars have approached the interrelatedness of the testaments through the principle of intertextuality, where the Old looks forward to fulfillment in the New in the person of Christ. The later prophets, for instance, express an expectation of one who would come to restore all things. The prophet Jeremi-ah envisions a future when God promises to make a new covenant with the house of Israel saying, "I will put my law in their minds, and write it on their hearts" (Jeremiah 31: 31 ff.). Isaiah describes a messianic age when the deaf will hear, the blind will see and the poor rejoice because "the tyrant will be no more" (Isaiah 29: 17 ff.). In fact, an entire section of Deutero-Isaiah contains many messianic oracles referred to commonly as the songs of the suffering servant.[35] Ellacuría examines the soteriological-ecclesiological significance of these "songs" in his noteworthy essay, "The Crucified People: An Essay in Historical Soteriology," insisting "historical soteriology not only thinks about salvation but actively promotes salvation, inviting Christians to embody a saving praxis."[36] Just as the innocent lamb was led to the slaughter, this figure of the suffering servant was considered to inaugurate a new age that will usher in the liberation of the afflicted and brokenhearted.[37] Hence, David Pleins asserts, there is in the writing of the prophets a clear "anticipation of future rectification of the oppressed."[38]

In 1 Corinthians 1: 30, Paul summarizes succinctly the Christian Scrip-ture's revelation of the mission of the Church in the world when he pro-fesses that Jesus has become wisdom, justice, sanctification, and redemption. This means that the mission of the Church in the world begins and revolves around the focal point of Christian faith, the center being Jesus. Edward Schillebeeckx states pointedly, "in the New Testament, the salvation which Christians experience in Jesus is often expressed by the Greek word *soteria* "salvation," (Luke 1: 71, 77)."[39] He dwells extensively on the theme of salvation in Jesus to mean being freed from servitude and from slavery; rescue from the hands of enemies or from various dangers, from nets or snares and oppressions (Psalms 68: 6; 107: 14; 31: 4; 107: 28; 143:11).[40] Agreeing with Schillebeeckx's perspective of salvation, Roger Haight, S. J., reviews a number of theological points of view in regard to the New Testament treatment of salvation and concludes, "in current theological interpretations of Jesus the genre of savior or liberator is most pronounced among the various forms of liberation theology."[41] Jesus' entire public ministry, beginning with his teachings, proclamations, healing miracles and wonders, and his entire life was dedicated to the inauguration of the kingdom of God, which consisted in giving people a new lease on life. Haight adds:

> "Salvation" denotes the deliverance of human beings from evil, physical, moral, political, or cataclysmic. It connotes a victory, a rescue of them from a state of negation and a restoration to wholeness or integrity. This broad concept of salvation allows one to incorporate into it analogously the many ways in which Jesus is the agent of salvation both during his historical life and from his position as the exalted one.[42]

In Jesus, according to Haight, the kingdom of God is not distant or unrelated to this world.[43] For those who "follow Jesus," bringing to life the things he went about doing in his ministry, salvation becomes an experienced reality of God's self-disclosure in him.[44] As I stated in the previous section, the primary meaning of salvation (what God does for God's people) in the Hebrew Scriptures is healing. The children of God are saved from the challenges they encounter over the course of history in the events of their daily lives. Despite their ups and downs, God visits them eventually with saving help. Salvation will be realized in this life through the recurring vindication of the people of God.[45]

Hence, the Gospels report the beginning of Jesus' ministry with the proclamation: "The kingdom of God is at hand. Repent" (Mk. 1: 15; Mt. 4: 17). The kingdom is proclaimed as a present reality, active in the world and calling for a response from the hearers (Mt. 3:2; 4:23; 5:3, 10; 9: 35; Lk. 10: 9; 11: 20; 17: 21: "The kingdom of God is in your midst"); at the same time, it is a future reality, the object of hope and prayer: "Thy kingdom come" (Mt. 6: 10).[46] While the kingdom was understood at one point in the Old Testament sense as the active exercise (Yahweh is king or reigns) of God's sovereignty, John R. Donahue counsels that such a view runs the danger of being overly spiritualized. He notes: "kingdom, while denoting the active rule of God, never loses its spatial dimension as active rule calling for a place or area in which this rule finds a home."[47] This view of the kingdom stands at the heart of this work, as a reality hoped for, which finds realization in the here and now. The famous Lord's prayer of Jesus implores, "Thy kingdom come, Thy will be done, on earth as it is in heaven," the phrase "on earth as it is in heaven" should be understood as applying not only to the will of God but also to the kingdom. By identifying the advent of God's kingdom with his ministry and teaching, Jesus proclaims the advent of God's justice to effect change and to create a more just society. The kingdom of God is therefore to be manifest in history, just as the proclaimer of the kingdom, Jesus, was incarnate in history.[48]

The Gospels provides the reader with a very clear picture concerning the thrust of Jesus' ministry. At the early stage of Jesus' public ministry, Luke places on his lips Isaiah's messianic prophecy (Is 61:1–3),[49] "The spirit of the Lord is upon me, because he has anointed me to bring glad tidings to the poor. He has sent me to proclaim liberty to captives and recovery of sight to the blind, to let the oppressed go free, and to proclaim a year acceptable to the Lord." [Luke 4: 18–19]. This understanding of his mission was the most basic to Jesus embodying his theology, so much so that later when the emissaries of John inquired if he was the anointed one or not, his response consisted simply of pointing them to the signs of his ministry which corresponded to what the prophets foretold would accompany the dawn of the messianic age.[50] He said, "go tell John what you have seen and heard—the blind see, the lame walk and the dead are raised to life" (Lk. 7: 22 ff.). This is consistent with the Old Testament view of the mission of God's chosen people in society, which Henrique Pinto corroborates, revealing that participation in the kingdom is not simply to offer hope for a future eschatological bliss. The experience of the kingdom must occur in the here and now, for if Jesus' teachings meant only the spiritual realities of poverty, "it would seem, in fact, that Jesus proclaims the resignation of the oppressed" whose consolation would be the prize of "God's glory in a postmortem state."[51] Indeed, Jesus' Sermon on the Mount presents a completely new set of values to those who seek justice, the peacemakers and those who suffer persecution in his name and for justice's sake to fashion a new world.

It is also quite instructive that immediately following his proclamation of the kingdom in the Gospels is Jesus' calling the disciples. Donahue notes, "Response to this call is not simply a hearing of Jesus' teaching but involves following and mission."[52] Through his call, Jesus enables the disciples to encounter and to draw strength from him to preach, to heal, and to confront the power of evil in the same manner that he did (Mk. 3: 13). Specifically, their encounter with

Jesus "gave them authority over unclean spirits," and the twelve "drove out many demons, and anointed with oil many who were sick and cured them" (Cf. Mk. 6:7–13). This call implies commitment to the kind and quality of life Jesus led and dedication to the cause of compassion for and mercy to the outcast accompanied by a prophetic stance to denounce and to confront the structures of evil in society. Hence, Jesus, as the proclaimer of God's kingdom, becomes a sacrament of God's salvation and a representative of the kingdom of God in the world. Donahue adds, "In Jesus' life this involved engagement with the social world of his time, the offer of mercy to the outcasts of his time, and the calling of others to continue this mission,"[53] a call that extends to the Church today. If the Church understands itself called by God to continue Jesus' mission in the world, then the reason for the Church's existence is implied in the call, namely, to uphold the actions and practices of Jesus in the world, to "drive out" demons of injustice and poverty, to "heal" humanity of sickness and hunger. In doing this, Christians are, therefore, not engaging in "secular" activities, but in fact, creating a dwelling place for the word of God that became flesh, Jesus, in human history.

On a whole, the writers of the Bible testify to concrete instances of what it means to be just, to live in harmony with concern for the common good, thus supporting the foundation of the church to have deeper relationship to the world. Rather than theorizing about justice, or goodness, or holiness in the abstract, the Bible illuminates stories of practical instances of good relationships and bad relationships, justice and injustice in the lives of people to point out specifically what God has done for God's people (as in the Old Testament), what God continues to do for all of humanity (in the event of Jesus' continued ministry in and though the Church), and God's call to the Church to continue what God does for humanity in Jesus, namely, put salvation into practice. Generally, any interpretation of biblical text is colored by the social context of the interpreter. Just as Martin Luther wrestled with the late medieval problem concerning what a just God and sinful creation meant, so the task of this contemporary time, particularly the Church in Nigeria, is just the reverse: to translate the love of God into doing of justice in the world.[54]

The Church's Mission in the World: Patristic Developments

To move beyond the biblical period and to review the Church's relationship with the world over time I will turn briefly to select representative sources relating how the early Church Fathers viewed the mission of the Church in the earliest stages of Christianity. Eric Plumer asserts that the writings of the

Apostolic Fathers are about the earliest Christian writings to win general acceptance in the Church besides the New Testament.[55] I will limit my research to consider only those writings that address specifically the concerns of the Church's relations to the world.

Although speaking of the "social teaching" of the Fathers is anachronistic, their writings reveal that even back then, they were already addressing issues relating to material things in day to day living as part of their concern for the burgeoning early Church. From his survey of the Fathers—from the Apostolic Fathers through the Cappadocians, Chrysostom, and Augustine—Justo L. Gonzalez draws the conclusion that "not one major Christian leader held that issues of faith and wealth should be kept separate."[56] To them, participation in the economic and social order was part and parcel of following Jesus. Gonzalez maintains, "in a Church beset by Gnostic notions about the evil of material creation, it was important to insist that all things, including those that are usually counted as wealth, are good."[57] Hence, the Fathers taught generally that things in themselves were not necessarily evil, but that unnecessary and superfluous accumulation and inordinate attachment to material things is one of the root causes of evil. On the whole, they embraced the principle that material things are meant to be shared and that the intended use of material things is for the common good.[58]

Suffice it to say then that Christianity at the beginning of the 2nd century still appeared to be a small Jewish sect, spread throughout the Roman Empire, which only won hearts of a sizeable population in the Empire with the passage of time. William J. Walsh and John P. Langan argue that although reasons for this success were largely social as well as theological, the radical sense of Christian community was the prime factor in its growth.[59] The flourishing sense of community and sharing in the early Church, which depended on the willingness of Christians to support those who were in need, made Christianity an attractive way of life to the followers. J. G. Gager observes:

> [This] radical sense of Christian community [was] open to all, insistent on absolute and exclusive loyalty, and concerned for every aspect of the believer's life. From the very beginning, the one distinctive gift of Christianity was this sense of community. Whether one speaks of "an age of anxiety" or "the crisis of the towns," Christian congregations provided a unique opportunity for masses of people to discover a sense of security and self-respect.[60]

In contrast to the individualistic and self-serving values of the pagan world that promoted personal might, the early Christian community upheld and promoted communal living as is reported in the Acts of the Apostles:

They devoted themselves to the teaching of the apostles and to the communal life, to the breaking of the bread and to the prayers. Awe came upon everyone, and many wonders and signs were done to the apostles. All who believed were together and had all things in common; they would sell their property and possessions and divide them among all according to each one's need. Every day they devoted themselves to meeting together in the temple area and to breaking bread in their homes. They ate their meals with exultation and sincerity of heart, praising God and enjoying favor with all the people. And every day the Lord added to their number those who were being saved. (Acts 2:42–47)

Sanks notes that the concern of the early Church was not with reforming the social structures of the Roman Empire. Rather, they emphasized, "followers of the Way should have different values and modes of behavior in the social and economic spheres of life than the surrounding pagan world."[61] Hence, Sanks continues:

Their teachings about material goods, wealth, its use, accumulation, and distribution were directed to other Christians. They did not understand Christianity to be merely a private or individual form of discipleship. Following Christ had social consequences and, hence, the Church had a social mission. The kingdom of God was their utopian symbol for a just and peaceful social order and their mission was to announce its presence, though not its fulfillment, among humans.[62]

In differentiating themselves from the rest of the society, it was implied that their lives ought to impact those who encountered or observed them. Only then would Christians be able to fulfill the charge of Jesus to be salt of the earth and light of the world, bringing light into the darkness of injustice, and oppression, becoming salt that adds a savory flavor to the bitterness of deprivation and want.

Indeed, according to Walsh and Langan, the basic view that "material goods are to meet the basic needs of all human beings" and the necessity to ensure "a fair distribution of this world's resources" was at the heart of the teaching of the Fathers.[63] Thus, the teaching of the Fathers can be understood to "constitute a message of solidarity and hope that the Church should strive to realize in its own life and that it can commend to the world as a response to the search for humane social values."[64] This solidarity and hope in the message of the Fathers should, therefore, form the basis of the Church's contemporary mission, especially in distressed circumstances of people's lives as I have outlined is the case in the situation of Nigeria.

So far, this review has attempted to answer the question: "What does the Church need to be and to do to fulfill its mission?" Biblical sources reveal that it is specifically to participate in ministries and services of healing, rescuing, restoring, and saving that Christians and, by extension, the Christian Church creates a dwelling place for the word of God in human history. This is the foundation on which the Fathers of the Church based their teaching: the sharing and community inspired by the following of Jesus should make the Church a new people with transformed values. As a result, it should become leaven in the society in which the church exists just as the early Church leavened the ancient Roman world. In the next section, I will examine briefly how this initial vision of Church became diminished, owing to the retreat of the Church from engagement with the world following the European Enlightenment.

The Church Retreats From the World: Post-Enlightenment and Post-French Revolution Developments

In the Middle Ages,[65] one of the defining feature of the church's self-understanding was "the growth of the papal monarchy and its struggle for independence from, if not domination of, the temporal power."[66] Haight states that the Gregorian reform during the second half of the eleventh century was the cap stone of this period. He notes, "The Gregorian reform provided a basis and a social historical impulse for the creation of Christendom, a unity of church, and society throughout Europe."[67] Generally, that period experienced a major influence of the papacy in civil matters and the Church assumed gradually the status of a socializing agent of society, providing and controlling services such as education. A significant development in this period for my consideration is the introduction into the Church's theology of "a mediaeval synthesis that would shape the self-understanding of Christians, especially Catholic Christians, through to the middle of the twentieth century."[68] To offer a succinct picture of the worldview this new synthesis brought upon the self-understanding of the Church in most of the Middle Ages, Haight identifies:

> Education as a socializing agency reflected and communicated to the elite the theological grounding of Christian civilization. One looked at the world theoretically and saw it organized hierarchically. The cosmos was understood to be arranged in order or levels of being that were related in a descending pattern ranging from the higher to the lower. Authority came from the top, from God and descended as it were through the ranks. For example, theocratic assumptions underlay the fact that both popes and kings justified their authority on the basis of God's will as mediated through revelation.[69]

With a well-developed bureaucracy, the Church at this time "constituted one organizational structure that effectively encompassed all of Western Europe."[70] The Western Christian worldview assumed its status at the center of all of human history—Western, including Western theological, culture.[71] In response, many countercurrents and movements in opposition to the wealth and power of the Church arose, including the Albigensians (or Pure Ones), the Waldensians (the Poor Ones of Lyons) as well as the Conciliarists who believed the church should be governed by a conciliar governance of bishops.[72] The resulting scandals of a church as its leadership was caught up in the allure of wealth and power began gradually to push it toward a call for reforms in the life of the Church. Sanks notes that the Avignon papacy and the Great Schism forced the cry for reform into a new and sharper focus, propelled by a revival of piety and spiritual movements as well as widespread discontent with the conduct of the leaders of the institutional Church.[73]

The Protestant Reformation ignited a chain of religious conflicts, especially between Protestants and Catholics, which lasted up until the time of the Vatican Council II.[74] Even as these wars raged, Europe was addressing more challenging crises posed by the "Age of Reason," or the "Enlightenment." The discovery of the New World coupled with advances in science and the consequent development of a new worldview that Europe was not the center of the world, independent of religious authority in a culture that was built on religious foundations were nothing short of declaring a revolution against the Church. "Empirical evidence and human reason replaced the Bible and church authority."[75] The emergence of rationalistic movements, scientific discoveries, and empiricism, which raged roughly from 1648 to 1789, not only alarmed Church authorities, but also sparked a siege mentality and an extremely defensive posture by the Church. This led the Church to view the world as hostile and so it began to withdraw significantly from its engagements with the world. Instead of finding ways to respond to the prevailing challenges by finding answers to the questions posed by scientific findings and historical critical method, the Catholic Church became smug and self-complacent, not regarding any need for renewal. Sanks notes:

> From the time of Constantine to the Reformation, Christianity and the culture of the known world had been integrated in the synthesis we have come to call "Christendom." With the Age of Reason, the culture began to develop independently of and even in opposition to Christianity. The church viewed this developing culture as hostile and threatening. . . . Condemnation of scientific discoveries, of philosophical movements, and of new forms of political life became the characteristic mode of ecclesial behavior.[76]

As a response to the challenge of Enlightenment, several pious and devotional movements sprang up within the Protestant and Catholic churches across Europe.[77] Pietistic communities and orders arose in Germany, calling for renewal of personal and devotional religion. In England, a similar movement broke away from the Church of England and formed the Congregational Church in the early 1600s, while another schism, in the Methodist Church, established itself in the United States by 1784.[78] Among Catholics, the most prominent of these movements, Jansenism stressed heavily personal conversion and holiness for members of the Church. Sanks emphasizes that the Jansenists, whose major opponents were the Jesuits, promoted rigorous morality and split eventually with Rome, springing forth as the "Old Catholic Church."[79] These new church-sect tensions and wars fueled by the independent worldview of the Enlightenment which raged up until the Vatican Council II, indicate the depths to which circumstances that led to a culture of the Church's withdrawal from the world, and how events of history shaped and continue to shape the self-understanding of the Church over the centuries.

The French Revolution, which to an extent, marked the end of the Age of Reason, was initially intended "to consider moderate reforms and solve financial problems."[80] However, the servant and peasant classes took this opportunity to press for more radical changes, including the abolition of "privileges due to birth and replacing the arbitrary government of the monarchy with one representing the rising middle class."[81] Since the Roman Catholic Church was an integral part of the established order, the reforms affected church life and some forms of ecclesiastical reform became incumbent. As part of the recommended reforms, in 1790, the law required "all bishops and clergy to take an oath to obey the Civil Constitution."[82] The Revolution became very anticlerical and divided the French Church between clergy who took the oath and those who did not, with an eventual effort to root out Christianity in France altogether, culminating in the enthronement of the goddess of Reason on the altar of Notre Dame Cathedral in 1793.[83]

Events of the French Revolution led the Church to view itself as being under siege; the capture of the Pope, persecution of its leadership, legality and church buildings, a vigorous anticlericalism, along with the spread of a secular worldview, all contributed to the Church beginning to believe in this siege mentality. Much of the ecclesial behavior of the time stemmed from these circumstances. Successive Popes did all they could within their leadership role to defend the Church from civil domination. However, over time, they became more preoccupied by "an increased concern with authority as a guarantor of certainty throughout the nineteenth century."[84] Amid this atmosphere the First Vatican Council was called in 1869. Not surprisingly, it basically defined papal infallibility and upheld the Syllabus of Errors.[85] This atmosphere would prevail until the death of Pius IX and the dawn of Vatican Council II.

Recent Developments in Papal Teachings: From Leo XIII to Francis

In this section, I will focus on select teachings from a sample of historical documents that are directly relevant to the mission of the Church, particularly those documents which anticipated the landmark document of Vatican Council II, *Gaudium et Spes*. I will approach them under four groupings along their historical timeline, beginning with the papacy of Leo XII, Post Leo/pre-Vatican II, *Gaudium et Spes* as a high-water mark of the Church turning and facing the world in her teaching, and lastly, Post Vatican II through Pope Francis.

An encyclical letter is derived from the Greek term, which means "a letter that goes the rounds."[86] From the letters of attestation Bishops wrote to their members while they were traveling to other places, to profess that they were in communion with their local Church, "since the sixteenth century, the title has been used to refer to papal letters concerned with doctrinal or moral matters, exhortations, warning or recommendations."[87] Encyclical letters have become a major means of passing on teachings and catechesis to the whole Church by successive popes, teaching in the name of Christ and guiding the universal church about specific issues and world events in general. I will begin by exploring the encyclicals from the era of Leo XIII.

Leo XIII

Sanks establishes that the selection of Leo as pope brought an air of openness into the Catholic Church. He observes,

> Although Leo XII himself could not be called a liberal Catholic, "his pontificate was one long and somewhat successful effort to place the Church on a new footing in regard to modern secular culture."[88]

Determined to break Catholicism loose from the rituals of medievalism and the siege mentality arising from its experiences during the Age of Reason and the French Revolution, Leo "discouraged the monarchist leanings among French Catholics, tried to restore good relations with Germany after Bismarck's attack on the church (*the Kulturkampf*), and tried to update the church intellectually."[89] Apart from allowing greater access to the Vatican archives for the purpose of research, he established a biblical commission to foster biblical research using the historical critical method.[90] Along with *Aeterni Patris,* which he penned in 1879 in which he outlined a new approach to seminary formation, instituting Neo-Scholasticism, and treating Thomism as the only acceptable Catholic philosophy/theology, Leo's *Rerum Novarum* of 1891 marked specifically a historical and a theological turning point for Catholic social thought and engagement. Leo wrote to address the inherent imbalances between the capitalist bourgeois class and the working urban proletariat class that prevailed the society in Europe at the time.

Thomas A. Shannon analyzes *Rerum Novarum* succinctly with these words:

> RN defended the right of private property (under attack by socialists), argued for a living wage for workers (rather than the contract most workers could not refuse), and affirmed the right of labor to organize and, when necessary, strike (against the major industrial interests of the day). The significance of this encyclical is not only that it spoke to the issues of the day, but also that it set in motion the tradition of popes continuing to address the social problems of the day.[91]

A specific novelty found in Leo's teaching was the clear indication that "doctrinal principles and social analysis must be used to illumine and shape social action."[92] Proposing a distinct role for the Church, Leo testifies, "It is the Church that insists, on the authority of the Gospel, upon those teaching whereby the conflict can be brought to an end, or rendered, at least, far less bitter; the Church uses her efforts not only to enlighten the mind, but to direct by her precepts the life and conduct of each and all."[93] Another novelty in Leo's teaching is that it legitimizes clearly workers' unions to serve as a bargaining tool for the rights of workers, thereby immediately blurring the line between what the Church should consider "secular social activities" versus "religious" concerns. This mode of thought has since become a more determining feature within Catholic social thought over the years.

Post Leo/Pre-Vatican II

Forty years after *Rerum Novarum,* Pius XI reiterated in *Quadragesimo Anno* (1931), the call for a fairer distribution of the world's resources which Leo had previously advocated, and furthermore, he articulated a new view that the human being be considered the measure and the center of any development and progress, calling for an integral approach to development.[94]

O'Brien and Shannon address the prevailing circumstances of the time from this perspective:

> When Leo XIII wrote in 1891, liberal capitalism was at the zenith of its power. Opting for reform rather than counterrevolution, Leo tried to nudge European Catholics away from an apparently hopeless alliance with monarchy and preindustrial feudal economic ideals toward a more promising strategy of political participation and social reform. In 1931 Pius XI faced a very different situation. World War I had shattered liberal confidence. Parliamentary democracy seemed almost helpless in the face of the mass movements of fascism and communism. And the economy of the Western world lay in the ruins of a worldwide depression. The church, better organized and more united than ever before, might be able to offer a credible alternative to a failed capitalism and a fearsome socialism.[95]

Among others, two of the most noteworthy ideas of *Quadragesimo Anno* include: the principle of subsidiarity and the notion of solidarism, or corporatism. The principle of subsidiarity insists that the state and all other associations exist for the purpose of the benefit of the individual. Societies should not assume what individuals can do, nor should larger societies undertake what smaller associations can accomplish.[96] Solidarism, or corporatism, the practical application of the principle of subsidiarity in the economic order of society simply:

> [Emphasizes] the mutual rights and duties of individuals and small groups within large, complex social organisms. . . . Just as it is wrong to take away from individuals what by their own ability and effort they can accomplish and commit it to the community, 'so, too, it is an injustice, and at the same time both a grave evil and a disturbance of right order to transfer to the larger and higher collectivity functions which can be performed and provided for by less and subordinate bodies.' This is because all social activity should 'prove a help (*subsidium*) to the members of the body social,' but never may destroy or absorb them.[97]

Solidarism has over the years been considered quite controversial, and this encyclical itself has been judged by some scholars and analysts to advocate an unsuccessful and largely ignored agenda, which attempt to "Christianize" the modern social and economic agendas.[98] Moreover, this encyclical articulated other influential forward thinking concepts, such as: social justice, the common good, and solidarity that had a great deal of influence on future developments in Catholic social thought.[99] Simply put, the overall importance of the document for its time was that society needed the Church to remember its moral obligation to challenge the day-to-day social, political, and economic conduct, which affects the daily lives of its parishioners.

John XXIII wrote *Mater et Magistra* (1961), to commemorate the seventieth anniversary of *Rerum Novarum*. This encyclical signaled a new era in Catholic social thought by pushing the discussion of social issues beyond the confines of the industrialized world of Europe and North America to include the circumstances of nonindustrialized nations, such as the Global South, and by stressing the specific necessity of the laity to take on leadership roles in living out the practical demands of the gospel message.[100] In the section of the document where John addresses specifically the "Contribution of the Church" (178–184), he indicates clearly what the role of the Church should be, and encourages active engagement of the Church for the purpose of advancing the cause of people living in weaker nations. He says, "To those sons of ours who, by promoting solicitously the progress of peoples and by spreading, as it were, a wholesome civilizing influence, everywhere demonstrate the perennial vitality of Holy Church and her effectiveness, we wish to express our paternal praise and gratitude."[101] Basically, *Mater et Magistra* emphasized distinctively "an increase of network of relations by which individuals are connected to each other," and also "argued for state intervention to ensure that property would achieve its social functions."[102] This served to affirm the principle of solidarity, a concept, which was on the cutting edge for its time.

In *Pacem in Terris*, John XXIII shared his conviction of the great potential of human beings to work together for peace on earth.[103] Issued in 1963, during the height of the Cold War between the United States of America and the Union of Soviet Socialist Republics, lived out in practice through the Cuban and the Berlin Missile Crises, this was generally a period of great international tension across the globe.[104] O'Brien and Shannon identify four key themes in the encyclical, which impacted Catholic teaching on morality and politics of peace and freedom: the rights proper to each individual, the relation between authority and conscience, disarmament, and the development of the common good.[105] Basic to these themes is the core implication that the Catholic social-ethical principle of the common good had now assumed global relevance, and individual nations discovered the spark of integrity to demand human rights, especially in nations with oppressive regimes. Most significantly "following the publication of the encyclical, Catholics in Chile, South Africa, South Korea, Poland, Guatemala, El Salvador, the Philippines, Mexico, East Timor, and elsewhere marched at the forefront of human rights movements."[106] Global world order is always in need of communities to take a stand on their behalf and this move of moral courage on the part of Catholic Church teaching in order to effectively advance the universal common good had a great deal of impact on the hearts and minds of its followers, transforming entire corrupt regimes.

Although some theological writers express disappointment in the failure of *Pacem in Terris* to address specific issues relating to nuclear deterrence, which was the preeminent burning issue at the time, this encyclical served to promote a distinct view of politics from a theological ethical perspective, and encouraged processes of persuasion and negotiation to emerge among men and women through reason and free will, in order for them to make moral choices for the common good.

Through Leo to John XXIII, the social doctrine of the Church emphasizes consistently that human beings are by nature social beings born into society with potential for development and self-actualization. The society on its part needs to be ordered in such a way that fosters the possibility of self-actualization of all humans with dignity and integrity. In simple terms, this translates as the necessity to preserve human dignity and to promote a sound social order, which results inevitably in a much-needed advancement of the quality of life and society throughout the Christian world, including in countries, such as Nigeria. These ideas became the background foundation of the remarkable tone that the Vatican Council II assumed, especially in the Pastoral Constitution on the Church in the Modern World, which called for more openness from the Church.

The Second Vatican Council, *Gaudium et Spes* (Joy and Hope), 1965

Gaudium et Spes, the Pastoral constitution on "The Church in the Modern World," marked a dramatic shift in the self-understanding of the Roman Catholic Church.[107] Emerging from the negativity of the siege mentality that characterized its ecclesial teaching and behavior throughout the 18th and 19th centuries, the document opens exhorting, "The joys and the hopes, the griefs and the anxieties of the men [sic] of this age, especially those who are poor or in any way afflicted, these too are the joys and hopes, the griefs and anxieties of the followers of Christ" (GS 1). In an unprecedented manner, a document of a council by the Roman Catholic Church "now addresses itself without hesitation, not only to the sons of the Church and to all who invoke the name of Christ, but to the whole of humanity" (GS 2).[108] In this new spirit of openess, *Gaudium et Spes* affirms the Church's "solidarity with the entire human family" and crafts an understanding of the mission of the Church in the world using specific terms to communicate its priority of continuing the work of Jesus Christ who "entered this world to give witness to the truth, to rescue and not to sit in judgement, to serve and not to be served" (GS 3).[109] Since human beings are created in the image and the likeness of God as an entity of creation that must be saved, the human person in body and soul should be the concern of the Church.

In continuing the mission of Christ in the world, therefore, the Church will no longer act of the assumptions of the past, concerned primarily with preserving the "purity" of faith content and practice, but, rather, be a Church of the modern age and of the modern humanity present in the midst of its modern social predicaments. The Church therefore, ought to seek and work to find answers to humanity's most pressing challenges: war, hunger, disease, and bad governance. Determined to move the Church's self-understanding out of its preconciliar view that conceived of the Church as a "Perfect Society" as opposed to the "City of Man," *Gaudium et Spes* crafts a more unique understanding of the Church as the People of God.[110] Specifically, this document calls the People of God, as they journey through life to become more actively involved in deciphering "authentic signs of God's presence and purpose in the happenings, needs, and desires in which this people has a part along with other men of our age" (GS 11). In order for the Church to accomplish this most effectively, the document expresses in a surprisingly profound way that the Church must be more open to "the dimensions of human culture opened up by advances in the historical, social, and psychological sciences."[111] Generally, the basic thrust of the first section of the document could be best defined as testifying to a transformation of the Council's theological anthropological understanding of humanity, and the world in which human beings live in relation to God who created humanity and the world.

The second part of the document, in acknowledging that the Church and humanity experience the same earthly situation (GS 40), it portrays that the Council Fathers were in effect recognizing that the Church indeed has the "duty of scrutinizing the signs of the times" (GS 4) in a world where scientific advancements and technology have greatly impacted the order of society and enhanced human dominion over space and time.[112] Jon Sobrino notes that the expression "signs of the times," indeed, had two meanings at the Council, saying "on the one hand, it had a *historical-pastoral* meaning: the sign of the times are 'events which characterize a period' (GS 4), and which are something new as compared with other signs of the past."[113] Significantly, he insists that the expression also "had a *historical-theologal* meaning."[114] According to him, "the signs are 'happenings, needs and desires . . . authentic signs of God's presence and purpose' (GS 11)."[115] This means, among other things, "God's presence or purpose has to be discerned in them."[116] In order words, Sobrino reveals the all-important potent elements of history that are able to manifest the presence of God in those actions that happen in the world, using the example of Latin America. The Latin American Church for Sobrino, integrated intentionally the historical-theologal approach in their ecclesial praxis. They linked the contemporary pain of the oppressed majorities of society with the pain that the suffering messiah took upon himself, and set about to work for their liberation. This offers a good example for the Nigerian Church to adopt in relation to Nigerian social reality.

While I do not intend to develop an exhaustive analysis of all the issues found in this document, it is significant to note that the document not only outlines the problems in the world, but also, most importantly crafts a path for human beings to follow in order to attain justice and equitable development in the modern world. In other words, this amounts to an inauguration of the Kingdom of God in the here and now, making manifest the presence of God in human history. Thus, the document advocates for the full participation of all people in the political life of the community:

> [It] is a duty most befitting our times that men, especially Christians, should work strenuously on behalf of certain decisions which must be made in the economic and political fields, both nationally and internationally. By these decisions universal recognition and implementation should be given to the right of all men to a human and civic culture favourable to personal dignity and free from any discrimination on the grounds of race, sex, nationality or social conditions.[117]

Encouraging the active participation of Christians in the temporal duties of society, the document says pointedly, "the Christian who neglects his temporal duties neglects his duties toward his neighbour and even God, and jeopardizes his eternal salvation" (GS 43). Unlike prior Church teachings, especially those from the eighteenth and nineteenth centuries that emphasized the "otherness" of the Church in relation to the world, *Gaudium et Spes* upholds the primacy of God's active presence in history. It emphasizes that through announcing the Kingdom of God, the Church is also called to perform certain specific tasks to aid in its coming through providing programs which enable integral development of social, economic, political, cultural and religious arenas of human life even as humanity awaits the eternal life to come (*Cf.* GS 43). This document has formed the basis of all subsequent teachings of the Church on questions related to social justice.

In retrospect, the question comes to mind as to how much the Church has adopted the intuitive framework of *Gaudium et Spes* into its praxis over the years. Sanks establishes an important caveat in the appropriation of the intuition of Vatican II using the Latin American Church as a case study. Making a distinction of that Church for taking the call of the Council seriously, he notes:

> By the time the second CELAM conference convened in Medellín in 1968, they had begun to read the "signs of the times" for the Latin American continent. They realized that the dialogue partner for the theology of Vatican II had been the nonbeliever of the Western European World. It became very clear that the situation in Latin America was quite different. There they were concerned not with the *nonbeliever*, but with the *nonperson*.[118]

Similar to the situation of the Church in Latin America, in which their Bishops "discovered," the "modern world" to be in need of addressing the root cause of abject poverty of their parishioners over and against the greed of their elite patrons, most of Africa today, especially in Nigeria, it is not the world of the nonbeliever controlled by science and technology but, rather, a world of refugees and orphans occasioned by violent sects, a world of poverty of the greater majority that makes them nonpersons when a tiny few wealthy play gods through their ill-gotten wealth. This is a world in which millions are dying from preventable disease and mass illiteracy. The review in chapter three, will expose a picture of Latin America to identify how Vatican Council II decisions were received there, especially the intuitive framework of *Gaudium et Spes*, in order to glean what lessons the Church in Nigeria can draw from it, especially in view of the many circumstances that these two parts of the world share in common. I will zero in on the Latin American nation of El Salvador to see how Vatican II inspired Archbishop Romero in his courageous ministry, as well as theologian Ignacio Ellacuría to articulate a practical theology of the church as a historical sacrament of liberation. Meanwhile, I will research universal level magisterial teachings from the time after Vatican II, exploring most especially those documents that appropriated the openness of *Gaudium et Spes* in engaging the social realities of contemporary society.

Post *Gaudium et Spes*: Paul VI, John Paul II, Benedict XVI, and Francis

Paul VI succeeded John XXIII when the pope who convoked Vatican Council II died in 1963. Following John XXIII, Paul VI issued the encyclical *Populorum Progressio* (1967), which expanded the scope of Leo XIII's treatment of the issue of inequality between rich and poor individuals as a reflection of the conflict between rich and poor nations.[119] His visits to Latin America, Africa, the Holy Land, and India opened his eyes to the reality of poverty and sub-human living conditions in those nations and this prompted him to call the attention of the international community to the painful reality of global poverty.[120]

Sketching a specifically Christian vision for international development, Paul insisted that the Church must seek to be an actor in that realm to challenge the powers that be to foster human progress in response to the Gospel of Jesus (PP 12). In a striking manner, the pope articulated clearly, "the Church was founded to establish on earth the kingdom of Heaven,"[121] emphasizing that development cannot be limited to economic growth but, rather, must look to encompass total and holistic human development.[122] To pursue the goal of the integral development of all people, the Church must exhort the nations of the world to join hands in collaboration and more particularly in the struggle against injustice, which was a common feature of many nations, especially in the two-thirds world.

In *Octogesima Adveniens*, written on the eightieth anniversary of *Rerum Novarum* in 1971, Paul VI directed this document specifically to Catholics, urging them to incorporate more seriously a new sense of Christian responsibility in the world into all phases of their lives.[123] Specifically, he stressed the role of individual Christian and local churches in responding to situations of injustice. Christine E. Gudorf notes that "this Apostolic Letter was an open letter to Cardinal Maurice Roy, then president of the Council on the Laity and the Pontifical Commission on Justice and peace."[124] Here, DeBerri, offers a succinct summary of the document:

> [The Apostolic Letter] initially reviewed the social teaching that had been developed in *Rerum novarum's* trajectory and then proceeded to examine recent changes in the world that required further development in the Church's social teaching. Virtually all analysts agree that the most distinctive innovations in OA revolved around a pronounced shift from economic to political perspectives in the pursuit of justice, accompanied by a related shift from claims of universal authority in the magisterium to expectations that solutions emerge from local contexts.[125]

At the heart of this document is an appeal for inclusion of individuals from all walks of life in decision-making processes that affect their lives in society.[126] This is an essential mark of the Church's call for a deeper sense of respect, which informs human dignity and freedom. Paul argues that the realities of political society demand that all people must have "a greater sharing in responsibility and in decision-making."[127] These foundations for the common good make integral development of the person more reasonable and more civil, and should become the characteristic of the basis for all human societies and political and economic governance. Besides this document revealing that the Church must provide a clearer openness to the world, the actual travels of Paul VI to various parts of the world were an important gesture to illustrate the universality of the Church in very practical terms. These travels enabled Paul to note, in person, the concerns of people beyond Rome and Europe. His realization was that the Church needs perpetually to go out and meet people where they are to become more aware of the actual lived contexts of their joys and pains.

The Synod of Bishops, established at the Second Vatican Council, issued the document *Justitia in Mundo,* in 1971 as a product of their reflections on the theme, "The Mission of the People of God to Further Justice in the World."[128] The document, apart from creating implicitly an illumination of the maturity of native leadership in the Churches of Africa, Asia, and Latin America post-Vatican II, affirmed the basic thrust of *Gaudium et Spes,* insisting, "Gospel principles mandate justice for the liberation of all humanity as an essential expression of Christian love. The Church must witness for justice through its own lifestyle, educational activities, and international action."[129] It is instructive that the document refers to structures of injustice and oppression in the language of sin and views the struggle for a just society as, indeed, part of Christian witness:

> Action on behalf of justice and participation in the transformation of the world fully appear to us as a constitutive dimension of the preaching of the Gospel, or, in other words, of the Church's mission for the redemption of the human race and its liberation from every oppressive situation.[130]

The entire document refutes consistently the tendency to separate "working to create a just society" from "religious" duties and obligations. Poignantly, the Bishops upheld the right and duty of the Church to proclaim justice on all levels and to denounce unjust situations.

On September 14, 1981, John Paul II issued *Laborem Exercens* to commemorate the ninetieth anniversary of the publication of *Rerum Novarum,* shifting the focus of the Church's reflection on the "social question" from the relationship between capital and labour, to the understanding of work as an integrative force that shapes an individual's identity, character, and dignity.[131] This encyclical views that the human person is the measure for determining the effectiveness and quality of work, insisting, "the sources of the dignity of work are to be sought primarily in the subjective dimension, not in the objective one."[132] Iber notes that the encyclical intended to develop a specific spirituality for work in order to enable the Church to uphold and encourage the role of individuals in the family, local workers unions, Churches, civil society groups as legitimizing these groups in building relationships to promote the dignity of persons in society.[133]

Ten years later, John Paul again recalled *Rerum Novarum*, on its centenary anniversary, with the encyclical *Centesimus Annus* (1991). This time, he offered "both a look back at the *res novae*, the "new things" that seized the attention of Leo XIII, and a look ahead at what "the new things" were at the end of the twentieth century and the turn of the third Christian millennium."[134] At a time when most Eastern Europe socialist states had collapsed with the end of the Cold War and the end of the Persian Gulf War, the current issue concerned the weakening of oppressive regimes in Africa, Asia, and Latin America and the hope for "new things" within the social order. In the encyclical:

> John Paul addresses both the dramatic changes undermining communism in Eastern Europe and the necessary choices by newly liberated nations concerning alternative economic systems. More thoroughly than any of his predecessors, he engages the arguments surrounding Western capitalism. He condemns Eastern European socialism but holds out hope for capitalism if it accords with the requirements of justice. He criticizes the consumerist culture in the West and the tendency of capitalism to take unfair advantage of working people. His encyclical is a strong call for both personal and institutional renewal.[135]

Outstanding in its empirical sensitivity, this encyclical shifted the discussion of social questions from material dimensions of the imbalances in wealth distribution to recognize the inherent good of the contribution of human creativity and imagination, and specifically to demand that political and economic systems support frameworks to unleash that creativity and imagination, rather than with "resources" per se.[136] Indeed, John Paul thought carefully about what does and does not work with regards to exercising a "preferential option for the poor" especially in these new democracies in the Third World

and in impoverished parts of the developed world. The Pope, therefore, outlined a more comprehensive overview of Catholic social teaching as well as
a practical application of these key points to address specific issues of concern.[137] His leadership offering wise counsel and practical steps for prudent
action underscores the role of the Church in offering a human face to political
and economic policies and institutions. These principles of social engagement
draw their inspiration from the basic teaching of *Gaudium et Spes*.

In line with his predecessors, Benedict XVI explored the interplay between love and commitment to social justice in *Caritatis in Veritate*, which
was issued in 2009.[138] To overturn the inherent imbalances and exclusiveness
characterizing the present global economy, nations of the world were challenged to join hands in solidarity, especially to create conscious development
efforts to address the disadvantages of poorer nations. He notes:

> In these countries, it is very important to move ahead with projects based on subsidi-
> arity, suitably planned and managed, aimed at affirming rights yet also providing for
> the assumption of corresponding responsibilities. In development programmes, the
> principle of the centrality of the human person, as the subject primarily responsible
> for development must be preserved. The principal concern must be to improve the
> actual living conditions of the people in a given region, this enabling them to carry
> out those duties which their poverty does not presently allow them to fulfil. Social
> concern must never be an abstract attitude.[139]

Building on the teachings of his predecessors, the document stresses the importance of personal growth of the individual as the heart of any meaningful
development; calling for a "shared commitment to working for justice and
peace of the human family" (CV 57) in order to promote human dignity. Ac-
cordingly, it maintains that while socio-economic matters may not be a direct
area of competence for the Church, "every economic decision has a moral
consequence" (CV 37), and so should concern the Church. Thus, Benedict
contends:

> Charity in truth, in this case, requires that shape and structure be given to those types
> of economic initiative which, without rejecting profit, aim at a higher goal than the
> mere logic of the exchange of equivalents, of profit as an end in itself.[140]

In very practical terms, he suggests that aid programs in developing nations
should involve the whole community in active participation at the grassroots
so that aid does not hurt those for whom it is intended.

Francis' first encyclical, *Lumen Fidei,* written in part by his predecessor, Benedict, dwells on the theme of faith as light with the function to illuminate human existence to distinguish between good and evil to help all people make right choices in society.[141] In assessing the world's economy, an echo of the call of *Gaudium et Spes,* he ascents that the Church should share the joys and sorrows of society. Francis explains that there is a valuable link between faith and the common good, which enables men and women to create an environment of love to nourish their life together, something much needed in the present world:

> Faith does not draw us away from the world or prove irrelevant to the concrete concerns of the men and women of our time. . . . Faith is truly a gift for everyone; it is a common good. Its light does not simply brighten the interior of the Church, nor does it serve solely to build an eternal city in the hereafter; it helps us build our societies in such a way that they can journey towards a future hope. The Letter to the Hebrews offers an example in this regard when it names, among the men and women of faith, Samuel and David, whose faith enabled them to "administer justice" (*Heb* 11:33). This expression refers to their justice in governance, to that wisdom which brings peace to the people (*cf. 1 Sam* 12:3–5; *2 Sam* 8:15).[142]

To create such a world, against the prevalence of contemporary individualism, Francis stresses the role of just forms of government that recognize that all authority comes from God. As God's agents on earth therefore, their role is one that must be dedicated to serving the common good, offering their leadership to open possibilities for forgiveness that lead people to overcome conflict and live in harmony. This premise the mediating role Francis has been playing in the Middle East and many other places across the globe where the Church is involved in peace-making.

In his latest encyclical, *Laudato Si,* Francis sheds light on the intimate, yet extremely complex relationship between integral human ecology and nature, reiterating that the choices of a consumer culture affect the poor most acutely; and when we fail to care responsibly for God's creation, the poor who are those who are the most affected (LS 16). The Pope emphasizes that the world is a gift: "We are not God. The earth was here before us and it has been given to us" (LS 67). So, all of us are responsible to preserve nature and to live responsibly so our choices do not degrade or destroy the sanctity of the environment, posing a danger to the life and health of others. In an obvious reference to world powers, who drive the global economy and power brokers, who push their agenda and interests even at the cost of the lives of the poor, the Holy Father cautions:

A spirituality which forgets God as all-powerful and Creator is not acceptable. That is how we end up worshipping earthly powers, or ourselves usurping the place of God, even to the point of claiming an unlimited right to trample his creation underfoot. The best way to restore men and women to their rightful place, putting an end to their claim to absolute dominion over the earth, is to speak once more of the figure of a Father who creates and who alone owns the world. Otherwise, human beings will always try to impose their own laws and interests on reality. [143]

Apart from spelling out the obligations of world powers that the comity of nations, multinational drivers of the global economy, and other organizations have toward overcoming the challenges of environmental degradation, Francis, above all, indicates the important contributions that individuals and organizations in civil society can make in this regard, especially in nations with weak enforcement of law and order. He notes:

While the existing world order proves powerless to assume its responsibilities, local individuals and groups can make a real difference … Because the enforcement of laws is at times inadequate due to corruption, public pressure has to be exerted in order to bring about decisive political action. Society, through nongovernmental organizations and intermediate groups, must put pressure on governments to develop more rigorous regulations, procedures and control. [144]

This is a clear demonstration of the need of the Church to be present in the society to face and address the concerns of society. Francis is calling the Church to meet people where they are in their day-to-day challenges.

Generally, concern for the plight of the marginalized—the outcasts—has been at the center of the ministry of Francis. At a mass to open the Vatican's *Caritas Internationalis* general assembly at St Peter's Basilica on Tuesday May 12, 2015, the Pope said, "We must do what we can so that everyone has something to eat, but we must also remind the powerful of the Earth that God will call them to judgment one day, and there it will be revealed if they really tried to provide for him in every person and if they did what they could to preserve the environment so that it could produce this food." [145] Earlier in his pontificate, the Pope lamented, "The times talk to us of so much poverty in the world and this is a scandal. Poverty in the world is a scandal. In a world where there is so much wealth, so many resources to feed everyone, it is unfathomable that there are so many hungry children, that there are so many children without an education, so many poor persons. Poverty today is a cry." [146]

Typical of Francis' sensitivity to those "excluded," the first group of Cardinals he appointed included those from small countries, such as: Haiti, Burkina

Faso, Nicaragua and Ivory Coast, indicating the Pope prioritizes embracing all parts of the world as equal children of God. In a statement on Tuesday November 26, 2013, Francis, in what appeared to be his agenda for the mission of the Church, said:

> I prefer a church which is bruised, hurting and dirty because it has been out on the streets, rather than a church which is unhealthy from being confined and from clinging to its own security. I do not want a church concerned with being at the center and then ends up by being caught up in a web of obsessions and procedures.[147]

His posture assumes a significant status when it is viewed within the larger context of the history of the mission of the Church in the world, at a time when the Church seems to have taken up defending its privileges and aligning itself with the established order and interested in benefitting from the many possibilities of earthly power.

A significant detail of Francis' pontificate has been his openness to identify the Church more concretely with the tenets of Liberation Theology, which gained its most significant following during the 1960s and 1970s among Latin Americans to protest inequality and bloody repression that characterized the experience of the people living on that continent. A key gesture in this direction was to invite Gustavo Gutiérrez, the founder of Liberation Theology, to serve as one of the main speakers at a recent gathering of the Vatican's charity arm, *Caritas Internationalis*, and to appear at an official Vatican press conference launching the assembly on Tuesday May 12, 2015.[148] Considering that the Vatican officials had overtly avoided associating with Gutiérrez and many other champions of Liberation Theology official church functions in the recent past in order to give a clear signal of the Church's disassociation with the movement, this was not an insignificant move on the part of Francis. Recently, not only did he beatify Archbishop Oscar Romero, but also, he declared openly that his own brothers, other Catholic bishops and clergy had persecuted Romero because he choose to stand on the side of his people in the midst of their pains while apparently those who persecuted him chose to stand with the oppressors.[149] Francis' ministry demonstrates to a greater degree one who is inspired by the call of the Vatican Council II to be a Church that serves, and not one that is served. This is the call to which this essay testifies, calling the Church in Nigeria to imbibe the spirit of Vatican II, most especially the openness of *Gaudium et Spes* in the seminary training program as well as in witnessing and living out the social gospel and liberation theology for Nigerians struggling from injustices.

What Lessons for Church and Salvation in Nigeria?

This review specifically indicates that to avoid or retreat from the world not only deviates from the initial drive of the Church, but also creates a dangerous and destructive Church practice. The early Christian community in Jerusalem for example, attracted followers precisely because of the attention it gave to the needy. Proposing that the Church engage more actively in the world enables its leaders to address some of the fears that diminish the Church's mission. This is what the Church in Nigeria needs to imbibe; the values of Christianity are meant so the Church serves as a leaven in society where all live as children of God and care for one another.

This vision of Church implies that its priority is to be in service to the world. When the Church turns to serve itself and to preserve its material privileges, then it misses the mark of its purpose in self-pursuit. To work to establish a just society that upholds the dignity of all, the Church must understand its call to be a sign in the world of what a truly just society can be, and this is the essential thrust of the social teachings of the Church. This was the call of the Vatican Council II, reflecting that the Church as a body and that individual Christians should connect their religious hope to hope and action for a more just world. The Latin American Church responded to this call at Medellín, and just such an understanding of Christianity has been maturing on that continent over the years since that time. To explore how the Nigerian Catholic Church ought to reconsider of the relationship between the Church to the world, I will now turn to reflect on a church whose experience bears some family resemblance to the situation in my homeland of Nigeria – the Catholic Church in El Salvador.

Notes

1. Cf. Norman Tanner, *The Church and the World: Gaudium et Spes, Inter Mirifica* Rediscovering Vatican II Series (New York: Paulist Press, 2005).
2. William T. Cavanaugh, *Migration of the Holy: God, State, and the Political Meaning of the Church* (Grand Rapids: William B. Eerdmans Publishing Company, 2011), 42.
3. *Ibid.* 43.
4. Archbishop Oscar Romero, *Voice of the Voiceless: The Four Pastoral Letters and Other Statements* Trans. Micahel J. Walsh (Maryknoll, New York: Orbis Books, 2001). Romero's second Pastoral Letter is entitled "The Church, the Body of Christ in History."
5. Avery Dulles, *Models of Church* (New York: Doubleday, 2002), 63.
6. DS. 1639.

7. DS. 3315, 3857–3860, 1262, 1312, 1617, 1660, 1529, 1608, 3544.

8. Dulles, *Models of Church*, 59.

9. J. G. Gager, *Kingdom and Community: The Social World of Early Christianity* (Englewood Cliffs, N. J. 1976), and William J. Walsh, S. J. and John P. Langan, S. J., "Patristic Social Consciousness—The Church and the Poor," in *Faith that Does Justice: Examining the Christian Sources for Social Change*. Edited by John C. Haughey (New York: Paulist Press, 1977), 113 ff.

10. Cavanaugh, *Migration of the Holy*, 57.

11. Henri de Lubac, *Catholicism and the Common Destiny of Man* (London: Burns and Oats 1950), 29.

12. Karl Rahner, *Foundations of Christian Faith* (New York: The Crossroad Publishing, 1978), 322.

13. Yves Congar, *The Church that I love*, translated by Lucien Delafuente (New Jersey: Dimension Books, 1962). Chapter two of the book is specifically titled "The Church, Universal Sacrament of Salvation" and treats in depth the view presented above. See also Edward Schillebeeckx, *Christ the Sacrament of Encounter with God* (New York: Sheed and Ward, 1987).

14. Ignacio Ellacuría, "The Church of the Poor, Historical Sacrament of Liberation." trans. Margaret D. Wilde, in Ignacio Ellacuría & Jon Sobrino, *Mysterium Liberationis: Fundamental Concepts of Liberation Theology* (Maryknoll: Orbis Books, 1993), 543–64.

15. Roger Haight, *Christian Community in History* Vol. 1, 2.

16. Vatican II Dogmatic Constitution on Divine Revelation, *Dei Verbum* no. 24.

17. See Ellacuría, "The Church of the Poor, Historical Sacrament of Liberation."

18. Reinder Bruinsma, *The Body of Christ: A Biblical Understanding of Church* (Maryland: Review and Herald, 2009), 20–27.

19. *Ibid.*

20. Bruinsma, *The Body of Christ*, 22.

21. See 1971 Extraordinary Assembly of the Synod of Bishops, *Justitia in mundo*.

22. Stephen Smith, *Saving Salvation: The Amazing Evolution of Grace* (Harrisburg, Pennsylvania: Morehouse, 2005), 12.

23. Ellacuría, "The Historicity of Christian Salvation." trans. Margaret D. Wilde, in Ignacio Ellacuría, & Jon Sobrino, *Mysterium Liberationis: Fundamental Concepts of Liberation Theology* (Maryknoll, New York: Orbis Books, 1993) 256.

24. *Ibid.* 256–59.

25. Ellacuría, "On Liberation," *Essays on History, Liberation, and Salvation* ed. Michael E. Lee (Maryknoll: Orbis Books, 2013), 42.

26. T. D. Hanks, *God so Loved the Third World* (New York: Orbis Books, 1984), 6.

27. See Bernard Anderson, *Understanding the Old Testament* (New Jersey: Prentice-Hall, 1975), 8–10; and Brevard Childs, *The Book of Exodus* (Philadelphia: Westminster Press, 1974), 240–53.

28. Smith, *Saving Salvation*, 13.

29. John R Donahue, "Biblical Perspectives on Justice" in *Faith that Does Justice: Examining the Christian Sources for Social Change*. Ed. John C. Haughey (New York: Paulist Press, 1977), 69.

30. David J. Pleins, *The Social Visions of the Hebrew Bible: A Theological Introduction* (Louisville, Kentucky: Westminster John Knox Press, 2001), 217. For a wider treatment of social ethics question, see Walter Rauschenbusch, *Christianity and the Social Crisis* (New York: Macmillan, 1910), and his, *A Theology for the Social Gospel*, Library of Theological Ethics edition (Louisville, Kentucky: Westminster John Knox Press, 1997).
31. Pleins, *The Social Visions of the Hebrew Bible*, 213–277.
32. Donahue, "Biblical Perspectives on Justice," 73.
33. Vatican II, *Dei Verbum*, # 16.
34. Cavanaugh, *Migration of the Holy*, 105. Cavanaugh here develops similar ideas as held by Gerhard Lohfink, *Deos God Need the Church? Toward a Theology of the People of God*, translated by Linda M. Maloney (Collegeville, MN: Liturgical Press, 1999).
35. Pleins, *The Social Visions of the Hebrew Bible*, 257–9.
36. Ellacuría, *Essays on History, Liberation, and Salvation*, 195.
37. Pleins, *The Social Visions of the Hebrew Bible*, 257–9.
38. *Ibid.* 259.
39. Edward Schillebeeckx, *Christ: The Experience of Jesus as the Lord*, Translated by John Bowden (New York: Crossroad Publishing Company, 1983), 477.
40. *Ibid.* 447.
41. Haight, *Jesus Symbol of God* (Maryknoll, New York: Orbis Books, 1999), 75. Part II of the volume is specifically dedicated to Biblical sources for appropriating Jesus in Christology and offers excellent analysis of Jesus' social ministry.
42. *Ibid.* 167.
43. *Ibid.* 80.
44. Much has been written about the earthly ministry of Jesus and the early Church's mission as a continuation of the kingdom that Jesus inaugurated, giving rise to intense debate on the "historical Jesus." Delving into that debate is beyond the scope of this work. I will rather limit myself to certain elements of the Jesus tradition, which scholars agree are connected legitimately to Jesus' earthly mission, especially its roots in the Old Testament's view of salvation as the heart of Jesus' ministry, and its connection with the here and now.
45. Smith, *Saving Salvation*, 24.
46. N. Perrin, *The Kingdom of God in the Teaching of Jesus* (London: SCM Press, 1963), 74–87 as quoted by John R. Donahue "Biblical Perspectives on Justice," 86.
47. Donahue "Biblical Perspectives on Justice," 86.
48. *Ibid.*
49. *Ibid.*
50. *Ibid.*
51. Henrique Pinto, "Isaiah 61: 1–2a in Liberation Theology," in *African Christian Studies* Vol. 5 no. 2 (June 1989), 20.
52. Donahue "Biblical Perspectives on Justice," 87.
53. *Ibid.*
54. *Ibid.* 86.
55. Eric Plumer, "The Development of Ecclesiology: Early Church to the Reformation," in *The Gift of the Church: A Textbook on Ecclesiology* (Collegeville, Minnesota: Liturgical Press, 2000), 23.

56. Justo L. Gonzalez, *Faith and Wealth: A History of Early Christian Ideas on the Origin, Significance, and Use of Money* (San Francisco: Harper & Row, 1990) 225.

57. *Ibid.* 226.

58. *Ibid.* 227–229.

59. William J. Walsh, S. J. and John P. Langan, S. J., "Patristic Social Consciousness—The Church and the Poor," in *Faith that Does Justice: Examining the Christian Sources for Social Change.* Edited by John C. Haughey (New York: Paulist Press, 1977), 113.

60. J. G. Gager, *Kingdom and Community: The Social World of Early Christianity* (Englewood Cliffs, N. J. 1976) 140, as quoted by Walsh, S. J. and Langan, S. J., "Patristic Social Consciousness—The Church and the Poor," 113.

61. Sanks, "The Social Mission of the Church: Its Changing Context" in *The Gift of the Church: A Textbook on Ecclesiology* (Collegeville, Minnesota: Liturgical Press, 2000), 271.

62. *Ibid.*

63. Walsh, S. J. and John P. Langan, S. J., "Patristic Social Consciousness—The Church and the Poor," 114–16.

64. *Ibid.*

65. I use this designation as employed by R. W. Southern, to include the period "from the age of Bede to that of Luther, from the effective replacement of the imperial by papal authority in the West in the eighth century to the fragmentation of that authority in the sixteenth, from cutting of political ties between eastern and western Europe to Europe's breaking out into the wider western world beyond the seas." See his *Western Society and Church in the Middle Ages*, Pelican History of the Church, Vol. 2 (London: Penguin Books, 1970), 24.

66. Sanks, *Salt, Leaven and Light*, 72.

67. Haight, *Christian Community in History*, Vol. 1, 280.

68. *Ibid.* 281.

69. *Ibid.* 282.

70. *Ibid.* 339.

71. David Tracy, *On Naming the Present: God, Hermeneutics, and Church*, Concilium Series (Maryknoll: Orbis Books, 1994), 3.

72. For a detailed treatment of these movements and their import in this period, see Sanks, *Salt, Leaven and Light*, 72–78.

73. *Ibid.* 86. *Cf.* Haight 415–6.

74. Sanks, *Salt, Leaven and Light*, 91–3. This section relies extensively on chapter two of Sank's account titled: "Recalling Our Story: Catholic Reform and Reaction."

75. *Ibid.* 192. Galileo's telescope in 1609 initiated not just a new way of viewing the cosmos, but most importantly the place of the human person in the cosmos.

76. *Ibid.* 94.

77. *Ibid.* 95.

78. *Ibid.*

79. *Ibid.*

80. *Ibid.* 97.

81. *Ibid.*

82. *Ibid.*

83. *Ibid.* 98.

84. *Ibid.* 100.

85. *Ibid.*

86. Iber, *The Principle of Subsidiarity in Catholic Social Thought*, 35.

87. Rodger Charles, *Christian Social Witness and Teaching, Vol. 2.* (Gracewing: Fowler Wright Books, 1998), 12.

88. Sanks, *Salt, Leaven and Light*, 110.

89. *Ibid.*

90. *Ibid.*

91. Thomas A. Shannon, "Commentary on *Rerum Novarum* (The Condition of Labor)," in *Modern Catholic Social Teaching: Commentaries and Interpretations* edited by Kenneth R. Himes, O. F. M. (Washington D. C.: Georgetown University Press, 2005), 127.

92. David J. O'Brien and Thomas A. Shannon, eds. *Catholic Social Thought: Documentary Heritage.* Expanded Edition (Maryknoll: Orbis Books, 2010), 9. All papal social encyclicals discussed in this chapter will be quoted from this text unless otherwise stated.

93. *Rerum Novarum* 13, as quoted by O'Brien and Thomas A. Shannon, eds. *Catholic Social Thought.*

94. Iber, *The Principle of Subsidiarity in Catholic Social Thought*, 43.

95. O'Brien and Shannon, eds. *Catholic Social Thought: Documentary Heritage*, 41.

96. See *Quadragesimo Anno* 79–80 for a full statement of the principle, and for a detailed treatment and analysis, see Iber, *The Principle of Subsidiarity in Catholic Social Thought*, particularly Chapter 2.

97. Christine Firer Hinze, "Commentary on *Quadragesimo anno* (After Forty Years)," in *Modern Catholic Social Teaching: Commentaries and Interpretations.* 160–161.

98. *Ibid.* 171.

99. *Ibid.*

100. Marvin L. Mich, "Commentary on *Mater et magistra* (Christianity and Social Progress)," in *Modern Catholic Social Teaching: Commentaries and Interpretations.* 191.

101. *Ibid.* 118–119.

102. O'Brien and Shannon, eds. *Catholic Social Thought: Documentary Heritage*, 85.

103. Iber, *The Principle of Subsidiarity in Catholic Social Thought*, 61.

104. O'Brien and Shannon, eds. *Catholic Social Thought: Documentary Heritage*, 135.

105. *Ibid.*

106. Drew Christiansen, S. J., "Commentary on *Pacem in terris* (Peace on Earth)," in *Modern Catholic Social Teaching: Commentaries and Interpretations.* 217.

107. Sanks, *Salt, Leaven and Light*, 129–33.

108. *Ibid.* 130.

109. *Ibid.*

110. *Ibid.*

111. Donald R. Campion, S. J., "The Church Today," an introduction to the constitution in Abbott, *Documents of Vatican II*, 185 as quoted by Sanks, *Salt, Leaven and Light*, 130.

112. Campion S. J., "The Church Today," 185.

113. Sobrino, *Jesus the Liberator* 25.

114. According to Burke, the *theologal* is related to but distinct from the *theological*. The latter deals with the study, formulation, and explication of the divine, while the former attempts

to express the implicit "God dimension" of reality. Basically, it implies the sense that through our sentient intellection, we apprehend real things that exist on their own apart from us. Cf. Burke, *The Ground Beneath the Cross*, 40 & 48.

115. Sobrino, *Jesus the Liberator* 25.
116. *Ibid.*
117. *Gaudium et Spes*, 60.
118. Sanks, *Salt, Leaven and Light*, 168.
119. Iber, *The Principle of Subsidiarity in Catholic Social Thought*, 67.
120. *Ibid.*
121. *Populorum Progressio* 13, as quoted by Edward P. DeBerri et al, eds. *Catholic Social Teaching: Our Best Kept Secret*, Fourth Revised and Expanded Edition (Maryknoll, New York: Orbis Books, 2003) 68–72.
122. *Ibid.* 68–72.
123. O'Brien and Shannon, eds. *Catholic Social Thought: Documentary Heritage*, 278.
124. Christine E. Gudorf, "Commentary on *Octogesima adveniens* (A Call to Action on the Eightieth Anniversary of Rerum novarum)," in *Modern Catholic Social Teaching: Commentaries and Interpretations*, 315.
125. DeBerri *et al.* eds. *Catholic Social Teaching: Our Best Kept Secret*, 73.
126. Iber, *The Principle of Subsidiarity in Catholic Social Thought*, 69.
127. *Octogesima Adveniens* 47, as quoted by Iber, *The Principle of Subsidiarity in Catholic Social Thought*, 69.
128. Synod of Bishops, *Justitia in Mundo*, 1971 as quoted by DeBerri *et al.* eds. *Catholic Social Teaching: Our Best Kept Secret*, 76.
129. *Ibid.*
130. *Ibid.* 77.
131. Iber, *The Principle of Subsidiarity in Catholic Social Thought*, 70. John Paul II issued several encyclicals but I am limiting my research to the two that share an overview of his treatment of the social questions. Detailed accounts of his numerous letters have been published chronologically by many others.
132. *Ibid.*
133. *Ibid.* 72.
134. George Weigel, "The Virtues of Freedom: *Centesimus Annus* (1991)," in *Building the Free Society: Democracy, Capitalism, and Catholic Social Teaching*, edited by George Weigel and Robert Royal (Grand Rapids: William B. Eeerdmans Publishing Company, 1993), 207.
135. Daniel Finn, "Commenatary on *Centesimus annus* (On the Hundredth Anniversary of Rerum *novarum*)," in *Modern Catholic Social Teaching: Commentaries and Interpretations*, 436.
136. O'Brien and Shannon, eds. *Catholic Social Thought: Documentary Heritage*, 469.
137. *Ibid.*
138. Benedict XVI, Encyclical Letter *Caritatis In Veritate*, (Vaticana: Libereria Editrice, 2009).
139. *Ibid.* # 47.
140. *Ibid.* # 38.
141. Cf. Francis, Encyclical Letter *Lumen Fidei*, (Vaticana: Libereria Editrice, 2013) # 4.
142. *Ibid.* # 51.
143. Francis, Encyclical Letter *Laudato Si*, (Vaticana: Libereria Editrice, 2015) # 75.

144. *Ibid.* # 79.

145. Holy Mass for the Opening of the General Assembly of Caritas Internationalis Accessed November 20, 2015; available from http://w2.vatican.va/content/francesco/en/homilies/2015.

146. Pope Francis, Meeting with Students of Jesuit Schools, June 7, 2013. Accessed May 12, 2015; available from http://www.vatican.va/holy_father/Francesco/speeches/2013.

147. Pope Francis, "No More Business as Usual" CNN's Belief blog http://religion.blogs.cnn.com accessed December 6, 2013.

148. "Caritas Internationalis briefs Journalists on General Assembly" http://www.news.va/en/news/caritas-internationalis-briefs-journalists accessed May 31, 2015.

149. See Nicole Winfied, "Pope Denounces Priests, Bishops who 'defamed' Oscar Romero," Associated Press, http://www.ap.org accessed November 20, 2015. Nicole reports that at the weekly general audience in St. Peter's Square at the Vatican, Wednesday, October 28, 2015, "Pope Francis strongly denounced the Catholic priests and bishops who 'defamed' Salvadoran Archbishop Oscar Romero after his murder in a campaign that delayed his beatification until earlier this year." Speaking off-the-cuff to a group of Salvadoran bishops and pilgrims who traveled to Rome to thank the pope for beatifying the champion of the oppressed, the pope said Romero continued to be murdered even in death by his colleagues, in what appears to be a tacit reference to the holding up of Romero's sainthood for years by the Vatican, "primarily due to opposition from conservative Latin American churchmen."

· 3 ·

INTERPRETING THE CHURCH IN ACTION

Icons and Martyrs

This chapter reviews the responses of the Catholic Church and other church bodies to the ferment of liberation that permeated Latin America from the late 1960s to present, comparing it with the experiences of parts of Eastern Europe, Asia, and Africa. It will illustrate the significant new social orientation of the Catholic Church towards the historical reality of Latin America in the past few decades, which I characterize as an active interpretation of the mission of the Church as the body of Christ in history.[1] The majority of the population of Latin America, which was once considered predominantly Catholic, is distinguished by the experience of entrenched poverty and injustice.[2] In response, the Second Vatican Council (1962–1965) inspired a spiral of changes in religious practices, belief systems, and political institutions across the region.[3] These changes altered the contours of that society and inspired new understandings and interpretations of the Christian Gospel. A combination of intra- and extraecclesial pressures compelled the Catholic Church to question its role as a pillar of support for oppressive regimes and the oligarchy in most of Latin America.[4]

Paul E. Sigmund notes the change in the Latin American Catholic Church from hierarchical to pluralistic orientation, in which there were, introduced a variety of political ideas, ideologies and movements based explicitly on the Christian message.[5] This new way of thinking sparked striking innovations, from liberation theology to progressive forms of grass-roots religious/social life, and an appreciable embrace of integrating religion and politics by religious bodies. This awakening gave rise to a transformed moral vocabulary. Thus, situations, such as: like inadequate housing, malnutrition, limited access to health care and education, the lack of clean drinking water, unemployment and underemployment, high infant mortality, and channels for political participation that characterize the poor living conditions in Latin America are no longer considered to be the will of God, but viewed as resulting from sinful human action.[6] I will take time later to comment on the comparable situation taking place in Nigeria.

Venezuelan professor, Otto Maduro, observes that no religion exists in a vacuum.[7] Since human beings sharing religion share at the same time, a collective life, which includes multiple dimensions such as: economic, affective, familial, linguistic, political, cultural, and so on—these dimensions, also, impinge primarily and significantly their whole life of faith and religion.[8] Hence, these concerns are not exclusively secular concerns set apart from religion, but are, in fact, integral to the good news of Christianity and, indeed, of any religion. In this light, therefore, after decades of neglect, during the years following Vatican Council II, the Church began to witness a growing awakening and interest in the political significance of Latin American Catholicism towards promoting social change on the continent.[9] Following the call of Vatican Council II, the Church in Latin America began to publicize the disparities of wealth in the continent and reveal the implications for the people who live there. John P. Harrison notes:

> In this most Catholic of the major world areas, groups within the Church have actively engaged in politicizing the mass of the previously inert and disorganized poor and in so doing have either consciously or inadvertently challenged the dominant social structure which the Church traditionally has championed as the binding element needed for the political stability in which the institutional Church best functioned. This challenge to the existing social order by "career religious" – Evangelical Protestants as well as Catholics – is peculiar to Latin America in the scale of action and in the degree of intensity and explicitness of expression.[10]

The Latin American Church sought to come to grips with this new reality of an unequal of society living amid the technological, economic, political, military, educational, and cultural transformations as Vatican II recommended. As a result, the Latin American Church found itself in conflict with existing governments,[11] compelling it to attempt to manifest a changing social orientation "which entailed open involvement in political issues on behalf of the poor."[12] When the Council of Latin American Bishops (CELAM) convened in Medellín, Colombia in August 1968, "the Church seemed to be changing its social and political attitudes so profoundly that reports of a revolutionary Church began to accompany discussions of the political situation in Latin America."[13] Indeed, these changes resulted in the impact of the Vatican Council II and the subsequent Medellín General Conference of Latin American Bishops.[14] The Medellín Conference has since generated much discussion on the part of the leadership to understand this change of orientation, often posing the question: "Can traditional religious institutions serve as sources of energy to drive change in society?"[15]

The period between 1960 and 1990 was a period of worsening economic fortunes in Latin America resulting in impoverishment of the masses. The 1990 Report of the Economic Council for Latin America (CEPAL) states, "by 1980 there were 135 million poor in the region, in 1986 there were 170 million, and in 1989 there were 183 million, including 88 million indigent people."[16] Three years after the Vatican Council II closed, the Latin American Bishops in 1968, describing the prevailing circumstances at the time, wrote:

> Latin America is obviously under the sign of transformation and development; a transformation that, besides taking place with extraordinary speed, has come to touch and influence every level of human activity, from the economic to the religious.
> This indicates that we are on the threshold of a new epoch in this history of Latin America. It appears to be a time of zeal for full emancipation, of liberation from every form of servitude, of personal maturity and of collective integration. [Medellín, "Introduction," 4].[17]

Gradually, Catholics of different orientations worked out the implications of Medellin in their individual and institutional lives, and consequently, they have been drawn increasingly into participation in the political arena.[18]

The review in this chapter will focus on the orientation of a historically conscious theology as it has been lived out in the Latin American Church and, in paying attention to the historical reality of the Africa, will ask, how the Church in Nigeria might learn from the experience of the Church in Latin America. To sharpen this enquiry, I will focus about the Church in El Salvador, drawing on the life and the witness of Archbishop Oscar Romero and two of his many collaborators, theologians Ignacio Ellacuría and Jon Sobrino. The experiences in diverse locations, such as: Poland, the Philippines, South Africa, Malawi, Rwanda, and others will also be captured in this review to suggest the extent to which those experiences can help my analysis of the relationship between the Church and the state in multiple religious and social environments.

The Icon of El Salvador

El Salvador, "the savior," is a densely populated tiny country of just over 21,000 kilometers' square.[19] Although it has experienced some economic growth in the recent past, which is traceable to the 1961 Alliance for Progress initiative of the Kennedy administration, the experiences of most of its people living in entrenched poverty and injustice have been common.[20] Teresa Whitfield offers a pointed description of the situation, writing:

> Between 1961 and 1975 landless peasants had increased from 12 percent to 41 percent of the rural population; 92 percent of the properties covered 27 percent of the cultivatable land while at the other extreme a mere 0.7 percent covered 39 percent. The "transformation" proposed by [President] Molina . . . was initially for an area of abject poverty in cotton-growing lowlands of San Miguel and Usulután. This area was dominated by five major landholders, each of whom had an income equivalent to that of almost 7,000 local families. Illiteracy was running at 65 percent, lack of sanitation at 98 percent, drinking water at 50 percent, and adequate housing at 35 percent. Employment expectations were about 141 days of work a year.[21]

This inequality and political crisis can be traced to the colonial history of the country, when policies of their Spanish and Portuguese overlords established skewed economic divisions and legalized concentration of scarce land in the hands of a few, even as the common people depended on farming for survival.[22] The percentage of landless rural families grew over the years even as the colonial economy relied heavily on forced labor of the indigenous people.[23] This injustice was maintained through a debt peonage system that established semi feudal social structures that persist in El Salvador today.[24]

The horrific slaughter of indigenous peasants in 1932 remains a crucial "dangerous memory" in Salvadoran history. Revolts, to protest transformation of farmlands into coffee plantations for the oligarchy, erupted primarily in the western provinces of Sonsonate and Ahuachapan.[25] About a hundred people were killed, including soldiers and civilians. A repressive response from the government and the oligarchy "massacred" *matanza* not only the rebels but also vast numbers of people not linked to the rebellion, in the range of 10,000 to 30, 000 deaths.[26] This event remains a central marker in recent Salvadoran history of oppressive rule.

Since the 1920s, a series of military regimes perpetuated a status quo of oppression, crushing ruthlessly any form of opposition. By 1960, moderate Catholics had formed the Christian Democratic Party (PDC) that could help the poorer population oppose the elite control over the government.[27] The

PDC adopted a moderate critical position and became quite popular in the 1960s.[28] This compelled the Salvadoran government to embark on small-scale agrarian reforms to appease the growing population, and served eventually as a build-up to the general election of 1972[29] that marked a turning point in popular opposition to the ruling Salvadoran government.

The Medellín Conference of 1968 awakened the Church in El Salvador to begin to stand with the people. This resulted in tensions and conflicts between the Church and the state because of the awakening of movements of the people to declare independence and liberation from both oligarchic rule and internal colonialism. The movement for liberation was nurtured by a new interpretation of the Christian Gospel in the light of the Vatican Council II, and reechoed particularly by Medellín. This became visible in El Salvador driving changes in the religious landscape as well as transforming society and politics across the entirety of Latin America.

The 1972 election, which brought in General Molina as president, was considered fraudulent. General Molina attempted minimal reforms, mostly in the form of handouts to the masses as a ploy to legitimize and to maintain fundamentally oppressive structures of the government.[30] Since the Catholic Church was known to be supporting initiatives to press for change and liberation, the government initiated violent repressive attacks against priests and members of religious orders.[31] Church institutions and organizations linked to the Church, including ministers and Church volunteers, such as catechists and ministers of the word were incredibly affected.[32] Describing the intensity of the persecution directed at the Church at the time, Ignacio Martín-Baró says:

> By the time Romero became archbishop of San Salvador, the archdiocesan printing press, the St. Paul Bookshop, and the Central American University had already been the target of bombs. The campaign of defamation in the press and on radio and television had reached unimaginable heights. Six priests had been expelled from the country, two of them after being tortured. The house of a diocesan priest had been raided by the security forces. Even Archbishop Chávez had been attacked by the media. He was accused of allowing and encouraging "communistic sermons," and of initiating the violence of *campesino* organizations, such as the UTC (*Unián de Trabajadores del Campo*, Farmworkers' Union).[33]

Amidst these challenges, grassroots political organizing intensified. Militant popular organizations emerged in the late 70s, some of these groups found existing Christian communities in the base, *cursillos*, *encuentros*, and other Catholic educational and pastoral programs as a stepping stone for social change.[34] Especially in the rural settings, such gatherings became a common ground for peasants and indigenous people to discover and to discuss their problems, and to work toward a plan of action to address their needs. Peterson captures the situation best:

> From the early 1970s on, especially in the archdiocese of San Salvador (including Chalatenango province), in the "para-central" region (mainly San Vicente province), and in the coastal and eastern parts of the country (especially Usulutan, Cabanas, and Morazan provinces), progressive Catholic projects were the primary gathering site and source of both material and ideological resources for the growing political opposition.[35]

Some Church leaders and pastoral agents viewed these movements as contrary to Catholic tradition, since Church leadership had a history of toeing the line of the elite establishment in most countries. However, many Catholic activists were committed openly to popular political organizations, such as: *Frente de Accion Popular Unificada* (FAPU) "United Popular Action Front" and *Federacion de Campesinos Cristianos* (FECCAS) "Federation of Christian Peasants," and some priests and nuns encouraged their faithful to participate actively in these and other opposition organizations.[36]

In organizing social justice movements in the Church, the leadership of the bishop of a diocese is very important. This was the case with Archbishop Luis Chávez y Gonzalez, who served as Archbishop of San Salvador from 1939 to 1977. Through his ministry, "the reforms of the Second Vatican Council encountered ground in El Salvador already fertilized to receive the idea that faith could call for social and even political action, and that this action could be in opposition to the established order."[37] Chávez in his leadership role, opened the doors for the local Church in San Salvador to apply directly the principles of Vatican II, and, later, those of Medellín after 1968, to the life of the archdiocese and motivated younger priests and nuns to implement new pastoral initiatives to address social issues at the local level.[38] When Chávez was about to retire, both the government and the Salvadoran oligarchy, however, wanted Church leadership that would be more concerned about keeping the peace than promoting Christian life of the people.[39] This was the atmosphere surrounding the emergence of Oscar Romero as the next archbishop of San Salvador.

Archbishop Oscar Romero and the Salvadoran Reality[40]

On February 3, 1977, the Vatican announced the appointment of Oscar Arnulfo Romero as archbishop of San Salvador. He took over as archbishop in a simple and private ceremony on February 22, 1977.[41] Romero's appointment was received with mixed feelings. Progressive clergy and laypeople thought that Auxiliary Bishop Arturo Rivera y Damas would have been a better fit to continue the progressive policies of Chávez. Conservatives in the Church, the government, the military, and the elite oligarchy supported Romero, who was perceived to be conservative, and considered more likely to reverse the trend of pastoral activism and to return the Church to its historical position as pillar of the Salvadoran status quo.[42] Thus, Romero's appointment was greeted with much jubilation by the Salvadoran government and the oligarchy, believing it signaled a victory for their conservative cause.

The choice of a private ceremony for Romero's installation as archbishop of San Salvador made a significantly good impression upon the clergy of the archdiocese, especially because the government was not invited to the ceremony.[43] According to Whitfield, the archbishop's "conversion" began on March 12, when Jesuit Father Rutolio Grande, along with peasants who rode with him on their way to celebrate Mass in the village of El Paisnal, was assassinated by automatic weapons fire.[44] Grande and other Jesuits in El Salvador incurred the wrath of the landowners because their pastoral work inspired the peasants to organize and to stand up for their rights. "Rutilio Grande's death was to prove a defining event for the Jesuits of Central America and for the Salvadoran Church under the leadership of Monsignor Romero."[45] This change on the part of Romero was so dramatic that many began to speak of "the miracle of Rutilio" as Whitfield notes.[46] "For the Jesuits, the internal disputes that had so characterized the painful years since the meeting in December 1969 were silenced by a unity born of persecution."[47]

In response to Grande's murder, Archbishop Romero ordered all Catholic Schools in the country to close for three days, and in an unprecedented action, canceled all Masses in the country on second Sunday after the incident, except for holding a single memorial service in the cathedral.[48] He wrote a letter to the Salvadoran government demanding an explanation for the killing, stating that he would not attend any government functions until perpetrator of crime had been apprehended.[49] This murder, similar to most political killings that followed, was never unraveled and in his three years as archbishop, Romero continued to not attend any government function.

In the face of the many death threats for his criticism of the government and the elite oligarchy, the Archbishop did not even accept offers of any sort of protection, including an armored car offered by the president in September, 1979.[50] In his diary, Romero notes:

I wouldn't accept that protection, because I wanted to run the same risks that the people are running; it would be a pastoral anti-testimony if I were very secure, while my people are so insecure. I took advantage to ask him [the President] for protection for the people in certain areas where military blocks, military operations . . . sow so much terror.[51]

While my research is not intended to cast aspersions on the hierarchy of the Church in Nigeria, my main concern is to make a simple comparison to the fact that most contemporary Nigerian bishops live in well-protected mansions manned securely by security personnel. A good number of Nigerian bishops drive cars politicians have offered them as gifts. Meanwhile, the thought of death never deterred Romero from his duties as a shepherd of his people, nor did he seek special protection for his priests. "It would be sad," he remarked in June 1979, "if in a country where people are being assassinated so horribly, we didn't count priests among the victims as well. They are the testimony of a church that is incarnated in the problems of the people."[52]

During Romero's time as shepherd of the Salvadoran Church, he witnessed an unprecedented fury, which was directed at all pastoral agents; catechists, nuns, and priests, perceived obviously as the practical and the symbolic leaders of the progressive social movement that inspired opposition. Peterson reports, "between February 18 and February 22, 1977, the Salvadoran government expelled or exiled eleven foreign priests, including two Belgian priests and Spanish Jesuit Ignacio Ellacuría (who was later murdered at the UCA with other Jesuits)."[53] Indeed, throughout that summer, flyers circulated with the slogan, "Be a patriot. Kill a priest."[54] Peterson provides a detailed account regarding how scores of priests, nuns and other church workers and faithful were killed in the series of attacks that greeted the leaders of the Church during that period.[55] Church personnel were assassinated precisely in retaliation for their participation in progressive pastoral projects aimed at liberating poor people from tyranny and oppression.

The transformation in Monsignor Romero's in the face of intensified persecution of the Church challenged his relationship with the Church he served and the government and powers he opposed.[56] "Throughout his three years as archbishop he would suffer not just the slander and abuse of the right-wing press, but also—and much more painful to him—the 'systematic and incomprehensible opposition' of the Papal Nuncio and the majority of the Salvadoran bishops."[57] The Jesuits, whom he opposed initially, later became key players in running the archdiocese and his closest collaborators. With this support, Romero garnered the courage of a shepherd who would risk anything for the life of his sheep. He wrote to Jimmy Carter, then President of the United States, asking on behalf of the Salvadoran people that the United States not send arms nor support any kind of repressive action by the Salvadoran military against the poor people.[58] This letter went public internationally, annoying and embarrassing not only the Salvadoran and US governments, "but the Vatican as well, which did not seem at all pleased with the archbishop's Christian sincerity, or his disregard of 'diplomatic niceties.'"[59] This response displays the Vatican's tendency to urge caution on the part of its national Church leadership by way of falling back on the practices of mediation and compromise in the face of controversy and conflict with states or governments. However, most of the time the Vatican operates in similar situations without having access to accurate or helpful information.

In time Romero, paid the price for taking sides with his most defenseless flock. On Monday, March 24, 1980, he was assassinated while celebrating Mass in a hospital chapel in San Salvador. Peterson notes that the immediate catalyst for the assassination was Romero's March 23 homily, in which he ordered soldiers not to obey orders to kill.[60] Clearly, these controversial three years of Romero's ministry as archbishop of San Salvador made him the ultimate target of the assassin's bullet, specifically because he had overtly denounced the oligarchy and had upheld the cause of the poor. His pastoral letters demonstrated clearly his deep passion to prioritize and stand up for the cause of the oppressed and to expose the causes of their suffering as Vatican Council II had taught. These actions cost Romero and many other Church leaders their lives.[61]

Arturo Rivera Y Damas succeeded Romero as archbishop of San Salvador from 1980 to 1994, and he followed some of the same progressive courses as Romero.[62] Throughout the 1980s, Rivera was at the center of negotiations between the Salvadoran government and the armed groups that were now united under a common front, the *Frente Farabundo Martí para la Liberación Nacional* (FMLN) just months after the death of Romero.[63] Both rebel leaders and government officials credited him with playing a key role in pushing the country toward crucial peace accords, which took place in January 1992. However, Romero was killed not only by gunfire of the enemy, but also continued to be "assassinated" by some of his fellow priests and bishops who did not approve of his pastoral strategy of active engagement with the forces of death in defense of the grassroots people.[64] According to Kevin Clarke, "Archbishops who have succeeded Rivera . . . have been notably resistant to the pastoral style and political direction set by Romero."[65] Some observers believe that some sections of Church hierarchy supported tacitly the persecution of Romero and others through systematic appointment of bishops who would frustrate all Romero stood for. Clarke continues:

> The current archbishop, José Luis Escobar, alas, caused widespread outrage in El Salvador when in September 2013 he abruptly closed Romero's legal aid office (now called Tutela Legal), issuing a statement that claimed its work was no longer relevant.[66]

However, Archbishop Romero continues to live in the hearts of the Salvadoran people. Salvadoran Father Daniel Santiago, considers the life and the ministry of Archbishop Romero to be a social miracle that changed the world, defying all known paradigms of human behavior, especially inspiring El Salvador's Christian base communities.[67] He notes:

> *Como Monseñor* is an expression frequently heard in the poor communities of El Salvador. It means "like Monsignor," a reference to slain Archbishop Oscar Romero. This expression is commonly used in situations which defy common sense and "laws" of human behavior. Frequently heard in meetings of Christian base communities, *como Monseñor* expresses the miraculous (contrary to the laws of social behavior and common sense) intervention of Oscar Romero in the lives of the poor.[68]

Indeed, Romero was killed, but the "Romero miracle" of his pastoral leadership inspired the masses to erupt through their actions in the history of El Salvador and to make their religion part of history by employing relevant religious rituals to develop a spirituality that strengthened their hope, and sustained their work for their liberation. As a bishop-martyr, Romero's prophetic leadership, which culminated in his death, induced a practical interpretation of the Christian gospel, and became so visible in El Salvador driving changes in the religious landscape and transformations in society. Likewise, the Church in Nigeria requires similar leaders who are willing to make just such a "prophetic stand," not only by offering ecclesiastical pronouncements, but also by developing a comprehensive and a decisive commitment to work with the masses to break the circle of oppression as Romero did. This calls for "conversion" on the part of the hierarchy in Nigeria, to make a conscious effort on behalf of those who suffer injustice perpetrated by powerful elite in structures of society. At the time of his death, Romero had the intuition that the Church's many collaborators would take up, making social justice mission an integral part in the life of the Salvadoran Church, including the efforts of Jesuit Father Ignacio Ellacuría, who is the focus of the next section.

Ignacio Ellacuría: The Church as the Historical Sacrament of Liberation[69]

In a similar manner to Archbishop Romero, Ignacio Ellacuría was a pioneer liberation theologian until he, too, became martyred in El Salvador for his convictions in 1989 along with five other Jesuits and two women.[70] After his initial studies in Ecuador, and a period of teaching in El Salvador, he also studied theology in Innsbruck in Austria, and then returned to El Salvador where he worked until his death in 1989.[71] His return to El Salvador coincided with a period of grave tensions and civil unrest. According to Kevin Burke:

> Both within the church and in the world at large. . . transformations were underway. As elsewhere in Latin America, the high expectations spawned by the Alliance for Progress were souring. Rather than redistributing wealth and improving the actual situation of the poor, the Alliance in fact only furthered the deep divisions already inherent to the continent. . . In El Salvador the political situation grew increasingly unstable and repressive. Grossly inequitable land distribution produced a steady increase in the number of landless *campesinos* during the 1960s, while chronic unemployment, inadequate housing, poor sanitation, lack of health care, illiteracy, and infant mortality gradually reached epidemic proportions. Poverty and injustice bred a uniquely Salvadorian discontent that invited radical change and exacerbated political repression.[72]

In his short but creative life, as editor, as political analyst, and most notably, as rector of UCA, Ellacuría played the role of Gramsci's organic intellectual.[73] Although he wrote on a wide range of theological topics, Ellacuría focused mainly on historicizing "the Christian understanding of salvation in order to produce what he calls a historical soteriology, a credible, morally challenging, and efficacious account of how the salvation mediated by Jesus continues to take flesh in history."[74] His special concern with soteriology appears in his first published collection of theological essays, *Freedom Made Flesh*.[75]

Per Ellacuría, "salvation history is a salvation in and of history."[76] "Salvation history" refers to the great saving acts of God played out actively in the history of the children of Israel and continued in the activity of Jesus and his followers. However, Ellacuría insists, "there is not only a salvation history, but salvation must be historical."[77] He notes:

> This is to see transcendence as something that transcends *in* and not as something that transcends *away from*; as something that physically impels to *more* but not by taking *out of*; as something that pushes *forward*, but at the same time *retains*. In this conception, when one reaches God historically—which is the same as reaching God

personally—one does not abandon the human, does not abandon real history, but rather deepens one's roots, making more present and effective what was already effectively present.[78]

Thus, Ellacuría, insisting that history is the richest place of God's presence and self-revelation, points to liberation as the specific form that salvation takes in history,[79] thereby identifying what the Church needs to do if it is to take on the role of mediating salvation, to work for liberation.

The historical character of salvation includes sin and liberation as its most essential themes. Invariably, liberation, if understood from the perspective of the historical dimension of sin, must take uniquely concrete forms that provide people with freedom and restore them to a new life. This, in the understanding of Vatican II, is an essential part of the Church's mission. "What the church contributes to the salvation of history is the constitutive sign of the history of salvation. The church belongs intrinsically to this history of salvation and carries within it the visible part that reveals and makes effective the whole of salvation."[80] Conceiving of the Church as the historical sacrament of liberation implies that the Church is able to fulfill this function: "(1) by devoting itself entirely to the reign of God that Jesus proclaimed, and (2) by choosing to be 'neighbor to the robber's victim' (Luke 10.36), that is, by entering into profound historical solidarity with the crucified peoples."[81]

The Nigerian Church must to learn from the Salvadoran Church that human faith confronts the reality of history, and so the Church cannot opt out of history. In practical terms, this requires the Church to dive into arduous process of social transformation in service to humanity. The Church in Nigeria, in parallel progress as the Salvadoran Church, should therefore, work for the liberation of the poor, the marginalized and the oppressed Nigerians, since liberation is the form in which salvation is realized in history. Summing up Ellacuría's understanding of church as the historical sacrament of liberation, Burke notes:

> The church fulfills the critical demand of God's reign when it prophetically denounces the crucifying powers of this world. It takes up its constructive task when—in deed even more than word—it announces that the reign of God draws near as salvation/liberation of the poor in relation to their terrible situation of captivity and death.[82]

Deepening his analysis of sin as social and structural evil, Ellacuría proposes the view that liberation is the necessary condition for the fullness of salvation to become manifest.[83] Humans, not animals, things, or social structures, always commit sins, but their sins cannot be limited to the individual in isolation. Personal sin, as well as all personal activities, has implications as real and as historical as the presence of evil in the world.[84] Hence, Ellacuría notes emphatically that one indication of salvation in history consists in communities willing to work together to unmask idolatries, the institutional structures that deify them, and the propaganda mechanisms that disguise them; a task to which he dedicated himself in El Salvador with the consequence of his brutal murder.

Ultimately, Ellacuría's concept that salvation is geared toward transforming reality and removing sin is reflected in his conviction that liberation is the ideal historical process in which people encounter the living God who saves human beings.[85] For him, therefore, liberation is a code word for salvation, a thought that colors the spectrum of liberation theology as a movement. It is precisely through the interaction of liberation and salvation that Christian liberation avoids two of its most dangerous tendencies: the tendency to view liberation as a purely immanent process, and the tendency to view liberation as a purely transcendental process.[86] Ellacuría's view of salvation has an original precedent in the Exodus experience of the people of Israel. Through this experience, the children of Israel encountered God as God, the liberator, who delivered them from their socioeconomic oppression at the hands of the Egyptians.[87] Thus, Ellacuría articulates strikingly the import of the events surrounding the Exodus, saying:

> They are used to confirm the historical action of the people themselves, who were invited to leave oppression and go to the Promised Land, and show in that action who their God was and how God acted. History thus becomes a proof of God because history is itself a demonstration of God; only in history is God understood in relation to humanity, and humanity in relation to God.[88]

In other words, the question of what constitutes salvation emerges from the concrete circumstances of people who are in need of salvation; It is not sufficient for theology or the Church to explore conceptual answers to these questions, but is necessary to discern the origins of the concrete hunger for salvation and the signs of salvation that satisfy that hunger concretely.[89] To a people living in the bondage of oppressive rule and exploitation, salvation will imply necessarily liberation from those exact conditions. Hence, in response to the exigencies to realize, to shoulder, and to take charge of the weight of historical reality as he encountered in El Salvador, Ellacuría became a living intersection between the world of power and the world of the powerless poor, and paid the price with his own life.

Ellacuría's shift in developing a new understanding of the nature of salvation opens new possibilities for how scholars think about the Church.[90] This entails employing tangible ways through which the Church in its ministry ensures that the children of God can have life more abundantly (Jn. 10:10). Thus, Ellacuría insisted that the Church in El Salvador during his time was required to "take on history" by naming and denouncing the powers of death that crucified the Salvadoran poor and by remembering the God of life who liberates and raises them to new life. Ellacuría lived this view of faith and Church and it was precisely amid these circumstances that his life was brutally cut short in the Salvadoran war—he lived the essence that the Church must give its life for the liberation of others. Specifically, as a "theologian-martyr," Ellacuría poses a challenge to Nigerian theologians, to employ the strengths of academic theology to address the lived challenges of faith experienced amid an unjust society. Theology can only be relevant when it addresses the life experiences and challenges of the people. If not, it will remain abstract, and potentially dangerous. Ellacuría's fellow Jesuits, who died with him, shared the same conviction along with many others masses of people who survived, including Jon Sobrino, who survived simply because he was not around when the others were killed. Sobrino's contributions to the view of faith and church as liberation from bondage and suffering will be my focus in the next section.

Jon Sobrino: Jesus the Liberator[91]

Jon Sobrino, in an analogous manner to his colleague Ellacuría, was born in Spain's Basque region (1938), and arrived in El Salvador as a novice in the Society of Jesus in 1957. Since then, he lived his entire life in El Salvador, with two notable interruptions: "five years in St. Louis studying philosophy and engineering, and seven years in Frankfurt studying theology."[92] He describes his return to El Salvador after his studies as a conversion experience that awakened him "from the sleep of inhumanity" to notice the pains and sufferings of the poor people of El Salvador. In his words:

> I must confess that until 1974, when I returned to El Salvador, the world of the poor—that is, the real world—did not exist for me. When I arrived in El Salvador in 1957, I witnessed appalling poverty, but even though I saw it with my eyes, I did not really see it; thus that poverty had nothing to say to me for my own life as a young Jesuit and as a human being. . . Everything which was important for my life as a Jesuit I brought with me from Europe.[93]

In other words, he did not view that he needed to respond to salvation as a historical reality as a fellow human being. Categorically, Sobrino terms his inability to see through the poverty of the people as a "dogmatic slumber."[94] Thereafter, he spends all his energy and writing to call the attention of the institutional Church to such a slumber that has been much too common in the ministry of the Church throughout history. In his estimation, to awaken from this slumber was not an easy experience; "it was as if layers of skin were being removed one by one."[95] When he returned to El Salvador in 1974, his interactions pushed him beyond awakening from dogmatic slumber to awaken in fact, from the sleep of inhumanity. He believed that the sufferings of his fellow human beings became a challenge that demanded that he respond in faith and develop a more human way to connect so would be touched by it and move towards action. His experience resonated with the transformation taking place in the Church in El Salvador at the time. Sobrino ascents:

> To my surprise, I found that some of my fellow Jesuits had already begun to speak of the poor and of injustice and of liberation. I also found that some Jesuits, priests, religious, farmers, and students, even some bishops, were acting on behalf of the poor and getting into serious difficulties as a consequence. . . among them Ignacio Ella-curía and Archbishop Oscar Romero, to name just two great Salvadoran Christians, martyrs, and friends.[96]

Through this awakening, Sobrino dedicated himself, henceforth, to view the world from the perspective of the poor, a practice that led him to pursue new insights into what faith is, and correlating innovative ways to respond to the mystery of God.[97]

One of the outstanding contributions of Sobrino to this new liberating interpretation and understanding of the Christian faith, as it is best expressed in Latin America and in his many writings, is his approach to Christology: "to put forward the truth of Christ from the standpoint of liberation."[98] Summing up the underlying impulse of Sobrino's Christological approach, Jorge Costa-doats notes:

> Sobrino's Christology strives to convince the reader that, in order to be Christian, it is not sufficient simply to confess faith in Christ, that we must recognize the anger of using his name for ideological purposes and that we need to return to Jesus of Naza-reth to reclaim his liberating power. We must not be naïve. All Christologies reflect specific interests, and among these, says Sobrino, we must distinguish between those that correspond to Christ and those that distort him.[99]

Indeed, the distinguishing mark of Sobrino's Christology is his specific articulation that salvation begins to appear now in its own history.[100] This is the type
of theology that Nigeria desperately needs, a theology that affects the social
reality of Nigeria and that leads to transform that reality precisely in the direction of the kingdom of God. In Sobrino's own words, "I endeavor to stress the
liberative, and so good-news, dimensions of both Jesus' mission and his person.
Jesus' mission is good news (the kingdom, God's mediation) and it is also good
news that it is this very Jesus of Nazareth (God's mediator) who carries it out."[101]
Thus, recognizing that there has been a specific historic distortion of faith in
Christ that has centered the Church's eyes on a Christ who is more divine than
human, Sobrino insists that such faith in a divine Christ has allowed the rich to
justify keeping the poor in their misery and has been used to justify their oppression instead of liberating them.[102] This is the kind of Gospel that most Nigerians receive from the institutional Church. "Against these serious distortions of
Christ, Sobrino focuses on the emerging figure of 'Christ the Liberator,' which
is derived from Jesus of Nazareth's humanity and historicity."[103] Such faith in
Christ, as indicated by Sobrino, shows that God, in fact, desires to liberate all
victims from the concrete prisons of historical evils.

In his second volume, *Christ the Liberator*, building on the previous work,
Sobrino takes up the Resurrection of Christ, the Christology of the New Testament, and, finally, the Christological formulae of the early church councils.[104] Throughout *Christ the Liberator*, Sobrino writes from the reality of faith,
as it was set in motion by the event of Jesus Christ, and from the situation of
victims—the "Crucified People" of history—particularly the poor of El Salvador, among whom he lives.[105] In his words, "I look at the resurrection of Jesus
from the hope of the victims—with the correlative revelation of God as God
of victims—and from the possibility of living already as risen beings in the
conditions of historical existence.[106] Explaining the resurrection of Jesus as
a spiritual challenge as presented by Sobrino, Roberto S. Goizueta explains:

> If Jesus' resurrection represents the victory of life over death, Sobrino suggests, this
> fundamental Christian belief cannot be adequately understood apart from its con-
> crete, historical connection to Jesus' own life and death; the one who is raised by
> God from the dead is the same one who was crucified unjustly for proclaiming and
> enacting God's reign. What we call "death," then, cannot be understood apart from
> its intrinsic connection to injustice: the one crucified was innocent. And what we
> call "life" cannot be understood apart from its intrinsic connection to justice: the
> innocent one who was crucified has been vindicated. Though the terms "death" and
> "life" embrace more than this, they necessarily include and demand the justification
> of the victim, the vindication of his life.[107]

Without limiting Jesus to a finite context in history, or reducing him to a symbol of believers' personal wishes, those who follow must decide, to choose life or death, to stand with the oppressed or the oppressors. The choices Christians make in this life will determine what decisions we make on behalf of the least of these, or not.

From Sobrino's perspective, faith and spirituality touch all aspects of human life and the way people relates to their reality.[108] The good news of the Kingdom becomes real in "liberation from material want" amid every challenge people face, poverty, destitution, hunger, disease, suppression, and misrule. Aspiring toward the fundamental values established by the reign of God as Jesus inaugurated it, therefore creates a vision for a society that ensures the dignity of all of humanity. God's reign will, thus, provide the basic direction for this historical project; the flourishing of all of creation, which is constitutive of the mission of the Church if it is to stay true to the reign of God.

Sobrino's Christology is relevance specifically for the experience of the Church in Nigeria, namely, his proposal of a new title for Jesus Christ, one that is a dynamic representation for what Jesus Christ means to the Christian believer in El Salvador. Jesus is "Good News," the "*euvangelium*." His own life was integral to the proclamation and the initiation of the Reign of God so for those to whom his message was directed, it was received as the good news of their liberation and freedom from the things, the people and institutions that held them captive. Other examples can be found in Rotilio Grande and Oscar Romero of El Salvador, and Nelson Mandela of South Africa, who lived their lives in a way that they became actual personifications of the proclamation of the reign of God to the people that represented an actual and real end to injustice, suppression, and violence. They, too, were the *euvangelium*. Furthermore, the criterion for determining if any proclamation is Good News or not is whether it produces joy. The joyful proclamation and the effect of joy in those who receive the news of God's reign are essential conditions of the proclamation of the good news, "something frequently forgotten in the mission of the Catholic Church, which is often more concerned with communicating a 'truth' that has to be given and received in an orthodox manner, without bothering to present it with joy and to check whether it has produced joy."[109]

In summary, I have endeavored to share the significance of the lives and ministries of Archbishop Romero and his collaborators Ellacuría and Sobrino as well as all those who took up similar challenges in other places in Europe, Asia, and Africa. These personalities converged on their understanding that the mission of Jesus was one of service towards liberating of God's children here on earth as it is in heaven. The writings of Sobrino, similar to those of Ellacuría point most particularly to the importance of the contributions of theology towards crafting a more practical understanding of faith in relation to the realities of society. It is my estimation that Nigerian Catholic theologians will be more relevant if their theology addresses the concerns of contemporary Nigerian society as Sobrino and Ellacuría did in El Salvador. Despite its limitations, the Church in El Salvador served more of a life-giving purpose. In the next section, I will widen my analysis of the relationship between the Church and the state to explore a variety of religious and social environments to discover how these diverse situations can apply to the Nigerian reality.

Martyrs of the Philippines

The Catholic Church in the Philippines, in collaboration with other religious and civil groups, ousted successfully the brutal and corrupt government of dictator Ferdinand Marcos, known at the time as "the Hitler of Southeast Asia."[110] In 1986, the Church, in liaison with other groups, organized continuous protests that became known as the "People Power Revolution," attracting millions of Filipinos to demonstrate against the government. Philippine Jesuit Antonio B. Lambino notes, "the Church, as a people and as institution, figured notably in the political upheaval."[111] According to him, "religious symbols like the cross, the rosary, images of Mary and of the child Jesus were prominently visible among the human barricades. The celebration of the Eucharist had already become a focal point of unity throughout the protest movement that proceeded the days of February."[112] Beginning with the assassination of the popular opposition leader Senator Benigno (Ninoy) Aquino in 1983, the movement against Marcos grew rapidly. This revolution coincided with mounting discontent over the corrupt administration of Marcos and his wife Imelda, who were supposedly good Catholics. It became widespread in the early eighties, spearheaded by both Communist insurgents and various churches throughout the country.[113] The regime, then, became repressive of the opposition and grossly violated human rights to suppress any form of dissent.

Aquino and other opposition leaders were compelled to flee, and he took refuge in the United States of America.[114] After three years in exile, news of his return became rife, and the opposition, more confident, intensified. Upon his return, August 21, 1983, however, he was assassinated as he descended from the aircraft that brought him home. His assassination sparked a popular revolt that brought the Marcos dictatorship to an end. From bishops to priests, pastors, nuns, ministers, brave students and farmers, people sprang into action, breathing new life into communities, forming new organizations to press boldly, but nonviolently for their liberation. Under these circumstances, the Cardinal Archbishop of Manila, Jaime Cardinal Sin, with the support of other bishops[115] rallied and united Evangelicals and other Protestant denominations as well as some communists in the fight against the tyranny of the regime.[116] Cardinal Sin had meanwhile convinced Corazon Aquino, the widow of the slain Benigno Aquino to run against President Marcos, who decided to call a snap election as the protests lasted. At least, one million Filipinos signed petitions supporting Corazon Aquino.[117]

In a buildup to the elections, the Catholic Church stepped up Mrs. Aquino's campaign to call for a change in the government through a series of pastoral letters. Nigerian Bishop and social analyst Matthew Hassan Kukah notes that a few of these letters stand out most clearly:

> A *Dialogue for Peace* (1983), *Let there be Life* (1984), *Message to the People of God* (1985). The bishops issued two letters in 1986. The first was: *A Call to Conscience* (1986). And then, the battle cry was heard in the most forceful latter of all, which was titled: *We must Obey God Rather Than Men* (1986). By that statement, the Catholic bishops indeed sent out signals that Mr. Marcos' time was up." [118]

Marcos lost the elections and attempted to subvert the results, but to no avail. When it became clear that he had rigged the elections, Cardinal Sin appealed to the masses on Catholic Church Radio Veritas, calling millions of Catholics to pray and to nonviolent resistance.[119] Indeed, a number of public officials defected, including the Minister of Defense, Ponce Enrile and General, Fidel Ramos, Deputy Chief of Staff of the Armed Forces Commander of the Philippine Constabulary as well as a few hundred troops. Their defection sparked courage for millions of unarmed people to take to the streets and protest, calling for the resignation of the Marcos regime.[120] Kukah reports, "the placement of a statue of the Blessed Virgin Mary behind both men during their press conference was not lost on anyone. These symbols of religion showed God's support!"[121] Facing the collapse of his support, Marcos, his family and an entourage of his inner circle fled the country. After two months in which the election contested, the dictatorship fell, and Corazon Aquino assumed power peacefully.

Although this event raised several interpretations, the role played by the Catholic Church in particular, in relation to the events that gave rise to the "People Power Revolution," resonates with the intuition of *Gaudium et Spes* that the Church should engage with society. This led to sustained efforts by the Catholic Church in the Philippines to ensure the entrenchment of more democratic values and institutions. In the 1990s, the Bishops of the country mandated that parishes form The Pastoral Parish Council for Responsible Voting (PPCRV) and "Voters Organization, Training and Education toward Clear, Authentic, Responsible Elections (VOTE-Care).[122] Besides encouraging people to cast their votes, these bodies above all ensured, "the votes are properly registered, counted, and protected."[123] Although these events in the Philippines may not have solved all fundamental problems of the society, such as poverty, its reality has indicated over all that the Church is a formidable force to mobilize public opinion and to protest for desired change in society. Specifically, effective leadership of the Church coupled with the appropriate use of religious symbols was useful in this case, and offer a crucial lesson for the Church in Nigeria.

The next section will reveal some examples from Africa, which indicate, on the one hand, that if the Church's mission is consistent with the understanding of the Gospel as an instrument of liberation, it can work to mediate acts of salvation with the children of God on earth as it is in heaven. On another hand, if the Church stands on the wrong side of history, it will, unfortunately become yet another agent of death rather than life as happened in the situation in Rwanda.

African Examples of Incarnated Christianity and Tragedy: Malawi, South Africa and Rwanda

Malawi

Malawi, a country of about 10 million people, is in southern Africa, bordered by Tanzania to the north, Mozambique to the east and Zambia to the West. It was the first country in southern Africa to gain independence from British colonial rule in 1964.[124] Unlike other countries in Africa in which different religious and ethnic groups competed for political power at the time of their independence, Malawi, a predominantly Christian colony, had fewer than a dozen ethnic groups, and transitioned to independence without violence. A predominantly Bantu-speaking people, the Chekwa, account for more than

90 percent of the population.[125] Politically, Malawi, like South Africa, is a member of the Southern African Development Community (SADC), along with other nations, namely Angola, Botswana, The Democratic Republic of Congo (DRC), Lesotho, Mauritius, Mozambique, Namibia, The Seychelles, Swaziland, Tanzania, Zambia, and Zimbabwe. Ecclesiastically, however, the Catholic Church in Malawi is a member of the Association of Member Episcopal Conferences of Eastern Africa (AMECEA), which gathers together the Catholic Bishops of Eastern Africa.[126]

Upon gaining independence in 1964, Hastings Kamuzu Banda was elected as president, and declared himself president-for-life in 1971.[127] Under his leadership, Malawi became a one-party state, instituting a dictatorship that lasted until he lost his bid for reelection as president in 1994. American Professor Sylvia M. Jacobs hints as to Banda's style of administration:

> On June 9, 1978, the country held its first parliamentary elections after independence. However, Banda required all prospective voters to take an English examination, thereby disqualifying 90 percent of the population from voting. Thus, Banda took control of parliament, and anyone who criticized him was imprisoned or expelled from the country. He crafted a one-party state system based on what he called 'law and order' and 'peace and calm,' which demanded complete loyalty and obedience to him. His enemies were hunted, detained, imprisoned, exiled and killed.[128]

Banda's administration was hostile particularly to religious groups. In his entire thirty-year rule, various religious groups were persecuted or treated harshly. The Jehovah's Witnesses due to their belief in distancing from politics, faced sustained and systematic violence encouraged actively by top political functionaries, who tagged them as traitors.[129] About 250,000 people were imprisoned in Malawi at the time, with over 10,000 tortured, killed, or vanished, according to an Amnesty International report.[130] The actual numbers could be more.

The increasing human rights violations continued for a long time despite criticism from various groups within the country. The Catholic Bishops of Malawi, in March 1992, "for the first time in the postcolonial history of Malawi, issued a pastoral letter openly condemning the one-party rule, the violation of human rights, and the lack of freedom of speech and democracy."[131] Prior to this point, the Catholic Church was viewed by the political elite as being less supportive during the period of the actual struggle against colonialism. The pastoral letter, entitled *Living Our Faith*, emboldened the opposition, as Mfutu-Bengo notes:

The pastoral letter of the bishops enabled the underground opposition to President Kamuzu Band's oppressive regime to become open, public and vocal for the first time. Students and workers went to the streets to demonstrate, to protest and to strike in support of the pastoral letter. At once, opposition to dictatorship became a popular mass movement, which could be stopped not by repression but by democratization and by the rule of law.[132]

Two days after the release of their letter, the bishops were arrested, detained, and interrogated for eight hours.[133] The government threatened to exterminate them, but they did not budge. Upon hearing of their courage, other churches joined them, as well. It is important to note that since the 80s and 90s, the churches started championing a stronger underground opposition to President Kamazu Banda, and were supported during this time by Western donors who suspended their non-humanitarian aid to Malawi in May 1992.[134] The fact that this effort took such a long time to develop reveals that in fighting corrupt regimes people and movements ought to be persistent and patient. At the same time, strong collaboration establishes a foundation to foster a mightier front to succeed in defeating dictatorships. In the case of Malawi, this partnership yielded results when, in 1992, churches and protest groups joined to form a Public Affairs Committee, an umbrella of religious and political groups calling for change in Malawi.[135] The Alliance for Democracy, led by Chakufwa Chihana, and the United Democratic Front, led by Kakili Muluzi, formed in September 1992, joining forces with the Public Affairs Committee in fronting opposition efforts against Banda's unpopular regime, all with the support of the church.[136]

Following the Bishops' arrest the people and the international community continued to mount pressure, which compelled President Banda to give in to the demands of the bishops' pastoral letter that proposed a multiparty democracy referendum. Just as a referendum was held in June 1993, and President Banda was defeated in the parliamentary elections held in May 1994, ushering in Bakili Muluzi as the new president of Malawi.[137] Although he was a Muslim, the bishops and, indeed, the people accepted the election results, believing Muluzi's campaign promises that he would work for the common good.

Significantly, other church bodies adopted the premise of the Catholic bishop's pastoral letter, giving it a national legitimacy. This letter became a working document for the platform of the opposition front, irrespective of denominational affiliation, desiring primarily to pursue just policies with the common goal to change a bad government.[138] Thus, Mfuto-Bengo concludes, while "the Presbyterian Church (CCAP) was credited with destroying the colonial government by educating the Malawian political elite, the Catholic Church ought to be accredited and celebrated for destroying dictatorship through the revolution of the word."[139] That the bishops acted at all at this time is the point I wish to emphasize. Most significantly, they accomplished joining forces with other civil society groups and pressed home successfully their demands for change. The Church in Nigeria, which is also living in a multiethnic/religious environment should borrow a leaf from Malawi in its drive to advance the cause for change.

This type of movement for the liberation of people is considered an authentic approach in Catholic theological terms. Pope John Paul II visited Malawi in 1989 and urged the bishops to act in accordance with the proposals found in *Gaudium et Spes* to correct Malawi's poor political and human rights conditions.[140] On the bishop's *ad limina* visit to Rome, the Pope insisted again on their action. Upon their return from Rome, it became clear that the bishops responded positively to the Pope's appeal and they began the new campaign for liberation of their people.

South Africa

In South Africa, "it is very difficult for the Catholic Church to influence governance directly,"[141] since the Church is in a minority and in decline. However, through collaboration with other church bodies and civil society organization, the South African Catholic Bishops' Conference Parliamentary Liaison Office (CPLO) is involved in portfolio committees with representatives of other religious bodies to make inputs on policy effectively since the time of its emergence from the authoritarianism of apartheid in 1994.[142] This body has served as the major organization of the Catholic Church, which is involved in the political life of the country since its return to democracy.

South Africa's government operates currently along the lines of a multiparty democracy, with separation of powers, a constitution, and one of the most liberal bills of rights in the world.[143] Anthony Egan explains the South African political machinery, saying:

> Breaking away from a "winner takes all" candidate-based system, it employs a party-list proportional-representation electoral system in which voters vote for a party, not an individual. Parties draft candidate lists in order of internal popularity . . . smaller parties have a greater chance of getting a few seats than in the old Westminster sys-

tem used before 1994. The advantage is that voting is clear; the disadvantage is that parties have inordinate control over who goes to parliament.[144]

The implication, as Egan explains it, is that in effect, "South Africa is a one-party-dominant situation, with the ruling African National Congress (ANC) virtually deciding what the country gets."[145] The Constitutional Court serves as a check and balance on the power of the ANC to curtail excessive abuses.

The ideology of South Africa's apartheid past, a consensus of scholars agrees, received its underpinning from the skewed theology of the Dutch Reformed Church.[146] A dubious application of Biblical texts, such as the separation of sheep from the goats in the last days, were used to prove that God had ordained the races to be different, in which case, the sheep were the whites and the goats, the non-whites.

The publication of the book *Let My People Go* by Albert Luthuli in 1962 signaled the arrival of meaningful opposition to apartheid. With Allan A. Boesak's *Farewell to Innocence*, published in 1977, chronicling most particularly the evolution of the church amid the struggle against apartheid, the stage was set for stronger opposition.[147] Besides Archbishop Desmond Tutu, the Anglican Archbishop of Cape Town, and others such as: Revs. Trevor Huddleston, Naude Beyers and Archbishop Dennis Hurley, the Catholic Archbishop of Durban, made enormous effort to raise awareness about the ills of apartheid and worked with the churches to organize resistance to it before Tutu.[148] In this initial stage, they concentrated on bringing church leaders of various churches together to unite and move forward with the task. Their struggles were not very publicized since this was before globalization of mass communications and CNN.

With the South African government banning the ANC and any other organized groups in civilian opposition to apartheid in the mid-seventies, the likes of Archbishop Tutu, Henry, Boesak, and other leading churchmen took to the streets, along with thousands of lay people and school children, who embarked on strikes, sit-ins and other actions.[149] These actions signaled the beginning of the involvement of the church in sustained campaigns against apartheid, which developed into a clearly ecumenical forum, thanks to the emergence of a clerical class indigenous to South Africa.[150] In 1985, the leadership of the World Alliance of Redeemed Churches referred to apartheid as an "aberration," marking a major crack in the power of the Dutch Reformed Church, the main theological bastion of apartheid, thus hastening the integration of the modern wings of the church.[151] The elevation of Bishop Desmond Tutu to the position of Archbishop of the important Anglican See of Cape Coast in the 1980s provided legitimacy and credibility to the church's struggle against apartheid. His reception of the Nobel Peace Prize boosted equally his international status along with that of the United Democratic Front, the organization that served as an umbrella to opposition groups in South Africa.

In the late 1980s, Church services, funeral ceremonies and other similar gatherings became alternative fora to denounce and call for intensified resistance to apartheid. This drew the attention of the international community to the inhumanity of apartheid, calling on world powers to sanction the South African government.[152] By the time, the churches vowed to make South Africa ungovernable, the white government had no choice but to commence negotiations with the ANC. The churches in South Africa, in similar manner to the Catholic Church in the Philippines, succeeded in exposing the ills of apartheid, and in educating the people to resist it, thus compelling the system to overheat and to grind to a halt in 1994. The involvement of the Church in South Africa in the struggle against apartheid is another instance of interpreting salvation in terms of liberation. The Church's involvement revolved around understanding its role as an agent of God's Kingdom to aid it to be enacted here on earth as in heaven following the call of Vatican II.

Rwanda

The approach used by the South African church was helpful in bringing down apartheid. In Rwanda, however, the story of church involvement rather ignited a tragedy. Rwanda, one of the most Christian nations in Africa, has a population composed of three social groups—the Hutus, Twa, and Tutsis—all of which share the same language, religion, and culture.[153] Missionary activities in Rwanda started in the early 1900s, while the country was already a German colony. After World War I, Belgium took over administration of Rwanda, and with the baptism of the local king, Rwanda was "consecrated to Christ the King and became a virtual Christian kingdom," with over 60 percent Catholic affiliation.[154]

African theologian Elisée Rutagambwa establishes that Catholic missionaries fractured Rwandan civil society by introducing a dualistic Manichean worldview in which people were either "saved or "damned."[155] This Judeo-Christian bipolar vision separated converts (*Bakristu*-Christians) from unconverted (*Bashenzi*-pagan) family members, thereby abolishing the role of their ancestors, who served traditionally as intergenerational "glue," that is, mediators between the living and the dead.[156] The new Christian vision replaced the traditional tripolar view (the living, the dead, and the ancestors) common to the African worldview. Christian converts *Bakristu* became a distinctive social group viewed as having little in common with nonconverts *Bashenzi*, even from members of the same family. Missionaries furthered this distinguishing typology by encouraging converts to relocate away from the nonbaptized, marking them with symbols and rites, such as wearing rosaries or religious medallions.[157] The colonialists adopted this practice, transforming it into a powerful ethnic ideological schema the Hutus and Tutsis used against each other later. Rutagambwa notes:

> According to this colonial ethnic ideology, all Tutsis were rulers and all Hutus were servants. Hence, just as the colonizers relied on the Tutsi chiefs to cement their political power, the missionaries chose Tutsi hierarchy as their tool for evangelization.[158]

With the support of the Church, the colonial officials appointed the Tutsi hierarchy to the new colonial administration. In addition, the now privileged Tutsi received private schools built for their children who would later work for the colonial power.[159] Rutagambwa maintains that traditional Rwanda was markedly different from this arrangement. In Rwandan culture, he explains, "cattle breeding was associated with wealth and prestige."[160] Hence, "a rich Hutu could become a Tutsi and a poor Tutsi could become a Hutu," if the latter acquired more cows for example, or if the former lost his breed of cows.[161] Thus, Rutagambwa points out that there would have been complications of the Rwandan Church missionaries' ethnic interpretations, creating and exacerbating socioeconomic divisions, which resulted eventually in the genocide.[162]

The Second Rwandan Republic of 1973 sanctioned the policy of ethnic and regional balances attempting to reverse the fortunes of the Hutus, who, until then were under the perpetual domination of the Tutsis in society.[163] Under this policy, each Rwandan was identified ethnically from birth, resulting in the Tutsis' being systematically excluded from all important areas of national life. According to Rutagambwa:

> Although this policy was clearly unjust, Church leadership justified it as a corrective measure for the former colonial exclusion of the Hutu. To the Catholic Bishops, Tutsis were still the oppressors of Hutus, even after thirty years of exclusive Hutu power.[164]

This "demonization" of the Tutsis preceded the 1994 genocide over a period of thirty years, with the Church collaborating actively with the political powers, ignoring all abuses against the Tutsis.[165] Up to the early 1990s, violence intensified against the Tutsis and moderate Hutus with these flagrant government-sponsored violations of basic human rights and with countless murders taking place in churches and Catholic school buildings without the Catholic Church making any protest. When the Church spoke out eventually, nonetheless it implicated cowardly the Tutsi RPF forces, "although the bishops knew that the Tutsi-dominated RPF troops were not involved in the genocide."[166]

During the genocide, besides the direct involvement of some priests and nuns as well as gathering Tutsis into church buildings, where they were slaughtered, Church authorities assisted priests and nuns to find safe havens in other countries to avoid facing trials in later years.[167] Rwanda is a case study of the historical involvement of the Church in leading people to death as opposed to the role the churches played in Malawi and South Africa to free the people from oppressive regimes. The Church, in the case of Rwanda, acted as an agent of death, rather than one of liberation, and shows that the Church, even as it can be a graced and spiritual body, it can also work against its own essence—giving life to the world. The Church in Nigeria will need to be proactive to minister in an environment similar to that of Rwanda, with its inherent ethnic divisions and consequent tensions. The Church should be mother and father to people of all ethnicities so to be true to its mission.

What Lessons for Church and Salvation in Nigeria?

This chapter reviewed several contexts in which issues of religion and politics allowed the Church to blossom in parts of Asia, Africa, and, especially, Latin America. The impact of the Second Vatican Council (Vatican II) and the subsequent Medellín Conference (in Latin America), inspired Christian communities to seek answers to the question: "What role can religious institutions play in the drive for change in society?" The answer to this question has proven to be rather very complex and no situation can be considered perfect. However, the Church can only fulfill its mission, not by running away from or avoiding history, but precisely by acting in history. It is difficult at times, especially if the Church wants to control the message. Although the Catholic

Church in the Philippines, Malawi, South Africa, and El Salvador could not take all the credit for the changes that took place in those countries, they happened because the church communities, even somewhat tardily, chose to dare history. The churches joined forces with other groups to press their governments for changes. Even in situations where their attempts did not address the core problems, it proved to be a step forward. These attempts underscore the importance of ecumenical action and collaboration with civil society groups to work for liberation and the common good.

Secondly, the experience of the Church in Philippine and El Salvador reveal the hidden resources and potential local churches possess during civil struggles. The Catholic Church in the majority role took the opportunity to galvanize support of other groups and pressed for the liberation of the Children of God on earth. In El Salvador, particularly, the Church embraced a style of theology and faith expression that enabled them to situate the mission of the Church more effectively to respond to the concrete realities within Salvadoran society. The pastoral leadership of Archbishop Romero inspired Salvadorans to articulate an understanding of their sufferings and persecution through a new interpretation of biblical stories from base communities. Romero's mastery at using political gestures and employing relevant religious rituals developed effectively into a spirituality that offered people strength to hope, and in fact, to work for their own liberation. The Church in Nigeria needs a Romero among the ranks of its leaders to move the understanding of the social mission of the church beyond simply charitable works and ecclesiastical pronouncements to action in service of society.

In Malawi and South Africa, where the Church was in the minority, it nevertheless joined forces with other church bodies, other religious groups, and various civil society organizations in charting a common front for liberation struggles. Such cooperation facilitates the church's response in society. The diverse plural religious and ethnic identities in Nigeria make it a necessity for the Church in its mission to collaborate with other religious bodies and civil society organizations to be more effective.

The case in Rwanda illustrates how the Church, by standing on the wrong side of history, not only affects the proclamation of the good news but also misrepresent what salvation involves in its mission. The Church in Rwanda acted as an agent of death, rather than one of life. The Church in Nigeria needs to rise above the limitations of its ethnic affiliations, to avoid the mistakes of Rwanda.

Change, liberation, freedom, salvation, always comes with a price, which in Christian terms includes martyrdom. Jesus paid the supreme price for the salvation of the world with his own life on the cross. Those who work for the salvation of others on earth, such as Romero, Mandela, Ellacuria, and many others take risks and sometimes pay the price with their lives. Church leaders in Nigeria today must also be willing to pay such price by sacrificing their privileges and risking their lives for the salvation of others in order to move out of remaining a self-serving Church.

Above all, although these churches and individuals did not and had no intention of endorsing political programs or specific public policies, they articulated a form of discipleship that could renew Christians individually and empower them collectively to respond to problems of society politically or economically. This is the value of their lives and theology for the Church in Nigeria. The Nigerian Church needs to recognize that its ministry connects with unmasking the root causes of poverty and oppression of the children of God and draws them to acts of conversion that place the Church on the side of the victims and against their oppressors.

Benedict XVI offers a more balanced statement proclaiming, "a just society must be the achievement of politics not the Church. Yet the promotion of justice through efforts to bring about openness of mind and will to the demands of the common good is something which concerns the Church deeply."[168] The African Synods I and II presents a unique opportunity to the Church in Nigeria to contribute productively and proactively to construct a society that embodies salvation of the children of God on earth as it is in heaven by proposing an understanding of faith that responds to the needs of people in the midst of the current challenges they face. To do this, the Nigerian Church needs to wake up from the slumber of neutrality and take up the challenge of Jesus himself, who says: "The spirit of the Lord is upon me, because he has anointed me to preach the good news to the poor. He has sent me to proclaim liberty to captives and recovery of sight to the blind, to set free the oppressed." (Luke. 4:18). More importantly, within the peculiar circumstances of the Nigerian nation today, responding to this call requires both ecumenical and inter-religious structures of collaboration, as I will discuss in the next chapter.

Notes

1. See Oscar Romero, *Voice of the Voiceless*. Romero's second pastoral letter as Archbishop of San Salvador, was titled "The Church as the Body of Christ in History," in which he noted that the concerns of the society were indeed the concerns of the Church, hence the actions of the Church in defense of the defenseless were at the heart of the Church's ministry.
2. Otto Maduro, *Religion and Social Conflicts,* trans. Robert R. Barr (Maryknoll: Orbis Books, 1982), 20.
3. *Ibid.*
4. Paul E. Sigmund, "The Transformation of Catholic Social Thought in Latin America: Christian Democracy, Liberation Theology, and the New Catholic Right," in *Organized Religion in the Political Transformation of Latin America,* ed. Satya R. Pattnayak (Lanham, Maryland: University Press of America, 1995), 41.
5. Sigmund, "The Transformation of Catholic Social Thought in Latin America: Christian Democracy, Liberation Theology, and the New Catholic Right," 41.
6. Jack Nelson-Pallmeyer, *War Against the Poor: Low Intensity Conflict and Christian Faith* (Maryknoll: Orbis Books, 1989), 10.
7. Maduro, *Religion and Social Conflicts,* 41.
8. *Ibid.*
9. John P. Harrison, "Preface," in *Churches and Politics in Latin America,* ed. Daniel H. Levine (London: Sage Publications, 1980), 7.
10. *Ibid.*
11. *Ibid.*
12. Michael Dodson, "The Christian Left in Latin American Politics," in *Churches and Politics in Latin America,* 111.
13. Dodson, "The Christian Left in Latin American Politics," 111.
14. Daniel H. Levine, "Introduction," in *Churches and Politics in Latin America,* 13–14.
15. *Ibid.*
16. C. Rene Padilla, "New Actors on the Political Scene in Latin America," in *New Face of the Church in Latin America,* ed. Guillermo Cook (Maryknoll: Orbis Books, 1994), 84.
17. Gustavo Gutiérrez, *A Theology of Liberation: History, Politics and Salvation,* 15th Anniversary ed. Edited and translated by Sister Caridad Inda and John Eagleson (Marknoll: Orbis Books, 1999), xvii.
18. Levine, "Introduction," in *Churches and Politics in Latin America,* 13.
19. Whitfield, *Paying the Price* 17.
20. *Ibid.* 32–33. Cf. Anna L. Peterson, *Martyrdom and the Politics of Religion: Progressive Catholicism in El Salvador's Civil War* (New York: State University of New York Press, 1997), 24.
21. Whitfield, *Paying the Price,* 67.
22. Peterson, *Martyrdom and the Politics of Religion,* 24.
23. *Ibid.* 25–29.
24. *Ibid.*
25. *Ibid.*
26. *Ibid.* Cf. Whitfield, *Paying the Price,* 18.

27. *Ibid.* 24.
28. *Ibid.*
29. *Ibid.* 24.
30. Ignacio Martín-Baró, "Oscar Romero: Voice of the Downtrodden," in *Voice of the Voiceless: The Four Pastoral Letters and other Statements*, 3.
31. *Ibid.* 3–4.
32. *Ibid.*
33. *Ibid.*
34. Peterson, *Martyrdom and the Politics of Religion*, 31.
35. *Ibid.*
36. *Ibid.*
37. *Ibid.* 49.
38. *Ibid.*
39. Martín-Baró, "Oscar Romero: Voice of the Downtrodden," 4.
40. James R. Brockman gives a detailed insight into the life and ministry of Archbishop Romero. See James R. Brockman, *Romero: A life: The Essential Biography of a Modern Martyr and Christian Hero*, 25th ed. (Maryknoll: Orbis Books, 2005). This section relies on Brockman's account.
41. *Ibid.* 4–5.
42. Peterson, *Martyrdom and the Politics of Religion*, 61.
43. Martín-Baró, "Oscar Romero: Voice of the Downtrodden," 5.
44. Whitfield, *Paying the Price*, 104.
45. *Ibid.*
46. *Ibid.* 102–103. Romero was generally perceived "as a timid and conservative man, a follower of Opus Dei whom the Papal Nuncio reportedly had recommended for the archdiocese after consultation with businessmen, government officials, military officers, and women of the upper reaches of Salvadoran society." In Rome in 1975, as an adviser for the Pontifical Commission on Latin America, he accused the Jesuits of complicity in political and agitative movements.
47. *Ibid.* 104.
48. *Ibid.*
49. *Ibid.*
50. Oscar Romero, *Su diario: del 31 de Marzo 1978 al de marzo de 1980* (San Salvador: Archdiocese of San Salvador, 1990), 75–76.
51. *Ibid.*
52. Romero, *La voz de los sin voz* (San Salvador: UCA Editores, 1987), 455.
53. Here and in the following sections, I rely on Peterson, *Martyrdom and the Politics of Religion*, 63 ff.
54. *Ibid.* 63.
55. *Ibid.* 64–65.
56. Whitfield, *Paying the Price*, 105.
57. *Ibid.*
58. Martín-Baró, "Oscar Romero: Voice of the Downtrodden," 18.
59. *Ibid.*

60. Peterson, *Martyrdom and the Politics of Religion*, 65.

61. Cf. Archbishop Oscar Romero, *Voice of the Voiceless: The Four Pastoral Letters and other Statements*.

62. Kevin Clarke, *Oscar Romero: Love Must Win* (Collegeville, Minessota: Liturgical Press, 2014), 134.

63. *Ibid.*

64. See Nicole Winfied, "Pope Denounces Priests, Bishops who 'defamed' Oscar Romero" Associated Press, http://www.ap.org accessed November 20, 2015. Nicole reports that at the weekly general audience in St. Peter's Square at the Vatican, Wednesday, Oct. 28, 2015, the pope said "Romero suffered martyrdom not only before and during his March 24, 1980, murder but afterward . . . even by his brothers in the priesthood and episcopate." Francis beatified Romero on May 23, 2015 in San Salvador.

65. Clarke, *Oscar Romero: Love Must Win*, 135.

66. *Ibid.* 137.

67. Daniel Santiago, *The Harvest of Justice: The Church of El Salvador Ten Years After Romero* (New York: Paulist Press, 1993), 93.

68. *Ibid.* 93–4.

69. Ellacuría, *Essays on History, Liberation, and Salvation*, 227–253. Burke says that the publication of the essay "Church of the Poor: Historical Sacrament of Liberation" in 1977 by Ellacuría marked a shift in his theological thought in that he began to pay more attention to ecclesiology and Church spirituality and practice henceforward.

70. Kevin Burke, "Reflections on Ignatian Soteriology: The Contribution of Ignatio Ellacuría," *Lonergan Workshop*, vol. 19, ed. Fred Lawrence (Boston College, 2006), 41. I rely in this section on Ellacuría's key essays: "The Historicity of Christian Salvation," and "Church of the Poor: Historical Sacrament of Liberation" as well as Burke's interpretation of Ellacuría's works.

71. For a detailed account of Ellacuría's life and works see Burke, *The Ground Beneath the Cross*; Ellacuría, *Essays on History, Liberation, and Salvation*.

72. Burke, *The Ground Beneath the Cross*, 16.

73. Aquiline Tarimo & William O'Neill, "What San Salvador Says to Nairobi: The Liberation Ethics of Ignacio Ellacuría," in *Love that Produces Hope: The Thought of Ignacio Ellacuría*, eds. Kevin F. Burke & Robert Lassalle-Klein (Collegeville, Minnesota: Liturgical Press, 2006), 237. "Antonio Gramsci, an Italian Marxist theoretician and politician defined an 'organic intellectual' as a person that counteracts hegemony by identifying with a group and trying to organize a social power within this group. An example of an 'organic intellectual' that comes to mind would be Martin Luther King Jr., who attempted to revolutionize racism and change the way people thought about the social construction of reality."

74. Burke, "Christian Salvation and the Disposition of Transcendence: Ignacio Ellacuría's Historical Soteriology," in *Love that Produces Hope: The Thought of Ignacio Ellacuría*, 173.

75. Ellacuría, *Freedom Made Flesh: The Mission of Christ and His Church*, trans. John Drury (Maryknoll: Orbis Books, 1976).

76. Ellacuría, "The Historicity of Christian Salvation," trans Margaret D. Wilde, in *Mysterium Liberationis: Fundamental Concepts of Liberation Theology*, 251–289.

77. *Ibid.*

78. *Ibid.* 254–255.

79. *Ibid.*

80. Ellacuría, *"Sacramento historico"* (1977) ML, Vol. 2, 141, trans. Wilde [554].

81. Burke, "Christian Salvation and the Disposition of Transcendence: Ignacio Ellacuría's Historical Soteriology," 178.

82. *Ibid.*

83. Ellacuría, "The Historicity of Christian Salvation." 254–55.

84. *Ibid.*

85. Ellacuría, *Freedom Made Flesh*, 96.

86. *Ibid.* 104.

87. Ellacuría, "On Liberation," 42.

88. Ellacuria, "The Historicity of Christian Salvation," 258.

89. *Ibid.*

90. *Ibid.*

91. Jon Sobrino's two-volume work on Christology is centered on the idea of Jesus Christ liberator"—the literal translation of the title from the Spanish, in which the term "liberator" functions as a soteriological "title." Sobrino articulates Christologically the "historical soteriology" that Ellacuía had already begun to explore. See Jon Sobrino, *Jesus the Liberator: A Historical-Theological View*, trans. Paul Burns and Francis McDonagh (Maryknoll: Orbis Books, 1993). The second volume in this two-volume "essay" in Christology—in Spanish, *La Fe in Jesucristo* [literally, The Faith in Jesus Christ]—takes up the postresurrection theological developments that gave rise to the very discipline of Christology. See *Christ the Liberator: A View from the Victims*, trans. Paul Burns (Maryknoll: Orbis Books, 2001).

92. Sobrino, "Awakening from the Sleep of Inhumanity," in *The Principle of Mercy: Taking the Crucified People from the Cross* (Maryknoll: Orbis, 1994), 1.

93. *Ibid.* 2.

94. Sobrino here alludes to the Hierarchy of the Church and its inability to perceive and feel the pains of the common people.

95. See Sobrino, "Awakening from the Sleep of Inhumanity."

96. *Ibid.* 3.

97. Sobrino, *Jesus the Liberator*, 12–13.

98. *Ibid.* 6.

99. Jorge Costadoats, "Central Themes in Sobrino's Christology," in *Jon Sobrino's Challenge to Christian Theology: Hope & Solidarity*, ed. Stephen J. Pope, 119–130. Maryknoll: Orbis Books, 2008.

100. *Ibid.* 119.

101. Sobrino, *Jesus the Liberator*, 6.

102. Costadoats, "Central Themes in Sobrino's Christology," 123–125.

103. *Ibid.*

104. See Sobrino, *Christ the Liberator*.

105. *Ibid.* 1–8.

106. *Ibid.* 1.

107. Roberto S. Goizuata, "The Christology of Jon Sobrino," in in *Jon Sobrino's Challenge to Christian Theology: Hope & Solidarity,* ed. Stephen J. Pope, 98–99.

108. Sobrino, "Presuppositions and Foundations of Spirituality," in *Spirituality of Liberation: Toward Political Holiness* (Maryknoll: Orbis, 1988), 23–45.

109. Sobrino, *Jesus the Liberator,* 78.

110. See David Wurfel, *Filipino Politics: Developments and Decay* (Quezen City: Ateneo de Manila University Press, 1988).

111. Antonio B. Lambino, forward to *Awakening to Mission: The Philippine Catholic Church 1965–1981,* by Pasquale T. Giordano (Quezon City, Philippines: New Day Publishers, 1988) iii.

112. *Ibid.* iii.

113. David Wurfel, *Filipino Politics: Developments and Decay* 71.

114. Giordano, *Awakening to Mission,* 8–11.

115. Bishop Francisco Claver, a Jesuit actually wrote the document that the entire bishops Conference adopted and issued.

116. Giordano, *Awakening to Mission,* 176.

117. *Ibid.*

118. Matthew Hassan Kukah, *The Church and the Politics of Social Responsibility* (Lagos: Sovereign Prints Nig. Ltd. 2007), 71.

119. Giordano, *Awakening to Mission,* 8–11.

120. Kukah, *The Church and the Politics of Social Responsibility,* 72.

121. *Ibid.*

122. Antonio F. Moreno, "Engaged Citizenship: The Catholic Bishops' Conference of the Philippines (CBCP) in the Post-Authoritarian Philippines," in *Development, Civil Society and Faith-Based Organizations,* eds. Gerard Clarke and Michael Jennings (New York: Palgrave Macmillan, 2008), 122.

123. *Ibid.* 124.

124. Joseph Matthew Mfutu-Bengo, *In the Name of the Rainbow: Politics of Reconciliation as a Priority of Social Pastoral Care in South Africa and Malawi* (Frankfurt: Peter Lang, 2001), 26–30.

125. Sylvia M. Jacobs, "Malawi: A Historical Study of Religion, Political Leadership, and State Power," in *Religion and Politics in the Developing World: Explosive Interactions,* ed. Rolin G. Mainuddin (Hampshire, England: Ashgate Publishing, 2002), 50.

126. Mfutu-Bengo, *In the Name of the Rainbow,* 28.

127. Jacobs, "Malawi: A Historical Study of Religion, Political Leadership, and State Power," 50.

128. *Ibid.* 60.

129. *Ibid.*

130. *Ibid.* 61.

131. *Ibid.*

132. *Ibid.*

133. *Ibid.*

134. *Ibid.*

135. *Ibid.*

136. *Ibid.*

137. *Ibid.*

138. *Ibid.* 223.

139. *Ibid.* 225.

140. Mfutu-Bengo, *In the Name of the Rainbow*, 29.

141. Anthony Egan, "Governance Beyond Rhetoric: The South African Challenge to the African Synod," in *Reconciliation, Justice, and Peace: The Second African Synod*, ed. Agbonkhianmeghe E. Orobator (New York: Orbis Books, 2011), 100.

142. *Ibid.* 100.

143. *Ibid.* 96–97.

144. *Ibid.*

145. *Ibid.*

146. Kukah, *The Church and the Politics of Social Responsibility*, 74; See also Mfutu-Bengo, *In the Name of the Rainbow*.

147. *Ibid.*

148. *Ibid.*

149. *Ibid.*

150. Egan says, "the 1996 and 2001 national censuses reveal a highly diverse church situation in South Africa. African Initiated Churches combined with Pentecostals and 'other churches' effectively constitute the 'mainline' churches in contemporary South Africa." (Egan, "Governance Beyond Rhetoric:" 99) Thus, it is difficult for the Catholic Church alone to make any meaningful impact on the political life of the country. The Church therefore, joined understandably forces with other church bodies and civil society organizations to pursue their desired changes in South Africa, which proved successful. This presents a veritable example to the Nigerian society, where, though the Catholic Church has a sizeable population, the highly diverse religious and ethnic divisions make it very difficult for one group to successfully drive the initiatives for change alone. I argue that collaboration at ecumenical and interreligious levels are necessary for the way forward in Nigeria.

151. *Ibid.* 76.

152. *Ibid.*

153. Elisée Rutagambwa, S. J., "The Rwandan Church: The Challenge of Reconciliation" in *The Catholic Church and the Nation-State: Comparative Perspectives*, eds. Paul Christopher Manuel, et al (Washington DC: Georgetown University Press, 2006), 173–189. This section follows Rutagambwa's account very closely.

154. *Ibid.* 174.

155. *Ibid.* 175.

156. *Ibid.*

157. *Ibid.*

158. *Ibid.*

159. *Ibid.*

160. *Ibid.* 176.

161. *Ibid.*

162. *Ibid.*

163. *Ibid.*

164. *Ibid.* 177.
165. *Ibid.*
166. *Ibid.* 179.
167. *Ibid.* 177.
168. Benedict XVI, *Deus Caritas Est*, # 232–5.

· 4 ·

"THE WORD BECAME FLESH"

Discerning a Pastoral Option for the Nigerian Church Considering African Synods I and II

The preceding chapters have advanced the argument that Christian religion is neither abstract nor esoteric. Indeed, at the heart of the Christian gospel is the profession: "the word became flesh and dwelt among us" (John1:1–18).[1] In the incarnation of Jesus is the most radical expression of God coming to meet humanity where humanity is, and in a form with which humanity can relate. The very conditions of daily life, the social context of the people constitute, in fact, the locus of God's self-communication, the place of the deepest form of divine encounter. Simply put, the incarnation implies that the Son of God became human so that children of men and women can live more fulfilled lives (John 10:10). This is the interpretation of the Christian gospel that lies at the heart of this study.

Building on the rich ecclesiological framework of Ignacio Ellacuría, as I explored initially in the previous chapter, I want to look at pertinent discussions of the African Synods I[2] and II[3] in 1994 and 2009, to advance my discussion for a paradigm shift toward a new pastoral option for the Church in Nigeria in the area of seminary formation, and a strengthening of ecumenical/interreligious structures of dialogue and collaboration with other arms of civil society as rapprochement in emancipatory praxis for the Church's ministry and witnessing, to be able to "become flesh" in the reality of people's lives.

African Synod I and II[4]

While this work does not pretend to undertake an exhaustive analysis of the African Synods I and II, the Synods deployed remarkable efforts and resources to articulate the interrelatedness of the personal and the social aspects of Christian faith. The First Synod echoed the necessity to bridge this gap, noting, "in Africa, the need to apply the Gospel to concrete life is felt strongly,"[5] even as the Second Synod dealt specifically with reconciliation, justice and peace, emphasizing the Church's theological and social responsibility and inviting the Church to reflect on its public role and place in Africa today.[6] In particular, the First Synod was an attempt to re-examine the Church's approach to evangelization in the face of dehumanizing conditions and failed leadership prevalent in Africa in spite of the Church's presence.

According to Pope John Paul II, the First African Synod of 1994 "was convoked in order to enable the church in Africa to assume its evangelizing mission as effectively as possible in preparation for the third Christian Millennium."[7] This Synod declared, "the main question facing the Church in Africa consists in delineating as clearly as possible what it is and what it must fully carry out, in order that its message may be relevant and credible."[8] Acknowledging the rapid growth of Christianity in Africa south of the Sahara, the Synod asks pointedly: "In a Continent full of bad news, how is the Christian message 'Good News' for our people? Amid an all-pervading despair, where lie the hope and optimism which the Gospel brings?"[9] Notably, the Synod, does not limit itself to proclaiming the good news to win new converts. It calls for religious imagination that can fashion concrete ideals to respond critically and prophetically to the restless desire for the Reign of God in Africa, noting:

> In Africa, the need to apply the Gospel to concrete life is felt strongly. How could one proclaim Christ on that immense Continent while forgetting that it is one of the world's poorest regions? How could one fail to take into account the anguished history of a land where many nations are still in the grip of famine, war, racial and tribal tensions, political instability and the violation of human rights? This is a challenge to evangelization.[10]

Underscoring the correlation between the quality of formation of agents of evangelization and outcome of the quality and content of evangelization, the Synod affirms the importance of sound pastoral agents in forming the people of God as "the most important resource," apart from the grace of Christ in meeting the challenges of Africa.[11] Chapter five of the Post-Synodal exhortation, "You Shall be my Witnesses in Africa," outlined the tasks expected of various agents of evangelization, such as vital Christian communities, laity, catechists, the family, young people, consecrated men and women, deacons, priests ordained and future, and bishops. Regarding future priests in particular, the Synod notes:

> Today more than ever there is need to form future priests in the true cultural values of their country, in a sense of honesty, responsibility and integrity. They shall be formed in such a manner that they will have the qualities of the representatives of Christ, of true servants and animators of the Christian Community . . . living simple lives as befits their milieu.[12]

While encouraging bishops to oversee proper formation of the priests, the document insists that formation programs should pay attention to wholesome values present in the priest's surroundings. In the Nigerian context, for example, this will imply a sound understanding of the nature and causes of poverty, the neglect of the masses and, in some regions of the nation, corruption.

In what appears to be a striking move to take responsibility for the life of society, the First Synod avers, "if the proclamation of justice and peace is an integral part of the task of evangelization, it follows that the promotion of these values should also be part of the pastoral program of each Christian community."[13] This is where the implication for seminary formation becomes most compelling for the Church in Nigeria as well as elsewhere in Africa, as John Paul II notes in the Post-Synodal document:

> That is why I urge that all pastoral agents are to be adequately trained for this apostolate. The formation of clergy, religious and laity, imparted in the areas of their apostolate, should lay emphasis on the social teaching of the Church. Each person, according to his state of life, should lay emphasis on the social teaching of the Church. Each person, according to his state of life, should be specially trained to know his rights and duties, the meaning and service of the common good, honest management of public goods and the proper manner of participating in political life, in order to be able to act in a credible manner in the face of social injustices.[14]

This responsibility, which is the obligation of every Christian, is particularly urgent and professes a unique implication in the life and the ministry of the priest as leader and animator of the Christian community in two related ways. First, priests need to be knowledgeable about the social implications of the Christian Gospel. Thus, seminary formation in Africa, particularly in Nigeria, must emphasize the fact that although pastoral letters, homilies, and witness to the gospel which characterized the social witness of the church over time are quite important efforts to make the Church the "salt of the earth" and the "light of the world," yet, it must be more strategic to realize its prophetic role in these times, through "witness of action." Again, Pope John Paul II says, "Today more than ever, the [C]hurch is aware that her social doctrine will gain credibility more immediately from witness of action than because of its internal logic and consistency."[15]

One of the outstanding contributions of the First Synod was the retrieval of the notion of Church as communion, highlighting role of the laity as legitimate sharers in the ministry of Jesus in the ecclesiological model of Church as family. Hence, John Paul II highlighted the urgency of training the lay people to take on leadership roles to transform society. In article 54 of *Ecclesia in Africa,* he poses:

> A last question must be asked: Has the Church in Africa sufficiently formed the lay faithful, enabling them to assume competently their civic responsibilities and to consider socio-political problems in the light of the Gospel and of faith in God? This is certainly a task belonging to Christians: to bring to bear upon the social fabric an influence aimed at changing not only ways of thinking but also the very structures of society, so that they will better reflect God's plan for the human family. Consequently, I have called for a thorough formation of the lay faithful, a formation which will help them lead a fully integrated life. Faith hope and charity must influence the actions of the true follower of Christ in every activity, situation and responsibility. Since "evangelizing means bringing the Good News into all strata of humanity, and through its influence transforming humanity from within and making it new," Christians must be formed to live the social implications of the Gospel in such a way that their witness will become a prophetic challenge to whatever hinders the true good of men and women of Africa and of every other continent.[16]

Without doubt, this Synod set forth uniquely innovative approaches to a self-understanding of the Church. The ecclesiology found in these discussions here follows the New Testament principle evident particularly in Pauline thought that considers participation the community of Christ as a metaphor for functioning as parts of the human body. Each part has a specific function within the body, hence, referring to the believing community as the "Body of Christ" (1Cor. 12:12–31). The *charismata* or "gifts of grace," exercised by individuals or groups of believers, are conferred by God and should be employed in God's service through Christian ministry. Such arrangements offer Christian believers the opportunity to develop a sense of their own importance and are cherished by women and youth, who, in traditional African societies and in the Church, appear to have no status.

However, the heavily accented notion of patriarchy in the African familial system that gives unfair advantage to the male over the female and children in many aspects of life signaled a major challenge to model of Church as family. This danger of patriarchy has a corollary in the clerical concept of ministry in Africa where the Church is identified almost exclusively with the hierarchy. Although the Synod recommended that African Episcopal conferences should champion the cause of the African woman and especially encourage research into the appropriate role of women in both the society and the Church, one only wonders how far this can go, since the bishops are themselves beneficiaries of patriarchy in Africa.[17]

The Second Synod, building upon the previous one, called specifically for "transformation of theology into pastoral care, namely, into very concrete pastoral ministry in which the great perspectives found in Sacred Scripture and Tradition find application in the activity of bishops and priests in specific times and places."[18] Pope Benedict XVI hinges his understanding and interpretation of the entire African Synod II on this realization:

> The three principal elements of the theme chosen for the Synod, namely reconciliation, justice and peace, brought it face to face with its "theological and social responsibility," and made it possible also to reflect on the Church's public role and her place in Africa today.[19]

Clearly, the Church in Nigeria as in most of Africa today faces complex interactive and overarching systems of injustice that call the Church to more active engagement in the structures that plague the living conditions of the Nigerian people. These systems have undermined every political and economic endeavor aimed at promoting the common good. The second Synod acknowledges this fact:

> [In Africa] situations demanding a new presentation of the Gospel, new in ardor, methods and expression, are not rare. In particular, the new evangelization needs to integrate the intellectual dimension of the faith into the living experience of the encounter with Jesus Christ present at work in the ecclesial community. Being Christian is born not of an ethical decision or a lofty ideal, but an encounter with an event, a person, which gives life a new horizon and a decisive direction.[20]

At the heart of the African Synod II therefore, include among other things, the call for a meaningful and enduring transformation of the structures of injustice is needed in Africa. In order to effectively carry this out, the Church will have to dialogue. It will have to develop a more active approach that engages with

the agents of power in a constructive dialogue for change. This will involve the
willingness and the disposition to struggle alongside the people, standing in solidarity with them and guiding them through the paths of peace, reconciliation,
and justice. In this light, the African Synod II poignantly stressed the necessity
of the churches to forge alliances toward creating a corresponding emancipator
spirituality and witness. Benedict XVI underscores this necessity inherently in
the representative participation at the Synod, implying:

> By inviting to this Synodal Assembly our fellow Christians – Orthodox, Coptic Or-
> thodox, Lutheran, Anglican, Methodist, and in particular His Holiness Abuna Pau-
> los, Patriarch of the Tewahedo Orthodox Church of Ethiopia, . . . – I wanted to make
> it clear that the path to reconciliation must first pass through the communion of
> Christ's disciples. A divided Christianity remains a scandal, since it de facto contra-
> dicts the will of the Divine Master (cf Jn 17:21). Ecumenical dialogue therefore seeks
> to direct our common journey towards Christian unity. . . I call upon the whole ec-
> clesial family – particular Churches, institutes of consecrated life as well as lay move-
> ments and associations – to pursue this path with ever greater determination. . . .[21]

To be able to dialogue about issues of common good, Catholics need to be
informed from the standpoint of their faith tradition. Yet, the Church in Nigeria prefers to continue to keep the social teachings of the Church a secret.
Pope Benedict XVI even decries this approach:

> Illiteracy represents one of the principal obstacles to development. It is a scourge on a
> par with that of the pandemics. True, it does not kill directly, but it contributes actively
> to the marginalization of the person – which is a form of social death – and it blocks
> access to knowledge. . . . I ask Catholic communities and institutions to respond to this
> great challenge, which is a real testing ground for civilization, and in accordance with
> their means, I ask them to multiply their efforts, independently or in collaboration with
> other organizations, to develop effective programmes adapted to people's needs.[22]

The faithful need to know that it is not an article of faith that they should
remain poor. They need to know that it is not an article of faith to be sub-
servient to self-serving leadership, but rather a legitimate demand of faith
to oppose bad leadership to bring about the common good of all. This understanding can form the basis for dialogue to foster common action among
different churches.

Sustained dialogue of understanding and cooperation is needed, not just
between various Christian denominations but equally between adherents of
other religious and social groups. This is necessary toward creating a culture of
peace. In the words of Benedict XVI:

As many social movements indicate, peace in Africa, as elsewhere, is conditioned by interreligious relations. Hence it is important for the Church to promote dialogue as a spiritual disposition, so that believers may learn to work together, for example in associations for justice and peace, in a spirit of trust and mutual help.[23]

The wealth of religious pluralism can be an asset to peace building and to the promotion of the common good. Openness to dialogue and the interaction between religious actors and with the political class and government functionaries around concrete social-political and economic issues are paramount toward building synergies for common action. The integrity of religious leaders involved in joint ventures for the common good is critical in ensuring the success of such endeavors. In an environment of distrust, hatred, and violence, virtues of reconciliation, justice and peace can be achieved only through dialogue.[24]

The apparent contradictions of violent conflicts, poverty, corruption and disease in Nigeria, pose an urgent need for the Church to fashion a strategic transformational approach to evangelization. Considering the African Synods I and II, such approach will involve two things: the formation of pastoral agents in a way that makes them sensitive to the need for the Church to contribute productively to construct a society that embodies the values of reconciliation, justice, and peace in Nigeria. This has a direct bearing on the style and approach to leadership, and so I call for a shift in the current trend of formation in the seminaries. Secondly, since the Church exists in society alongside peoples of other faiths and orientations, the Church needs to be in dialogue, which is not to be viewed as a specialized function suited only for a few specially trained clergy and laity, but, rather, must serve as an integral part of the entire process of evangelization. The next section will consider the needed shift in the formation of agents of evangelization.

A Paradigm Shift in Seminary Formation and Ecclesial Imagination

A Paradigm Shift in Seminary Formation

As far as this work is concerned, the overly theoretical style of seminary formation offered in Nigerian seminaries is correlative to poverty of leadership, which has hindered a praxis-oriented witness of the faith in the Nigerian Church. Since leaders of the Catholic Church are products of the seminaries, the call to update practices of seminary formation in this study is done in hope of addressing leadership practices, which are often neo-patrimonial in approach, to embrace a leadership of service based in transparency. Such a leadership will enable the Church in Nigeria to first, embrace best practices in its internal structures, and then to step into the organizational vacuum of a failing state and weak forms of government and provide space for a virile civil society, by actively joining in the social struggles of the people toward realizing the coming of the kingdom here "on earth as it is in heaven." This call is not in opposition to the mission of the Church, but it is in fact, inspired by the call of the African Synods, I and II. This modest attempt re-echoes simply this call of the Synods that seem to have been glossed over in Nigeria. Despite the spread of western education in Nigeria today, in most rural communities where priests minister, the priest is often the smartest, most educated person in the community. With this comes some form of moral authority. His role in forming public opinion becomes crucial in animating the community toward credible engagement in social life.

Elochukwu E. Uzukwu, like Downey, recognizes the anomaly in a seminary training that results in poverty of leadership, noting that the effects of transplanted West European Church structures conditioned Church leaders in Nigeria to operate in medieval feudalistic manners with their actions originating from an interest very much concerned with power.[25] To perpetuate this hierarchical pyramid pattern of ecclesiastical administration, the Church in Nigeria employs a style of training that keeps seminarians completely out of touch with realities of life and challenges that people face.

> In Nigeria, for example, people struggle to beat a neo-colonialist politico-economic arrangement in order to survive. But the issue in the church is power. Among the qualities required to function as a good priest or religious, obedience comes out on top. In a continent where 50% live in absolute poverty, and an estimated 400 million (according to United Nation Development Programme) will be living in extreme poverty . . . candidates for the priesthood and religious life are assured of food and other material necessities of life by foreign agencies and the local contribution of the laity. They are thus rendered incapable of appreciating in a practical way the lot of majority of Africans; also the root cause of our poverty escapes them at a practical level.[26]

Indeed, as it happens with any group of people, physical exclusiveness, and esoteric preoccupations breed their own sub-culture. Thus, the seminary, feeding upon long years of institutionalization indoctrinates future priests with a theoretical view of ministry and Christian life, which is over academic.[27] Seminaries in Nigeria, operating in the manner of total institutions, control practically every aspect of the lives of those being trained, thereby discouraging initiative, critical thinking, and suppressing creativity to preserve and defend "orthodoxy." Part of the effect is that "the seminarian, whose contemporaries devote themselves, sometimes with considerable sacrifice and initiative, to their families or their businesses, is preoccupied with matters of personal comfort, trifling luxuries, minor acquisitions, and so on," to the neglect of serious pastoral issues affecting the lives of the people to whom they will be ministering.[28] Thus, poverty of leadership, that plagues the Nigerian Church, can be identified rightly as a consequence of a mentality imparted through seminary training. In practical terms therefore, poverty of leadership and seminary training, are two sides of the same coin, which have hindered the kind of praxis found in the Church of El Salvador, for example, through the visionary leadership and witness of Archbishop Romero and Ignacio Ellacuría.

Premised on the foregoing, Downey calls for a reassessment of values in seminary training, where theological and pastoral training are taken in perspective:

> To begin with, one could visualize a more rigid distinction between the more strictly theological ministry and the pastoral ministry in the conventional sense of the word. But within each area, there would be more specific fields of specialization and therefore of ministry. We would therefore witness a departure from the system whereby all ministers follow the same rigid pattern of training, life style, and so on.[29]

The implication of Downey's call, which is at the heart of this work, is that the contemporary Nigerian reality and unfolding world-view and how these affect the day-to-day lives of Nigerians should form a basic component of priestly training. "The strictly defined course, specified for all seminarians, would be seen for the anomaly that it is," bearing in mind the basic question in each case, "for what type of ministry is the candidate being trained?"[30] Relatedly, the very structure of training will need to be reconsidered so that other options like in-service training, the university system, and the apprenticeship system options can be adopted in training for the priesthood. This is where the call of the African Synods I and II become very pertinent for seminary formation in Nigeria today, especially the First Synod that specifically reiterated the need to concretely apply the Gospel to life situations. This concern and commitment should be reflected in the curriculum of study in Nigerian seminaries.

Vincent J. Donovan, corroborates Downey's thought, noting "Evangelization is a process of bringing the Gospel to people where they are, not where you would like them to be."[31] Like Downey, Donovan argues for a peculiar formation for leadership and the priesthood in the Church on the African continent. Considering the current understanding of the priesthood to have evolved from specific cultural settings, he declares: "most of the development to the priesthood we know today did not take place in the New Testament, but rather outside of it, what we have here is a perfect example of culturization, an element of the Gospel taking on the flesh and blood of the culture in which it was preached, a true cultural interpretation of the Gospel."[32] Without making traditional Nigerian or African values the exclusive yardstick for doing theology in or exercising ministry in Nigeria, Donovan's experience among the Massai demonstrates how important it is for Church in Nigeria to "have an equal right to respond with its valid form of priesthood," since according to him, the present form of priesthood "is indeed a cultural interpretation of Christianity."[33]

As leaders of the Christian community, the teaching role of the priest is vital to help form the consciousness of the community to whom he ministers in the important impulse of witnessing the Gospel message to the community to ignite action. This cannot be achieved with a training that stifles creativity and critical thinking in defense of orthodoxy. Paul Gifford has indicated that in regard to attaining the desired levels of change in the style of leadership, "the lesson both of Asia and Latin America is that the path to change begins in the minds of its indigenous thinkers."[34] In Latin America for example, Ignacio Ellacuria took up the challenge of articulating the Christian claim of salvation through an explicit attention to the context of the poverty in El Salvador, whose majority population experienced extraordinary violence and repression in any attempt to improve its lot. He insisted that the church in El Salvador of his day had to "take on history" by naming and denouncing the powers of death that crucify the Salvadoran poor and by remembering the God of life who liberates and raises them to new life. The Nigerian Church needs theologians who view the obligation to participate in shaping the moral character of society as requirement of faith, and who are ready to offer leadership that stings both Church and society to this consciousness.

Frances Fox Piven and Richard A. Cloward have identified three necessary aspects for change in consciousness:

> First, 'the system'—or those aspects of the system that people experience and perceive—loses legitimacy. Large numbers of men and women who ordinarily accept the authority of their rulers and the legitimacy of institutional arrangements come to believe in some measure that these rulers and these arrangements are unjust

and wrong. Second, people who are ordinarily fatalistic, who believe that existing arrangements are inevitable, begin to assert 'rights' that imply demands for change. Third, there is a new sense of efficacy; people who ordinarily consider themselves helpless come to believe that they have some capacity to alter their lot.[35]

The change in consciousness which is stimulated by human agency can be found in all societies and among all groups-classes, including the Church. It enables human actors to act to make a difference in their world, shaping extant structures and forging new and adaptable systems in coping and improving the parameters of their societies uniquely. This is the unique role that theology needs to play in the current context on Nigeria to achieve the desired ecclesial leadership.

Effective change begins from below, from among the people. To get to the consciousness that they can work for change, the people need to be informed and formed. This is where Catholic social teaching becomes a handy tool in the hands of the Nigerian theologian today. When people are thus formed, they can ask questions which call the leadership to accountability and the attendant consequence of reform comes easily. The Catholic Church in the United States of America today, for example, has stringent checks and balances to issues around sexual abuse because a small group of informed Catholics at a parish in Wellesley, Massachusetts organized and started the advocacy for change. The Church in Nigeria will get at the point of overcoming the current poverty of leadership if Catholics are well formed and informed to ask questions and demand accountability from the hierarchy. In addition, this can best begin with the formation of priests in the seminaries.

Formation programs in seminaries will specifically need to prioritize teaching that focuses on helping priests understand the complex nature of the systems of injustice, which are inherent even in Church and the society so that they can become more aware and more capable to deal with these issues as they assume their ministry with the people. Such analysis is sometimes beyond the scope of the philosophical and the theological background the seminaries propose to offer to young priests, hence, in some cases, Church leaders have rushed in to condemn or otherwise to comment on issues without understanding the complexity of the issues at hand. Although the African Synods offer a unique call to update the methodology of the formation and training of pastoral agents, it does not provide detailed instructions as to how to incorporate the relevant tools of social analysis and contemporary history. This study offer some detailed recommendations regarding seminary training.

Nigerian seminaries and houses of formation will need to borrow from universities, colleges, and other institutions of higher education outside and inside Nigeria in terms of curriculum development. The current situation where too many general courses are offered without emphasis and concentration to ensure depth and proficiency accords little mastery of specific fields of study. Rather than offer so many courses, less courses with more depth and concentration should be the target. Seminarians should also be more exposed to the social reality in which they are eventually going to minister, by having more contacts with people and experiencing for themselves what the people face outside the seminary walls.[36] Seminarians thus trained, will become more attuned to contemporary history, and their social, political, and economic circumstances, gaining, in turn, a deeper ability to discern the "signs of the times," being able to read them with the eyes of faith and theology, and discerning the paths of sin and the avenues of grace.

Importantly too, seminary faculty should design specific courses to facilitate integration of social studies and theological studies, prayer life, and active life of service in light of faith. These tools will enable priests to develop a more fitting schedule of pastoral activities partnered with suitable techniques of social action and community organizing in consonant with Catholic social teachings. Every part of the curriculum—bible, sacraments, liturgy, ethics, homiletics, church history, etc. should integrate this aspect of seminary education, and this topic should not be confined to a single course on social justice. This calls for good visionary leadership with smart policy measures that ensure a radical structural transformation from a Catholic Church that talks to one that acts for the salvation of people in the Nigerian Church. All these needs to be pursued over a sustainable period by successive leadership committed to same objectives; a sustainable culture of honest, clean and transparent Church leaders as bishops, priests, religious and lay leaders.

A Paradigm Shift in the Liturgy and Ecclesial Imagination

Over the years, the liturgy has formed and reformed the life of the Church, since nothing is more evidently at the core of the Christian life than its public worship—which in fact, is precisely what liturgy means.[37] Thus, at Vatican Council II, for example, the liturgy was the first subject to be examined and the first, too, in a sense, in its intrinsic worth and importance for the life of the Church. Significantly, the placement of the liturgy as the first item on the agenda of the Council signaled the prioritization of the pastoral dimension of the entire Council as well as its place as a proving ground for how to conduct the remainder of the Council.[38]

The renewal and the reform of the liturgy at the Vatican II Council can, therefore, be said to have been undertaken with the realization that the Church's goal is to reach beyond itself. Indeed, the liturgy assumes a fitting and a privileged status as a moment of communion and participation for an evangelization that can lead to integral, authentic Christian liberation.[39] Liturgical celebrations provide the Church with unique opportunities to reach Africans with the word of God in a manner that they are able to heed, to assimilate, to incarnate, to celebrate, and transmit the Gospel message of hope to their brothers and sisters. In this way, the liturgy invites Christians to take up the commitment to serve their brothers and sisters, as the bishops of Latin America note: "The community, which joyfully celebrates the Lord's Pasch in the liturgy, has a commitment to bear witness, catechize, educate, and communicate the Good News through all the means at its disposal."[40]

Thus, the revelation of God's power and might, the message of God's holiness and justice, the truth about God's mercy and goodness, and the mystery of God's love and compassion must find expression in the liturgical celebrations of the Christian community. These truths will necessarily mean different things to different people in consonance with the age, historical experience, and the socio-political and economic circumstances of the bearers and of the recipients.[41] Essentially, it must be a celebration of the Good News, the news of new life in Christ, and the news of their earthly liberation and salvation.

However, in Nigeria, every religious activity—whether it is a matter of ritual, a public statement, or any other religious function—is carried out mostly with inherent conflictive and unequal relationships of power between the different classes that constitute the social structure of the society.[42] This sometimes disposes members of the clergy, especially those who share the privileges of power and its many opportunities with the elite, to perceive reality in a manner, which corresponds to justify their social condition and opposes significantly that of the poor, including their own parishioners in the same society. In many cases, the liturgy then becomes a tool in the hands of some politicians and some Church leaders in ways that disfigure its original evangelizing value. Often, some Nigerian religious leaders tend to use liturgical gatherings unconsciously to produce, to preserve, to reproduce, to propagate, and to inculcate religious teachings and practices that perpetuate and legitimatize oppression and suppression of the poor, who are the clear majority of the population.

Emphatically, Christians, who suffering, are exhorted not to worry about "this passing world," since their true home is in heaven. Christians are encouraged to obey their leaders even when the means of becoming leaders has been overtly fraudulent and the leaders, themselves, are clearly benefitting from systems of oppression and material greed, since as they are convinced, "all authority comes from God" (Romans 13:1). Thus, the liturgy becomes an avenue to create consent to the institutions of established dominance and oppression, while rejecting simultaneously any form of opposition to bad governance, corruption, and repression. With references to supernatural and metasocial forces as the basis of these claims, the elite in Nigeria, thus, have the advantage of holding on to power and establishing cohesion of the public. Events leading to the last general elections in Nigeria illustrate this reality.

As political campaigns mounted toward the last general elections of April 2015, a Catholic priest, Father Ejike Mbaka, renowned for his gifts of healing and prophecy, delivered a New Year Oracle against President Goodluck's bid for a second term, claiming that Goodluck was would lose at the polls since his governance brought much suffering for the people.[43] Mbaka's prediction attracted so much national interest specifically for his daring the unthinkable in Nigeria—to say something contrary to what the ruling government would be pleased to hear. Significantly, Nigeria's most senior Catholic clerics—John Cardinal Onaiyekan and the President of the CBCN Archbishop Ignatius Kaigama—came out swiftly to distance publicly the Nigerian Catholic Church from Mbaka's oracles.[44] Some Nigerian media reported that Cardinal Onaiyekan called for Mbaka's bishop to reprimand him.

While it is true that the Catholic Church always cautions its leaders against name-calling in the context of liturgical homilies, sometimes this is necessary—as the Prophet Nathan would tell David: "You are the Man!" (2 Samuel 12:7). Besides, one may ask what alternative voices are coming out of the churches to dare governments in power, whether at state, local, or federal levels even when every indication is that all is not right? Clear indications are that most of church leaders across denominational lines have been too acquiescent to the establishment. Excessive donations of money, cars, private jets (a former president of the Christian Association of Nigeria, CAN owns one), or landed property from those in power have demeaned the capacity of church leaders to speak up for the suffering masses or to condemn the failed ruling class who are responsible for the suffering and pain of most Nigerians. Our celebration of the liturgy needs, therefore, to be restored as a celebration of good news: good news of new life in Christ, and good news of the liberation and the salvation of the children of God from bad governance, as Mbaka noted.

By excluding any mention of the political and social, the Church evades her historical identity and mission. This scandalous silence has brought about a liturgical nonimagination among Nigerian Christians that colors a very negative and passive attitude of the people toward their immediate social reality, in the belief that "this world is not our home," as they are told. Among the Tiv of central Nigeria, for example, a sizable number of their very common and popular liturgical hymns are couched in a language that casts the historical reality of this world in very mean and insignificant terms.[45] Here is an example:

Figure 4.1: TAR NE KA TAR WASE NE GA (This world is not our world.)

Refrain: Tar ne ka tar wase ne ga angbianev mzamber ne, umbur nen ka ken shir se lu ye se mba va wundun u.	**Refrain:** This world is not our world I am pleading with you brethren, always remember we are pilgrims and shall be leaving this place
1. Tar a awuha nan, tar u a engem nan kpa I de saren se ga.	No matter how beautiful or glamorous the world might be don't desire it
2. Sea lu a inyaregh, shin tar ne kua akondu kpa umbur nen er tar ne ka shir, se mba va wundun u.	Even if you have money or clothes remember that the world is a pilgrimage and we shall be leaving it
3. Se kera ver asema sha mlu u inyar ga, umbur nen angbianev ka mlu u inyar yange naYuda hingir u teen Yesu ye.	Let us not desire money, remember brethren it was desire for money that made Judas to betray Jesus
4. Sea timber ashe sha mlu u tar yo, se mba vihin uma asev yo angbianev se mem u timber ashe sha imiondun mba tar ne se mba va wundun ve.	If we waste time on the glories of this world, we are wasting our lives brethren, let us stop wasting our time on the glories of this world because we are leaving them.

Source: Composed by Alfred Iho, Katsina Ala Diocese, Nigeria

A sample of similar popular liturgical songs of the Tiv Catholics is shown in appendix II. These songs, like many others, make the poor people feel impotent. They convey a feeling that Christians should avoid the world and wait for a better life in heaven.

Instead of giving the impression that Christianity should have nothing to do with creating hope for a better society and being involved in the struggle for justice and full civic participation, the Christian liturgy in Nigeria needs to imbibe the hope that Jesus came so that we might have life and have it to the fullest (John 10:10). Earlier I identified that seminary formation needs to address the root causes of poverty. Moreover, I called for reform of ecclesial imagination so that it can attend to the present needs of the people, and that seminarians must learn how to do this within the context of the liturgy. Seminary education and ecclesial imagination will need to be attuned to awaken people to the causes of their pains and to empower them to develop actions to reject those causes. Such education and ecclesial imagination will help the Church dialogue with other Christian churches as well as other religions, since the pains that Christians experience in their lives are not peculiar to Christians alone but to all Nigerians. Hence, there will be need to create common ecumenical and interreligious initiatives.

Systemic Reconciliation: Effective Ecumenical/ Interreligious Structures for Dialogue and Healing

Nigerian Professor Akintunde E. Akinade advocates for a specific Nigerian form of dialogue among Christians and between Christians and Muslims:

> In many parts of Nigeria, there is a form of dialogue of life that operates on practical and day-to-day terms. Christians and Muslims live next to each other, mingle freely in all aspects of human endeavor, meeting in the market place and on the streets, in schools and other learning institutions. . . . Christians receive Christmas and Easter greeting cards from their Muslim friends, neighbors, and relatives. Muslims are present in the church for the baptism, wedding, or burial of relatives and friends. In this dialogue of life, Christians and Muslims are enriched by each other's experience and spirituality, and strengthened by certain features of the faith of the other.[46]

According to Akinade, studies and paradigms in ecumenical/interreligious dialogue have always tended to focus "on theological concerns, or have explored the ideological dimensions of religion."[47] However, he opines that the lived character of dialogue in indigenous ethnic communities in places, such as Ghana, Yorubaland in western Nigeria and Gambia offers a more effective pattern for Nigeria as a whole, in contrast to Western theories of dialogue that tend to be text-centered, doctrinally oriented, and centered on issues of the lex credendi.[48] Such experiences can be replicated to other parts of Nigeria as a model. In the next section, I will focus on these much-needed initiatives, which can be enacted between the Christian churches in Nigeria.

Effective Ecumenical Structures for Dialogue and Healing

Earlier, I noted that modern Nigeria was created by the installation of a British colonial administration in the country. Consequently, the historical forces that shaped colonial Nigeria continue to shape the politics of contemporary Nigeria, especially given that its religious formation and religious struggles are grounded in colonial structures. According to Nigerian social political analyst Iheanyi Enwerem, the colonialists and the Christian missionaries were products of the New Enlightenment Age that spawned the evolutionary world of Darwinism, holding a firm belief in progress.[49] Indeed, he continues, the British colonialists in Nigeria shared the beliefs of Darwinism, and so perceived the north of the country, in contrast to the south, as the location of the finer races, from which the lighter-skinned Fulani race was chosen specifically, not only as superior to other ethnic groups, but also as having the right leadership as well as the right religion. Islam, therefore, was considered to be a better form of paganism than the fetishism of the savage south.[50] This created the local basis of state power in Nigeria, where the colonial state, supported by Europeans who were engaged in commerce, opted to work with and through local Muslim rulers rather than through Christian missions.

Because of this colonial attitude, Christians in the north, especially the northern indigenous Christians from the minority tribes, became targets of injustice and oppression at the hands of what was known as the "Northern System"—the Anglo-Hausa-Fulani Islamic hegemony. In this atmosphere, Christian missions needed a common ground to survive the hostile environment, marking the birth of ecumenical activities in Nigeria. Enwerem notes in this regard: "Part of their survival mechanism was to undertake ecumenical meetings either to counter the restrictions imposed on the missions by the Indirect Rule Policy or to seek avenues of compromise with the colonial administration."[51]

Since this threat was more pronounced in the north, Christian churches there were more determined to make forays into challenging the political status quo, and by 1948, the Rahol Kannang Meeting[52] of Christians from various churches formalized their ecumenical meeting into the Northern Christian Movement. Specifically, that meeting resolved to begin a campaign of political consciousness among Christians and to mobilize them against the political challenges posed by the Islamic ruling class in the north.[53] Since the imperatives of Indirect Rule on Christian missions were not as strict in the south as in the north, the need for ecumenism in the south was based more on intrareligious differences, largely those of mainstream Protestant churches against the more viable Roman Catholicism in Nigeria at the time.

By the end of the Nigerian civil war, the Federal Government initiated a policy of reconciliation, rehabilitation, and reconstruction, to help the people to heal from the ravages of the war. This served as a good opportunity for united and ecumenical witnessing by the different Christian churches. In the words of Enwerem:

> The Christian Council of Nigeria (CCN) seized the opportunity to impress itself positively upon Catholics, especially in the way the CCN helped to rehabilitate the mostly Catholic Igbo after the trauma of the war. This kind gesture by the CCN and the openness of the Catholics . . . brought about the trust necessary for the two Christian groups to establish the first national ecumenical project in 1971 – the National Institute of Moral and Religious Education. . . Its purpose was teacher training in Moral and Religious Education.[54]

This venture proved very rewarding and registered such successes that these bodies were inspired to establish another joint venture, the Christian Health Association of Nigeria, which was responsible for coordinating the provision of medical facilities, especially drugs, donated to the churches for their work in healthcare in Nigeria.

On August 27, 1976, the then Federal Military Government of General Obasanjo invited several church leaders to a meeting at Dodan Barracks—the seat of the military government.[55] From this meeting, the Christian leaders moved to the Catholic Secretariat just across the road to hold a private meeting. Per Enwerem, attendance at this meeting included thirty-three church leaders from thirteen denominations:

> Roman Catholics, Anglicans, Baptists, Methodists, the African Church, Presbyterians, the Salvation Army, the Lutheran Church of Christ in Nigeria (LCCN), the Apostolic Church, United African Methodists (UAMC), the Evangelical Church of West Africa (ECWA), the Church of Christ in Nigeria (COCIN), and the HEKAN churches.[56]

This meeting at the Catholic Secretariat was the origin and beginning of the Christian Association of Nigeria (CAN), since the decision to form a national association was made at this meeting.[57] At the moment CAN has expanded its membership from initially three groups to five blocs today: (1) The Catholic Church, (2) The Christian Council of Nigeria, (3) The Organization of African Instituted Churches (OAIC), (4) The TEKAN/ECKWA Fellowship, and (5) The Pentecostal Fellowship of Nigeria. The current constitution of the association requires that churches seeking admission to the body be committed to the teachings of the bible, especially to the worship of One God in the Trinity: The Father, Son, and Holy Spirit.[58]

Over the years, the drive for ecumenism in Nigeria has concentrated mostly on the churches agitating for the rights of Christians to freedom of worship and religion within the realm of Nigerian polity and for fairness to Christians within the skewed power structure that advantages Muslims. At the height of military dictatorship in Nigeria in the mid-1980s, CAN adopted a more dramatic posture through peaceful protests and demonstrations registering the discontent of the general populace. Following the reshuffling of the Federal Government Cabinet by the General Ibrahim Babangida regime in December 1989, protests erupted among Christians Nigeria, beginning with the Kaduna-based CAN in January 11, 1990, which Enwerem reports:

> It was alleged by CAN's national President that about 80% of the then present cabinet were Muslims. The other 20% were just the insignificant ones. Salifu [long-serving secretary of CAN] was more specific. According to him, of the total number of thirty-five ministers, twenty-seven were Muslims, only five [were] Christians, [with] three others. National CAN denounced the government in unequivocal terms and instructed that everybody should go out and do something and at the same time.[59]

Thus, from opposing in very strong terms Nigeria's move to full membership in the Organization of Islamic Conference (OIC) in 1986, the establishment of the Islamic legal system through the provision of the Sharia in the country's constitution, and the establishment of the Islamic banking system in Nigeria to the overt exclusion of Christians in the most sensitive areas of Nigeria's national life, CAN has consistently opposed and delayed the long-standing intention of the Hausa-Fulani Islamic ruling class and its scions to establish an Islamic theocratic state in Nigeria.

Despite these efforts, one of the major problems confronting CAN's inability to have a more effective ecumenical witness in the current historical reality of Nigeria hinges on the irony that while it is engaged in political activities, yet it is unable to extricate itself from the apolitical mindset in which Nigeria's Christianity has been enveloped since its introduction by European missionaries. There appears to be some equivocation arising from CAN's political identity and intent, with some leaders and member-churches desiring to remain purely an ecumenical (religious) association, while others are advocating having a more pronounced social role. Over the years, successive CAN leadership has

claimed mostly neutrality, but in fact, it always appears to support the establishment against the interest of the masses, and so these actions call to question its
ideological and intellectual honesty. According to Enwerem, this posture on the
part of CAN explains its unwillingness and coldness toward forming strategic
linkages with other human forces—albeit non-religious or non-Christian—that
are opposed to the same abuses about which CAN leadership speaks.[60] Thus,
besides the unwillingness of different Christian churches to cooperate with each
other toward the achievement of goals for the common good, the churches, and
by extension CAN, find it even more difficult to ally with non-Christian groups
for doctrinal and ideological reasons.

The failure on the part of CAN to translate their intellectual weight into
establishing linkages with other progressive forces in the nation remains a major drawback. Enwerem cites an example of this, pointing out that northern
Nigeria, the local regional CAN fought successfully for the return of mission
schools to the churches, but ended up with its member school's tuition being
financially out of the reach of the common people on whose behalf the CAN
leadership claims to speak.[61] The private universities owned by various Christian denominations are simply unaffordable for the children of the poor. This
tuition rate applies to high schools, such as the Loyola Jesuit Colleges in Abuja
and Lagos as well as other private grade schools. This fee-based system of access
to education, thus, undermines CAN's witness value nation as well as its ecumenical import in Nigeria.

Another challenge posed to CAN's ability to witness effectively in the current historical reality of Nigeria is the limitations of the ethnicities it encompasses. Similar to every other group in Nigeria, CAN operates within a Nigerian
context in which individuals still identify themselves, and are identified, and
valued according to their ethnicity rather than their national character; a context without a social security system; a context in which the elite and those in
power crush their opposition by harassing relatives of the critics.[62] In January
2013, Nigeria's Catholic bishops withdrew from CAN. The bishops charged the
umbrella body with polarization and partisanship. Hence, they were no longer
confident that CAN could still serve as the voice of the voiceless in Nigeria. In
a letter signed by the President of the Bishops' Conference, Archbishop Ignatius
Kaigama, entitled *Our Concern for Christian Unity*, the bishops said:

> We are suspending our participation in CAN meetings at the national level until
> such a time the leadership reverses back to the original vision, mission and objectives
> of CAN. At the moment, CAN is being dragged into partisan politics thereby com-

promising the ability to play its role as the conscience of the nation and the voice of the voiceless.[63]

Accusations that CAN had made overt political statements in support of the People's Democratic Party (PDP) government, and then President Jonathan Goodluck, were common.[64] The many contradictions among Nigerian church leaders, ranging from close alliances with corrupt politicians, to their ostentatious lifestyle, the opulence of some church functionaries and the doctrinal differences between the many church denominations, have all undermined the value of ecumenical witness of the Christian church in Nigeria. Above all, the inherent ethnic segregation of Nigerian society creeps into the ranks of church leaders and translates into ethno/religious disagreements and non-cooperation on very vital issues affecting the common good.

In the spirit of the African Synods I and II, and in the light of the ongoing discussion, all church bodies in Nigeria have potential to develop emancipatory ideas beyond those which individual churches can implement on their own, and, therefore, individual church bodies must call for a strategic alliance of progressive forces in the churches to forge and to articulate a common cause of action among the entire body of Christ. John Paul II noted this fact when he counseled that divisions among churches in Africa need to be healed through honest dialogue. In his words:

> Within the borders left behind by the colonial powers, the co-existence of ethnic groups with different traditions, languages, and even religions often meets obstacles arising from serious mutual hostility. Tribal oppositions at times endanger if not peace, at least the pursuit of the common good in society. They also create difficulties for the life of the churches and the acceptance of Pastors from other ethnic groups. This is why the Church in Africa feels challenged by the specific responsibility of healing these divisions. For the same reason, the Special Assembly emphasized the importance of ecumenical dialogue with other churches and ecclesial communities.[65]

There is need for the Christian community in Nigeria to become more proactive rather than reacting constantly to policies. The training of the agents of evangelization in Nigeria across all church bodies should strive to ground their practices and articulation of spirituality in an ecumenically based emancipatory religious outlook. Christians in positions of authority and government need to be properly educated concerning their roles as leaven in society, and above all, they need first to work for the common good against the current practice of the quest for personal and communal enrichment, chieftaincies and craving recognition. This is critical so they can avoid suspicion from one another in all ecumenical endeavors, and so win the support of all denominations in the effort to work for the common good and the coming of the kingdom on earth as it is in heaven. This same cooperation and witnessing is required in regard to linkages with people of other religions, which I address in the next section.

Effective Interreligious Dialogue and Healing

American theologian Roger Haight asserts, "we live in a world of wild pluralism which calls into question every tradition and notion of truth itself."[66] Indeed, the contemporary world, in the words of Akinade, "is characterized by an amazing plurality of ideologies, cultures, and religion."[67] This awareness creates an imperative for efforts toward human solidarity and unity despite differences.

In Nigeria, Islam and Christianity are the two dominant religious groups. "With a population of over 170 million people, Archbishop Teissier of Algiers once described this country as the greatest Islamo-Christian nation in the world."[68] Hence, Akinade explains, "Nigeria provides an excellent context for understanding the cultural, social, economic, and political issues that are involved in Christian-Muslim encounters,"[69] since many Christians live side by side with so many Muslims in Nigeria. Thus, engendering a dialogical framework that safeguards pluralism, freedom, and justice presents the most crucial challenge for Nigerians.

The colonial precedence of the British preserved, purified, and expanded Islam in Nigeria, and formed simultaneously the basis of legitimacy for the ruling class.[70] The concept of the North predominantly Muslim and the South as predominantly Christian, reinforced successive events of conflict and established a basis for bargaining in politics, resulting in what Nigerians refer to as the North-South dichotomy.[71]

Multiple factors, coupled with experiences of minority tribes with the Sokoto caliphate and the colonial administration, occasioned incessant ethno-religious conflicts, especially in Northern Nigeria.[72] In the face of this challenge, it was necessary to bring the two major religious bodies to the table for dialogue: The Jamalat-ul-Nasril Islam (JNI) for Muslims and the Christian Association of Nigeria (CAN) for the Christians. Thus, the Nigeria Interreli-

gious Council (NIREC) was established in September 1999, as a brainchild of
Muslim and Christian leaders, with the support of the Federal Government of
Nigeria.[73] The aims and objectives of the council include the following:

- To foster dialogue to understand the true teachings of the two religions,
  Christianity and Islam.
- To create a permanent and sustainable channel of communication and
  interaction, thereby promoting dialogue between Christians and Muslims.
- To provide a forum for cooperation between Muslims and Christians
  and to address issues of conflict violence.
- To serve as a platform to express cordial relationships among various
  religious groups and the government.[74]

Nigerian priest Thaddeus Byimui Umaru surveyed numerous efforts of the NI-
REC to enhance prospects for a more peaceful coexistence, and believes they
have been successful.[75] Among other things, Umaru recognizes that the initiatives of the NIREC has provided, even if minimally, over the years the necessary space for meetings, discussions and avenues for peace-building initiatives,
which helped minimize or avert some of the most violent clashes. Through
joint ventures such as: the Interfaith Mediation Center/Muslim-Christian Dialogue Forum (IFMC/MCDF), which a local Imam and a Pentecostal pastor
in Kaduna jointly initiated, an initiative that led to the formation of interreligious councils across the states of the Nigerian federation as well as mediated
among many troubled communities with resulting peace accords, these initiatives have yielded some positive results, despite challenges.[76] The Department
of Mission and Dialogue at the Catholic Secretariat of Nigeria co-ordinates
the activities of the Interreligious Dialogue Commissions existing in each diocese as well as the Justice Peace and Development Commission (JDPC),
which operates at the national, diocesan and parish level.

In spite of these efforts, however, "the predominant exclusivist approaches to religion, its sources, and teachings, as found among the majority of both
Muslims and Christians in Nigeria"[77] have created a sharp divide between
adherents of the two faiths. Fundamentalist groups, such as Boko Haram occasioned the gradual destruction and erosion of the hard-earned good relations,
which good-hearted Nigerian Christians and Muslims managed to build up
over the years.[78] With politicians manipulating the socio-economic root causes of Nigeria's crisis under the guise of religious differences, these efforts often
give rise to social instability. Religion should itself with "learning to live with

the other in the daily rhythm, including the shared joys and difficulties, of work, school, and play; learning to work with the other to overcome poverty, illiteracy, health issues as well as corruption and the many other social evils plaguing Nigeria today."[79] This is the challenge that contemporary society poses on the ecclesial practice of the Church as it strives to experience the kingdom of God on earth as it is in heaven in present-day Nigeria. This is what should be captured adequately in the process of forming pastoral agents in the seminaries.

Jonathan Sacks asserts, "religion is about identity, and identity excludes."[80] He further notes, "one belief, more than any other is responsible for the slaughter of individuals on the altar of the great historical ideas. It is the belief that those who do not share my faith—or my race or my ideology—do not share my humanity."[81] Examples of this are extensive throughout the history of the Crusades, the Inquisitions, the jihads, the pogroms, and the blood of human sacrifices through the ages. From this experience—substituting "race" for "faith"—emerged the horror of the Holocaust. In Rwanda, Cambodia, the Middle East, the Balkans, and currently, in Nigeria, there have been, and there will also be more horrors. This is the greatest challenge of all, and much will depend on whether the community of faiths is equal to this challenge united in common action, or not.

I emphasize that the root-causes of the violent crisis in Nigeria are too often rendered in religious colorations, when, in fact, they also often arise from concrete, unbearable hardships inherent in the Nigerian economy and society and in its wider African and world context. This, in my view, has a direct consequence on the increasingly violent and volatile environment in the Nigerian state. Kukah argues in the same direction when he says:

> We have such killings because we live in an environment of a severely weak architecture of state which allows evil to triumph. It is this poverty that produces jealousy and hatred which leads to violence. We live in a state of ineffective law enforcement and tragic social conditions. Corruption has destroyed the fabric of our society. Its corrosive effect can be seen in the ruination of our lives and the decay in our society. The inability of the state to punish criminals as criminals has created the illusion that there is a conflict between Christians and Muslims. In fact, it would seem that many elements today are going to the extremes to pitch Christians against Muslims, and vice versa, so that our attention is taken away from the true source of our woes: corruption.[82]

International and national media have "fed the propaganda of the notorious Boko Haram and hides the fact that this evil has crossed religious barriers."

The fact though is that millions of Christians and Muslims are peace-loving followers of their respective religions, and what the media reports is mostly the work of manipulators.[83]

Indeed, as Tanzanian theologian Festo Mkenda notes, in an intrinsically plural religious setting, such as Nigeria, the Christian church as well as other religious communities have to be equal partners in dialogue with others, and dialogue itself becomes indispensable to that endeavor.[84] The African Synods I and II, Mkenda continues, imply clearly that human beings can live together irrespective of their different religious beliefs. He observes:

> Properly understood, faith does not uproot people from their communities but establishes them there as "salt" and "light" in the form of reconciled lives in justice and peace. Such faith does not advance facile tolerance but promotes vibrant communities in which life is genuinely shared.[85]

This is the kind of religion that Nigerian faith communities needs need to imbibe and to practice, especially amid its current circumstances.

Recurring violence in Nigeria, often colored in terms of religious or ethnic differences, should be viewed against the background of lack of access to economic resources of the majority poor compared to the lavish life-style of government officials (both Muslim and Christians) who perpetuate systems, which create poverty for the larger population. This problem is fostered by the subordination of the judicial process to the interests of the rich, especially those with roles of authority and power in the social and the administrative structures of the country. The real authors of violence in Nigeria are those who, to protect their privileges, prevent justice by maintaining the structures of oppression, hiding it under the cover of religion. Corporate human suffering posed by poverty, hunger, disease is truly the result of structural arrangements of society in Nigeria, as they are in the rest of the world. These are potential areas for all religions, especially Islam and Christianity, to discern jointly the necessary degrees of common self-understanding and to form the bases for common praxis that resist such suffering.

The absence of strategic alliances between the progressive forces in all religious bodies to forge and to articulate a common cause of action continue to undermine the positive value of religion in the life of Nigerian and global society, since no one religion can do it alone. Religious dialogue and collaboration should translate into sound education of respective followers from the cradle to shape their thought processes toward ideals of peaceful co-existence and human progress. Such a development can occur without prejudice for the faith of the individual, whether Muslim or Christian, across ethnic and political lines toward building a viable foundation for a democratic nation, as against a nation, which is neither Muslim nor Christian. Under the current circumstances, therefore, it is imperative that the seminary formation program of the Catholic Church in Nigeria as well as other church bodies and Islamic clerics be attuned to this consciousness process. Seminarians and agents of formation need to be exposed to situations that bring them into contact with colleagues from other churches as well as other faiths. Courses on ecumenical and interreligious dialogue should emphasize areas of common interest and agreements and open students to the possibilities of collaboration using functional examples from Yorubaland in Nigeria as well as places, such as Ghana, where Muslims and Christians are not just living side by side, but are, in fact, often members of the same family.

An Alternative Pastoral Option for the Church in Nigeria: Linkages With Arms of Civil Society and the Formation of Self-Help Associations

The ubiquitous corruption of the political class, made up of both Muslims and Christians, and the unwillingness or the inability of the government to control this corruption, have been both the cause and the effect of most of Nigeria's current ills. In the face of a failing state with weak forms of government, religious bodies remain the only meaningful expression of civil society, where opposition can take shape, and where the ruling party and the state will not be able to lord their supremacy over the masses. It is vital, then, to ask the question: How, amid the current circumstances of Nigeria, can all religious traditions partner with local communities to design realistic alternatives to the unjust structures being challenged, and in fact, begin the process of bringing about those alternatives?

This is where the Catholic Church's social teachings, which coalesced into the concept of the common good, and have as its focal point the dignity of the human person comes into play.[86]As outlined in chapter two of this study, Catholic social thought bases the dignity of the human person on the fact that humanity was created by God in God's very image. Describing the basic orientation of the body of Catholic Social teachings, Nigerian theologian Joseph Ogbonnaya reveals:

It critiques development in terms of mere economic growth for promoting a dehu-
manized form of development. It points to a hierarchy of values upon which human
life should be organized. Its theological anthropology is holistic without neglecting
the socio-economic as well as political, cultural, and spiritual dimensions of human
existence. These principles of Catholic social teaching include the principle of the
common good, of the universal destination of the earth's goods, of solidarity and of
subsidiarity, etc.[87]

Ogbonnaya continues that the principle of "the common good" hinges on the
promotion, not only of one's own personal and individual good, but also, rather of the good of other members of the community and, indeed, of all humanity. Furthermore, the principle of the universal destination of the earth's goods
implies that the resources of the earth belong to everybody and so they should
not be the preserve of a privileged few, which Pope Francis describes as "a
golden rule of social conduct and 'the first principle of the whole ethical and
social order.'"[88] As human beings with common descent as creatures of God,
we all need to support one another as is stated in the principle of solidarity,
which reinstates the reality of our interrelatedness and our interdependence
toward realizing the common good, happiness, and wellbeing.[89] As humans
created equally in the image and likeness of God, for any of us to prevent
anybody deliberately from participating fruitfully in community life or from
expressing their community membership demeans their human dignity. The
principle of subsidiarity, therefore, insists that all earthly governments should
support their citizens to realize themselves without taking over the running of
other people's lives.[90] I argue, therefore, that linkages with civil society organizations can provide the safest place for all religions in Nigeria to work toward
the common good, since the principles of the common good are not bound by
any religion.[91] How will it be possible to achieve this linkage between religion
and civil society?

According to Uzukwu, the Association of Member Episcopal Conferences
of Eastern Africa (AMECEA) "has instinctively put its finger on the solution
to the problem of local churches in Africa—grass-root mobilization.[92] Besides
making the formation of small Christian communities a key pastoral priority,
he also calls for reform of faith leadership structures by breaking their models
with feudalism in order to present an alternative pattern of building community.[93] While it is true that the initiative of small Christian communities as
bishops in East Africa have championed has yielded fruits by way of creating
more active and responsive church communities, the Church in Nigeria needs
to go one step further. I believe "the hope of a bright future in Nigeria lies in

community-based self-help associations"[94] that can nurture and support people in the communities to work toward self-actualization.

It is critical for the Justice Peace and Development Commission (JDPC) of the Catholic Church in Nigeria, which operates from the national to the parish level, to nurture "the many existing ethnic, social, gender, development, economic, cultural, human rights, grassroots, voluntary associations in the villages, towns and urban centers to be able to help themselves and to participate in fashioning the type of society which would support the nation's citizens."[95] Such efforts should not be viewed as issues for lay or "secular" people, but primary to the mission of the Church. These associations will serve to educate people at the grassroots about their rights as well as to legitimate ways of mobilizing for developmental projects.

The churches in Nigeria are filled with many college graduates and other professionals in different educational and technical fields with no jobs and no means of sustenance. It is, therefore, crucial for the Church in Nigeria to employ the use of the self-help associations as a means of providing a measured intervention to support people seeking job placement in both the public and private sector. This is where the specific orientation of the Latin American Church, which resulted in awakening movements of independence and of liberation of the people from both oligarchy and internal colonialism, becomes crucial for the church in Nigeria.

Through the instrument of self-help associations, the Church in Nigeria can nurture farmers' associations, market women, youth groups, artisans, and other groups to demand fair prices for their produce, to organize cooperatives for community development, and self-sustaining ventures. The Jesuits in El Salvador, for example, inspired peasants to organize and to stand up for their rights. The rich ecclesiological framework of Salvadoran theologian, Ellacuría, who considers liberation as the practical form of salvation in history, becomes a powerful impetus for Nigerian church leaders to proclaim the Kingdom of God in a manner that means good news for the people: "food for the hungry, health for the sick, home for the refugee, peace for the troubled, and justice for the oppressed."[96] Community-based self-help associations, as they gain strength, will become better dialogue partners with other civil society organizations that work for freedom and liberty of Nigerians.

In an extensive study of the importance of civil society organizations in the evolution of democratic societies, Polish Professor Wlodzimierz Welowski indicates the most salient aspects of the ties that bind civil society.[97] The daily lives of individual members of society are regulated by their membership in associations of civil society and their community ties. A careful look at the models of classification by Welowski reveals the possibility and the space for all people to belong somehow, communitarian ties become a dear treasure for all those who participate in religious traditions to emphasize to guarantee the trust and cooperation of all and in the quest for the common good. The Church in Nigeria can creatively make use of communitarian ties between its members and people of other faiths who share the same social milieu to engage in social change for the good of all.

Ecumenically, different denominations of the Christian church can work toward co-ownership of institutions, such as schools, hospitals, agro-based companies or industries and other self-help institutions that benefit all of humanity. The sport of soccer is curiously one avenue that defies even the religious and ethnic lines in Nigeria. Christian churches can use soccer and other sports as avenues to build trust and draw ties across the board. Recently, the Lagos Province of the Redeemed Church of God announced in the local media its plans to start a Football Academy for youth. Such an initiative will have multiple effects if it is replicated and even adopted by the national body of CAN for youth development. Furthermore, various Christian churches should encourage their members to participate in politics based on the values of justice, equity, and fairness that ensure a just society for all. This can form the basis for united political action in keeping with other arms of civil society. Equally, the formation of professional associations of Christians in various fields will help form more responsible citizens to assume leadership roles in church and society. Therefore, bodies such as the Christian Lawyers Association, Christian Teachers Association, Christian Union of Journalists, and the Association of Christian Nurses and Midwives, etc., are critical in helping form the thought processes of citizens toward the ideals of the common good that will benefit all people, irrespective of their denominational or religious affiliation. When this is overlooked, individual Christian denominations can often end up going their separate ways, straining mutual trust, and festering suspicion. Such efforts can only be sustained by organizing serious ecumenical dialogue among churches.

Interreligious alliances between Islam and Christianity are equally key in bringing to clear focus the emancipatory potential of religion, specifically by means of engendering communitarian ties. Specifically, since the same individuals who are members of the various organs of civil society are the same ones who are adherents of the different religions, there is no doubt that contemporary religion has a vital role in strengthening the functioning of the various organs of civil society for the common good. With religion being such a delicate issue in Nigerian national polity, it is possible for political parties, for example, to make conscious efforts to include members of both religions in their membership and, especially, in their leadership. Although sometimes this is done mainly as a matter of political convenience—to garner votes from both sides—on occasion it results in a genuine commitment to work for the common good based on common religious convictions.

I will identify briefly some of the most important civil society organizations: professional, student, and labor in Nigeria and what positive influence religion can bring to bear through them toward attaining a dynamic Nigeria that guarantees good and safety for all, irrespective of religious affiliations. There is a need for agents of evangelization to be formed in a new direction that shapes their consciousness to be oriented toward the prevailing challenges of the society. It is equally important for pastoral agents to understand the workings of other arms of civil society that work toward attaining the common good, and to be able to collaborate with them, since people who make up these civil society organizations are the same ones that are members of the churches and mosques and live in the same environment as their faith traditions.

The Nigerian Bar Association

The Nigerian Bar Association (NBA) was established in 1959 as a nonprofit, umbrella professional association of all lawyers admitted to the Bar in Nigeria.[98] As an association of attorneys, its membership is professional and national in scope, and not tied to any ethnic group or religion. The NBA has branches in every state of the Nigerian federation and the Federal Capital Territory.[99] Despite the challenges this body faces, George Ehusani establishes that members of the Nigerian Bar distinguish themselves as the foremost defenders of civil rights in Nigeria.[100] To buttress his point, Ehusani uses the example of Chief Gani Fawehinmi, who became synonymous with protest activities in Nigeria, especially in the darkest years of the military dictatorship, when most Nigerians, including religious leaders, chose to be cautious. Ehusani states:

> As a lawyer, he institutes several charges in court against the government wherever he comes across cases of gross violation of human rights. . . Shall the Church which perceives itself as the light of the world and the conscience of the nation, and one which wields enormous power over millions of people in our society, sit back and

watch, as it were helplessly, while Gani's National Conscience Party, and the civil rights groups, such as the Campaign for Democracy and the Civil Liberties Organization, spearhead the struggle for freedom in our land?[101]

As professionals, whose calling obliges them inherently to promote the rule of law, the NBA should become a haven for links through the formation of bodies, such as: the Association of Christian/Catholic Lawyers and the Association of Muslim Lawyers, where members across the faiths will view their practice in the legal profession as an instrument of witness to the courses of justice and truth, which are common to all religions. In the long run, a strong alliance between the religious bodies within the NBA will lead equally to reform the entire judiciary where, under present circumstances, justice seems to be at the beck and call of the highest bidder.

National Association of Nigerian Students (NANS)

Historically, Nigerian students have staged major interventions and played critical roles in some of the most important struggles that have one way or the other shaped the destiny of this Nation.[102] Kukah establishes that Jamaican Professor, Patrick Wilmot, who came to Nigeria toward the end of the civil war of 1967–1970, was instrumental in constituting students into a body of change agents in society.[103] A product of Jesuit education, Wilmot viewed society through the prism of struggle and justice, and believed that meaningful change would come to Nigeria if students played a vanguard role. From the time of the invitation of the student body to Nigeria's Constituent Assembly in 1977, the suppression and the abolition of student unionism through successive military regimes, to the reality of the inherent limitations of student unionism, students continued to hold fast to their ideals and stop governments from resting on their oars.[104] According to Kukah, some of the significant moments of students' struggle include:

> The demonstrations against Murtala's death, the *Ali Must Go* demonstrations of 1978, which shook even a military dictatorship, the *Ango Must Go* demonstrations of 1986 which shook Ahmadu Bello University, the anti-SAP and removal of oil subsidy riots of 1989, 1990 and 1991 and the demonstrations against the annulment of the June 12 elections in 1993 were all spasms that made Nigeria sit up on the issues of the day.[105]

However, despite their agitations in the quest for popular education, "the struggle of NANS [has] never [been] fully given the moral support by a wider spectrum of society."[106] This is particularly the case because the absence of centralized coordination of the various struggles being waged on individual campuses in defense of the right to affordable education and independent students' unionism has required leadership of the student demonstrations in Nigeria to be ad-hoc, chaotic and lacking clarity and focus, without cohesive power to hold on for a reasonably longer time. These student organizations could have become more unified and, therefore, be more successful in their struggles had they received support of the religious bodies.

This will forestall the situation where students have to align themselves with institutions, agents, and individuals of sometimes dubious interests and credentials to remain afloat or even to avoid bad governments co-opting student bodies to distract them from calling for changes. Since all students practice one religion or another, promoting good religious life and harmony in the campuses through a more effective and efficient chaplaincy system could provide a platform to solving the problems of the country's universities, since this could enhance interfaith relations and strengthen the moral fiber of the universities. Chaplaincies, if well situated and managed, can be places where university students with their various faiths can nourish their spiritual sides, can seek and find purpose for their intellectual and other human quests and can contribute meaningfully to Nigerian national development. Priests and pastoral agents who will eventually staff these chaplaincies will need to be formed with this base contextual consciousness to be most effective. After all, seminarians are students, too. They should be eager to work with other Christian and secular students.

The Nigerian Labor Congress

Trade unionism in Nigeria, has always been conceived in political terms.[107] The Nigerian Labor Congress (NLC) was constituted formally as the umbrella body for various Nigerian trade unions in 1978. Prior to this time, four labor groups existed, including the Trade Union Congress (TUC), which was founded in 1943, the Labor Unity Front (LUF), the United Labor Congress (ULC), and the Nigeria Workers Council (NWC).[108] The emergence of the NLC ended decades of rivalry among the four bodies and other unions became affiliated with them. These unions, numbering over 1,000 were also restructured into 42 industrial unions.[109]

From its earliest beginnings, the NLC was the one movement that had clear political motives, working between labor and employer on the one hand, and between workers and government on the other. Kukah provides the clearest example of the Enugu Miners' strike of 1949 as an area of one of the most significant contributions of labor to the independence struggle in Nigeria.[110] In fact, one of the initial labor groups, the TUC, joined the National Council of Nigeria and Cameroon (NCNC) at the time of its formation in a buildup to independence. After independence, the labor movement shifted its politics to the need for equitable distribution of the nation's resources, basing their demands primarily on the need for a just living wage.[111]

Despite these favorable beginnings, conflict with military governments, dissonance created by the differences in the ideological orientation within its leadership, as well as inducement and cooption by the government contributed to a checkered history for the labor struggle in Nigeria.[112] Yet, the enormous potential of organized labor as a driver of change in society was demonstrated recently when then Nigerian President, Goodluck announced on New Year's Day of 2012, the withdrawal of fuel subsidies and threw an already angry and frustrated nation into convulsions.[113] Nigerians took to the streets for a week of protests of this decision by the President. However, as with similar attempts, lack of will power and logistics to sustain the protest forced most people to back down due to hunger and sickness with no sustainable support.[114]

The training of the agents of evangelization by various religious bodies in Nigeria, therefore, needs to emphasize the importance of collaborating with labor unions toward realizing these objectives. Labor union actions, such as strikes and demonstrations will be more successful if religious bodies support them. Specific areas of support will be in raising consciousness and in providing back-up and contingency arrangements for challenges and emergencies. Above all, the conspicuous presence of religious leaders in their clerical attire, marching with the people will not only add legitimacy to such actions but also serve to prevent such actions degenerating into violence. Labor leaders need to have the moral support of their religious bases to avoid the temptation of being induced and co-opted by the government. This is where the government has always succeeded in beating organized labor to the game, despite the numerical strength of the labor unions. This is how religious bodies can nurture organized labor, a practice that should be taught in the formation houses.

The Academic Staff Union of Universities

The Academic Staff Union of Universities (ASUU) was formed in 1978, as a successor to the Nigerian Association of University Teachers, which was formed in 1965 to involve academic staff in all Nigerian Federal and State

Universities.[115] ASUU became more active in struggles against the military regime during the late 1980s and, in 1988, the union organized a nation-wide strike to obtain fair wages and university autonomy. Thus, the ASUU was proscribed on August 7, 1988 and all its property was seized. It could resume operations in 1990, but another strike was banned on August 23, 1992. However, an agreement was reached on September 3, 1992 that met several of the union's demands, including the right of workers to collective bargaining. The ASUU organized further strikes in 1994 and 1996, protesting against the dismissal of staff by the General Sani Abacha regime.[116] Since the return to civilian administration in 1999, ASUU has been determined to pursue quality education in Nigerian universities and the welfare of her members, embarking on numerous strikes for a wide range of demands, including improving the salary scheme, reinstating lecturers who were sacked illegally, and funding and revitalizing Nigerian public Universities, which have all yielded considerable results.

Kukah studies the distinction with which ASUU, under the leadership of Professor Attahiru Jega (1987–1994), waged an ideological war against the military government. According to him, "Jega believed that the educational sector was very crucial to national development and as such, the struggle had national implications since there was a connection between the students themselves and their parents who were caught in the vortex of oppression arising from unemployment and poverty."[117] Continuing, he asserts categorically that Jega "shattered many myths which have limited the power of many an association in the face of military manipulation"[118] which has been the bane of social activism in Nigeria. Stressing how Jega struck a balance between his religious background as a Muslim in an environment of religious suspicion, and his integrity as an academic and a unionist committed to the common good, Kukah continues:

> Jega was president of ASUU at a time when he could have succumbed to pressures to be a "good Muslim" a "good Northerner" or a "good prince." Apart from General Babangida being a northern Muslim, Prof. Jubril Aminu, Alhaji Aliyu Mohammed, Secretary to the Government of the Federation and Sultan Dasuki were all powerful men with whom Dr. Jega could have struck a deal—being himself a blue blood.[119]

Jega's case is a solid example of a leader who is committed to his faith and, in the process, someone who is using his work and office to contribute to peace, reconciliation, and justice, toward the ideals of peaceful co-existence and human progress.

The formation of all religious leaders in the various faith traditions need to be well articulated in the direction that such development can occur without prejudice to the faith of the individual, whether Muslim or Christian. This should also be the case to make an effort to build bridges across ethnic and political lines toward creating a viable foundation for a democratic nation, against a model for a nation that is neither solely Muslim nor solely Christian, as present dangers portend. It is little wonder that Professor Jega, in his time as head of the Independent National Electoral Commission of Nigeria (INEC), conducted the last general elections in March 2015 that won national and international applause. ASUU remains one of the most credible organs of civil society in Nigeria today, and will be more successful with the support of religious bodies, by keying into the legitimate demands of ASUU.

The Council for Women Societies in Nigeria

Women's social role in Nigeria differs per religious and geographic factors. Generally, Nigerian scholars, however, agree that in pre-colonial Nigeria, women played more prominent roles in the social life of the major ethnic groups, particularly among the Hausa, the Yoruba and the Igbo.[120] Nigerian women farmed, fished, herded, and produced and marketed pottery, cloth-making, and crafts alongside Nigerian men. This indigenous form economic freedom was different from that of many western societies, where women had to fight for the right to work. With the mid-nineteenth century, Christianity as we know it today was introduced to the southern part of Nigeria, which also introduced women, especially among the Yoruba peoples, to Western-style education. Although many households, including those professing Christianity in southern Nigeria, like the north, were polygamous, women held traditionally economically important positions in interregional trade and markets, working on farms as major sources of labor, and occupying influential positions in traditional systems of local organization and governance.

Kukah reveals that the high points of women's participation in Nigeria's national life have always been traced to the spectacular flashes of the Aba and Egba Women's rebellions, which happened in 1929 and 1947, respectively.[121] Lately, the heroic efforts of women, such as Mrs. Ransome Kuti, Margaret Ekpo, Hajiya Gambo Sawaba, and Dora Akunyili have begun to get the attention they deserve. The formal organization of women groups as players in national development occurred in 1953 after the National Women's

Union metamorphosed into the Federation of Nigerian Women's Societies (FNWS).[122]

However, inclusion of women in Nigerian national life does not seem to have been treated with the urgency it deserves, even though women constitute 49% of the total population in Nigeria, as was reported by the 2006 census.[123] For example, the 1995 constitutional conference in Nigeria had only eight women out of a total of 369 delegates. Much of women's work remains invisible, unremunerated, and unrecognized. In Nigeria, as is the case elsewhere, religion and tradition are instruments of oppression of women.[124] They constitute, among others, the ideology of the society, which is a superstructure on the socio-economic foundation of any class society. Many religious beliefs and traditions are designed to justify and sustain private property, and dictated the relationship between men and women for centuries, entrenching male domination as the structure of social organization and institution at all levels of leadership.[125] Despite the obvious overwhelming numerical strength of women in church attendance in Nigeria, the face of the Church in public is nevertheless thoroughly male, just as are all the mosques. Women constitute close to 60 percent of Christian congregations, with nearly 70 percent of monetary contributions made by women, and they virtually keep the churches alive through their active participation in ministries.

Religious institutions will be more successful in promoting the course of women's participation in social life, first by giving women more space in the religious assembly, since the suppression of women has been constantly supported by religious practices. The seminaries and houses of formation will be more suitable places to begin this initiative, where pastoral agents are taught, not only to talk about the recognition of women, but also to portray actually through their actions as they minister in the community, the respect and place that should rightly be given to women. Here lies the key to the success of religion as an agent of change.

What Lessons for Church and Salvation in Nigeria?

Pope John Paul II, promulgating the Post-Synodal Exhortation, *Ecclesia in Africa* in Nairobi, September of 1995, said "The Synod is over; the Synod has just begun."[126] This implied a continued invitation to a practical implementation of the Synod's orientations to the unique circumstances of life in parts of Africa. This equally holds true for the second Synod, as it invites the Church

in Africa to reappropriate the social teachings of the Church to new circumstances of life. A new pastoral option for the Church in Nigeria in the light of
these Synods requires: (a) a reform in the training program of agents of evangelization to particularly imbibe the tenets of catholic social teaching, (b) a
strengthening of ecumenical/interreligious structures of dialogue, (c) formation of community-based self-help associations, and (d) collaboration with
civil arms of the society. Among the lessons to be drawn are the facts that:

- Knowledge is power. To be true to her mission as a sacrament of historical liberation, the Church in Nigeria will need to educate people about
  the true causes of their pains.
- The Church in Nigeria can rely on the mutual inspiration of Catholic
  social teaching with a variety of social movements to develop a fitting
  spirituality of social engagement to inspire the people to work for their
  liberation.
- Since liberation is in fact, the code word for salvation, the task of social transformation and renewal in Nigeria is a legitimate task for the
  Church and not some "worldly" concern. The Church in Nigeria can
  act in solidarity and union of interests with other faith and civil society
  groups to propose alternative actions through transforming actions and
  practices.
- Formation programs of the Catholic Church in Nigeria will need to
  expose leaders of faith to the workings of civil society and to dialogue.

These propositions for living religion in the words of eminent liberation theologian Gustavo Gutierrez, imply:

> An understanding of religion which does not stop with reflecting on the world, but
> rather tries to be part of the process through which the world is transformed ... in
> the protest against trampled human dignity, in the struggle against the plunder of
> the vast majority of people, in liberating love, and in the building of a new, just, and
> egalitarian society.[127]

Though religious belief consists in believing in one's own religious truth, it is
the universalization of one's religious truth claims that become problematic,
especially as they exclude the truth claims of others. In the next chapter, I will
make suggestions and propose ways of following Christ in a religiously plural
Nigeria that will contribute to the salvation of the children of God on earth
as it is in heaven.

Notes

1. Smith, *Saving Salvation*, 17–28.
2. Under the theme, "The Church in Africa and its Evangelizing Mission towards the Year 2000: 'You will be my witnesses' (Acts 1:8)" the Synod opened in St. Peter's Basilica on Sunday, April 10, 1994, and lasted for a month. John Paul II issued *Ecclesia in Africa* as the Post-Synodal exhortation to this Synod.
3. The Second Special Assembly for Africa of the Synod of Bishops (Second African Synod), held from October 4th to 25th 2009, had the title "The Church in Africa in Service to Reconciliation, Justice and Peace: 'You are the salt of the earth . . . You are the light of the world (Mt 5: 13, 14)." Benedict XVI issued *Africae Munus* as the Post-Synodal exhortation to this Synod.
4. Given the limited scope of this study, I draw rather selectively on sections of the ensuing papal exhortations from the Synods that are pertinent to advance my proposals on the review of seminary formation in response to leadership failure, and the need for dialogue and collaboration with other religions and organizations of civil society. The First Synod specifically dealt with areas such as the respect for human life and family with emphasis on the right of women to be actively involved in Church ministry and decision making process, the promotion of dialogue with African traditional religions, developing a theology of the African Church as family, and the denouncement of arms sales to Africa. The Second Synod dwelt specifically on the need to work toward reconciliation, justice, and peace. To achieve this, the Church necessarily has to dialogue, especially in Nigeria where the religious and social reality is overly plural.
5. John Paul II, *Ecclesia in Africa*, # 51.
6. Benedict XVI, *Africae Munus* # 17.
7. John Paul II, *Ecclesia in Africa*, # 141.
8. *Ibid.* # 21.
9. *Ibid.* # 40.
10. *Ibid.* # 51.
11. *Ibid.* # 52.
12. *Ibid.* # 95.
13. *Ibid.* # 107.
14. *Ibid.*
15. John Paul II, Encyclical Letter, *Centesimus Annus*, # 57. (May 1, 1991 AAS 83, 1991: 793–867).
16. John Paul II, *Ecclesia in Africa*, # 54.
17. See Proposition # 9, in *The African Synod: Documents, Reflections, Perspectives*. Maura Brown, ed. Maryknoll: Orbis Books, 1996, 89–92.
18. Benedict XVI, *Africae Munus* # 10.
19. *Ibid.* # 17.
20. *Ibid.* # 165.
21. *Ibid.* # 89.
22. *Ibid.* # 76–77.
23. *Ibid.* # 88.

24. Festo Mkenda, "Language, Politics, and Religious Dialogue: A Case Study of Kiswahili in Eastern Africa" in *Reconciliation, Justice, and Peace: The Second African Synod*, ed. Agbonkhianmeghe E. Orobator (New York: Orbis Books, 2011), 38.

25. Elochukwu E. Uzukwu, "The Birth and Development of a Local Church: Difficulties and Signs of Hope," *Concilium* 1992/1, eds. Guiseppe Alberigo and Alphonse Ngindu Mushete (London: SCM Press Ltd), 17.

26. *Ibid*. 19.

27. Downey, "The Creeping Curriculum," 330.

28. *Ibid*. 331.

29. *Ibid*. 333.

30. *Ibid*. 334.

31. Vincent J. Donovan, *Christianity Rediscovered*. 25 Anniversary ed. (Maryknoll: Orbis, 2003), xii.

32. *Ibid*. 112.

33. *Ibid*. 110.

34. Paul Gifford, *Christianity, Development and Modernity in Africa*, (London: Hurst & Company, 2015), 130–131.

35. Frances Fox Piven and Richard A. Cloward, *Poor People's Movements: Why they succeed, How they fail*, (New York: Vintage Books, 1979), 3–4.

36. Equally important will be for seminary education to be open to lay members of the Church to be educated alongside those training for the priesthood. If the lay members of the Church are as informed on theological matters, especially the social teachings of the Church just like their priests, the tendency to mislead them will be minimized. Now, only the Dominican Institute in Ibadan, The Spiritan International School of Theology Atakwu and the newly founded St Albert the Great Institute in Kafanchan are open to lay members of the Church for education.

37. The word "liturgy" itself derives from the Greek *liturgia*, meaning "the work of the people."

38. Rita Ferrone, *Liturgy: Sacrosanctum Concilium*. Rediscovering Vatican II Series, (New York: Paulist Press, 2007), 1–18.

39. John Eagleson and Philip Scharper, eds. *Puebla and Beyond: Documentation and Commentary*. trans. John Drury (Maryknoll: Orbis Books, 1979), 240.

40. *Ibid*. 139.

41. I have argued elsewhere for a more socially conscious liturgy, in a manner like the Pentecostal/Charismatic churches that offer people the opportunity to develop a sense of their own importance and interact as equals, against the structured authority patterns of the traditional churches. This atmosphere is particularly cherished by women and youth, who in traditional African societies and the mainline churches have no status. See Gabriel Terzungwe Wankar, *Towards the New Evangelization: Lessons from Pentecostal/Charismatic Christianity to the Catholic Church in Africa* (Unpublished STL Thesis, JST Berkeley, 2013).

42. Maduro, *Religion and Social Conflicts*.62–3.

43. Stan Chu Ilo, "Fr Mbaka and the Prophetic Voice in Nigerian Politics," *Premium Times* (January 7, 2015). http://www.blogspremiumtimesng.com (accessed September 12, 2015).

44. *Ibid*.

45. In Benue State, the Tiv number about 2.5 million out of a total population of some 5.2 million based on a breakdown of the last Nigerian population census that was conducted in 2006. Also found in Nassarawa, Plateau, Taraba and Cross River States, the Tiv population number somewhat more than 5.6 million, though concentrated in the state of Benue, where they are the majority. Ecclesiastically, the Catholic Dioceses of Gboko, Katsina Ala and Makurdi in Benue State are all 97 percent Tiv-speaking. The Catholic Diocese of Jalingo in Taraba State is 40 percent Tiv, while Lafia Diocese in Nassarawa State and Ogoja Diocese in Cross River State are each 20 percent Tiv speaking.

46. Akintunde E. Akinade, introduction to *Fractured Spectrum: Perspectives on Christian-Muslim Encounters in Nigeria*, ed. Akintunde E. Akinade (New York: Peter Lang, 2013), 5.

47. *Ibid.*

48. *Ibid.*

49. Enwerem, *A Dangerous Awakening: The Politicization of Religion in Nigeria* (Ibadan: IFRA, 1995), 24.

50. *Ibid.*

51. *Ibid.* 30–31.

52. Citing C. Logams, who is a Birom, one of the minority Christian tribes in north-central Nigeria, Kukah notes that *rahol kannang* is a Birom expression, which means 'the hill of secret conclusions.' He further notes that the idea of secrecy regarding the meeting could have reflected the fear, on the part of the participants, of possible reprisals by the Northern Islamic ruling class. See M. H. Kukah, *Religion, Politics and Power in Northern Nigeria* (Ibadan: Spectrum Books 1993), 62 and 79.

53. Enwerem, *A Dangerous Awakening* 31.

54. *Ibid.* 76.

55. *Ibid.* 79.

56. *Ibid.*

57. For a detailed account of the early beginnings of CAN, its leadership and development see particularly chapter three of Enwerem's account, titled "Origins of the Christian Association of Nigeria" (CAN), 75–100.

58. Enwerem, *A Dangerous Awakening,* 104. See the Constitution of the Christian Association of Nigeria (CAN), Art. X. hereafter cited as CAN's 1988 Constitution for a detailed organizational structure of CAN.

59. *Ibid.* 122.

60. *Ibid.* 192.

61. *Ibid.* 193.

62. *Ibid.* 185.

63. Archbishop Ignatius A. Kaigama, "Our Concern for Christian Unity," a letter to Pastor Ayo Oritsejafor, then President of CAN, September 24, 2012.

64. A dramatic incident occurred in late 2012, when Pentecostal Pastor Ayo Oritsejafor, at the time president of CAN, who comes from the same region as Jonathan Goodluck, received a new private jet as a gift from "unknown" donors at his birthday celebration, where President Goodluck was in attendance. In September of 2014, the same jet belonging to Ayo was widely reported in the media to have been intercepted by South African officials with USD $9.3 million aboard, believed to have been part of an arm deal for the Nige-

rian government. Pastor Ayo explained that he only leased the jet to the government. That CAN has become entangled with corrupt influences from the government is no news. During my tenure as an assistant secretary of the Executive Council of the Christian Association of Nigeria, Benue State Chapter (2005 and 2011), the national body of CAN under Pastor Ayo in collaboration with the Chaplain to the Presidential villa had embarked on a nationwide tour of state arms of CAN. The tour was done with monetary inducements to ensure the election of Jonathan Goodluck as president in the elections of April 2011. In addition, this by no means is an isolated case.

65. John Paul II, *Ecclesia in Africa*, # 49.
66. Haight, *Dynamics of Theology* (Maryknoll, New York: Orbis Books, 2001), 17.
67. Akinade, introduction to *Fractured Spectrum*, 3.
68. *Ibid.*
69. *Ibid.*
70. The British adopted the administrative and power structure of the caliphate, leaving out the missionaries, whose Western education was feared to be an instrument of protest by the emerging Southern elite against colonial rule, as well as undermining the role of Islam in the conquered caliphate. Cf. Matthew Hassan Kukah, *The Church and the Politics of Social Responsibility*, 177.
71. Matthew Hassan Kukah & Kathleen McGarvey, "Christian-Muslim Dialogue in Nigeria: Social, Political, and Theological Dimensions" in *Fractured Spectrum: Perspectives on Christian-Muslim Encounters in Nigeria*, ed. Akintunde E. Akinade, 12–29.
72. *Ibid.* 183. Kukah has written extensively on this subject, for details; see Matthew Kukah, *Islam and Christianity: Dialogue or Confrontation?*" Unpublished M. A. Thesis: University of Bradford, 1980. Matthew Kukah, *Religion, Politics and Power in Northern Nigeria* (Ibadan: Spectrum Books, 1993. Matthew Kukah & Toyin Falola, *Religious Militancy and Self-Assertion in Nigeria* (London: Avebury Press, 1996). Mathew Hassan Kukah, *Democracy and Civil Society in Nigeria* (Ibadan: Spectrum Books, 1999).
73. Fr Anthony Kenny OP, credits the official inauguration of Christian/Muslim dialogue in Nigeria in 1974 to the efforts of Fr Victor Chukwulozie, one of the first indigenous priest of the Kaduna. This work relies on the more readily available account of Thaddeus Byimu Umaru, *Christian-Muslim Dialogue in Northern Nigeria: A Socio-Political and theological Consideration* (San Bernardino: Xlibris LLC, 2013), 187.
74. *Constitution of the Nigeria Interreligious Council* (Abuja: NIREC, 2001), 1–7. Over the years, people have expressed fears about item d, that it suggests the possibility/temptation of collusion with corrupt governments as experiences have shown, rather facilitating a religious response to corruption. As a representative body of the two umbrella bodies of the two religions—JNI and CAN—NIREC aims to achieve her objective of mutual and peaceful co-existence in a plural religious Nigeria through continuous dialogue, meetings, religious and peace education, discussions, conferences, seminars and workshops. As an independent organization of fifty members drawn from the main representative bodies of the of the two religions, NIREC operates under the co-chairmanship of the Sultan of Sokoto as the leader of the JNI, and the President of CAN, with each group producing twenty-four other members each, making up the membership of fifty for the council.

75. Umaru, *Christian-Muslim Dialogue in Northern Nigeria*, 164–207. He chronicles efforts, such as the December 2007 religious crises in Bauchi, the numerous ethno/religious crises around parts of Plateau State, the 2009 Muslim-Christian youth summit in Minna Niger State to the February 2000 dialogue conference on Islamic Sharia.

76. John Campbell, *Nigeria: Dancing on the Brink* (Lanham, Maryland: Rowman and Little-field Publishers, 2011), 45. Campbell, a U.S. Department of State Foreign Service Officer, served twice in Nigeria, as political counselor from 1988 to 1990, and as ambassador from 2004 to 2007.

77. Kukah and McGarvey, "Christian-Muslim Dialogue in Nigeria: Social, Political, and The-ological Dimensions," 23.

78. Between 2009 and 2015, Boko Haram is said to have killed more than 13,000 civilians and displaced over 1.5 million people, mostly in northeastern Nigeria.

79. Kukah and McGarvey, "Christian-Muslim Dialogue in Nigeria: Social, Political, and The-ological Dimensions," 22.

80. Jonathan Sacks, *The Dignity of Difference: How to Avoid the Clash of Civilizations*, revised edition. (New York: Continuum, 2009), 46.

81. *Ibid*. 46.

82. See Bishop Matthew Hassan Kukah, "Be Still and Know that I am God (Ps 46:10)," an appeal Letter to Nigerians by the Catholic Bishop of Sokoto, Nigeria, January 2012.

83. Emmanuel Aziken, "Presidential Polls: The untold story of the peacemakers," *Vanguard*, April 6, 2015, http://www.vanguardngr.com (accessed January 18, 2016). The incidence reported here and some recent events in Nigeria have demonstrated that despite the bar-ricades erected by the manipulators of religion to breed violence, these challenges are not insurmountable. Aziken reports that recently, a Peace Committee successfully worked around the clock to ease the tension that had gripped the polity in Nigeria. The credibility of the members of the committee was the single strength, which was brought to bear on both the candidates and heads of institutions in the nation. Besides General Abdulsalami Abubakar, Commodore Ebitu Ukiwe, Alhaji Aliko Dangote, John Cardinal Onayiekan, and Sultan Alhaji Sa'ad Abubakar—who were seen in public projecting the decisions of the larger body—other members of the committee were Bishop Matthew Kukah, Al-haji Muhammad Musdafa, Lamido Adamawa; Primate of the Anglican Church, Most Rev. Nicholas Okoh; then President of the Christian Association of Nigeria, Pastor Ayo Oritsejafor, and Justice Rose Ukeje. Others are Prof. Ibrahim Gambari, a former Minister of Foreign Affairs, Prof. Bolaji Akinyemi; Publisher of *Vanguard* Newspapers, Mr. Sam Pemu-Amuka, Prof. Ameze Guobadia, Prof. Zainab Alkali; and a former President of the Nigerian Bar Association, Dame Priscilla Kuye. The fears from concerned stakeholders, including some international organizations, about the possibilities of uncontrollable vi-olence during and after the elections gave rise to the concept of this committee. In the previous general elections in 2011 as many as 600 persons were said to have died on account of the violence that followed the declaration of the results of the presidential elections. Through the mediating role of this committee, it turned out that in the history of Nigeria, the last elections marked the first time a contestant has called his rival to congratulate him, and this had a spiral effect as various contestants for different positions at the last elections followed Goodluck's gesture of a phone call to congratulate his oppo-

nent Muhammadu Buhari, and concede defeat. This committee, made up of Muslims and Christians, has continued to meet with the present government to suggest the way forward for Nigeria in her current circumstances for a better tomorrow.

84. *Ibid.*
85. *Ibid.*
86. Kukah, *Democracy and Civil Society in Nigeria* (Ibadan: Spectrum Books, 1999), 235.
87. Ogbonnaya, *African Catholicism and Hermeneutics of Culture*, 124.
88. *Ibid. Cf.* Francis, Encyclical Letter *Laudato Si, # 93.* Section VI of Chapter Two of the encyclical is titled "The Common Destination of Goods."
89. *Ibid. # 66.*
90. Ogbonnaya, *African Catholicism and Hermeneutics of Culture* 124. *Cf.* Kukah, *Democracy and Civil Society in Nigeria,* 236. Throughout the history of its evolution, the one aim of Catholic social thought has been to contribute to resolving the contradictions of the social question centering on the contradictions arising from the immoral cohabitation of wealth and poverty, life and death, too much and too little. These are issues that concern all religions, including Islam and Christianity, since the destitute and oppressed in Nigeria cut across all religions and tribes. It is therefore imperative for both religions to seek and promote common grounds for the building of a Nigeria for all, even as we identify and cope with our intra/interreligious differences in a spirit of respect.
91. Kukah, *Democracy and Civil Society in Nigeria,* 240.
92. Uzukwu, "The Birth and Development of a Local Church: Difficulties and Signs of Hope," 19.
93. *Ibid.* 20–21.
94. Iber, *The Principle of Subsidiarity in Catholic Social Thought,* 188.
95. *Ibid.* Iber offers an extensive analysis of the role of self-help grassroots associations as agents of social, ethical, and developmental change in Nigeria, and outlines guidelines for the formation of such associations. For details, see 185–190.
96. Orobator, "The Idea of the Kingdom of God in African Theology," *Studia Missionalia* 46 (1997):335.
97. For a detailed listing and treatment of various models of ties, especially communitarian ties, see Wlodzimierz Welowski: "The Nature of Social Ties and the Future of Postcommunist Society: Poland After Solidarity," in *Civil Society: Theory, History, Comparison,* ed. John Hall (Cambridge: Polity Press, 1995), 120–122.
98. See the Nigerian Bar Association, www.nigerianbar.org.ng (accessed August 10, 2015), *Cf. Constitution of the Nigerian Bar Association,* 24. As quoted by Mathew Hassan Kukah, *Democracy and Civil Society in Nigeria,* 129. According to the Constitution of the Nigerian Bar Association, the association established these goals: 1. Ensure the maintenance of the honor and independence of the Bar; 2. Defend the Bar in its relation with the Judiciary and the Executive; 3. Promote legal education in Nigeria; 4. Ensure the maintenance of the highest standards of professional conduct, etiquette and discipline, 5. Encourage, ensure and protect the public right of access to the courts and of representation by counsel before courts or tribunals, 6. Promote the principles of the rule of law.
99. Kukah, *Democracy and Civil Society in Nigeria,* 141.
100. Ehusani, *A Prophetic Church,* 116.

101. *Ibid.*
102. Kukah, *Democracy and Civil Society in Nigeria,* 141. Kukah notes that the precursor of student unionism in Nigeria, initially known as the National Union of Nigerian Students (NUNS), was the West African Students' Union (WASU), founded in Britain as an umbrella body for students from various West African countries. From inception, the goals of the association were anchored on decolonization, attaining total independence and sustaining the ideals of nationalism.
103. *Ibid.* 142.
104. *Ibid.* 151.
105. *Ibid.* 153. By 1978 NANS had to pick the gauntlet against the military regime of General Olusegun Obasanjo which had decided to commercialize education by introducing and increasing tuition fees in Nigerian Universities. That struggle is what is famously referred to as "Ali-Must-Go," since the then Federal Commissioner for Education was General Ahmadu Alli, one of the recent chairmen of the People's Democratic Party (PDP) that lost the 2015 general elections to the opposition.
106. *Ibid.* 151. The experience that people acquire from student unions is vital to any meaningful change in a struggling democracy, as examples in Russia, China as well as South Africa have shown. The revolution in Russia, for example, was made possible because yesterday's revolutionary students had now become professionals, just as student unionism became the nursery for leadership. Religious bodies have a unique advantage as institutions of trust to fill in the gap of giving direction, clarity and focus to the aspirations of the students, to translate them into meaningful issues to engage the government. Besides mentoring the thought processes of the students to fashion out useful ways of registering discontent, religious bodies necessarily need to support student bodies with logistics and contingency arrangements in times of protests so that the students are not overwhelmed by the challenges they encounter and are forced into abandoning their struggles in the middle of the road. Especially in a time of the revolution of the mass media of communications, student bodies are a veritable and indispensable group in raising consciousness, mobilization, and resistance through instantaneous use of the media with the advantage of their energies and talents.
107. Owei Lakemfa, "The Trade Union Movement: Travails and Struggle" in *Trade Unionism in Nigeria: Challenges for the 21ˢᵗ Century,* ed. Funmi Adewumi (Lagos: Friedrich Ebert Foundation, 1997), 99.
108. See the Nigerian Labour Congress, www.nlcng.org (accessed August 17, 2015).
109. *Ibid.*
110. Kukah, *Democracy and Civil Society in Nigeria,* 154.
111. *Ibid.*
112. *Ibid.* 155–7. Cf. The Nigerian Labor Congress, www.nlcng.org (accessed August 17, 2015). In 1988 for example, General Ibrahim Babangida, appointed state administrators to the NLC, and dissolved its national organs due to NLC's opposition to the anti-people Structural Adjustment Program (SAP) of the government. Also, in 1994, the regime of General Sani Abacha was irritated with the labor movement's agitation for the restoration of democracy. As in 1988, the military government dissolved NLC's National Executive Council and appointed a Sole Administrator. The same treatment was meted to the two

unions in the oil and gas industry, Nigeria Union of Petroleum and Natural Gas Workers (NUPENG) and Petroleum and Natural Gas Senior Staff Association of Nigeria (PEN-GASSAN). Despite these setbacks, there were significant accomplishments. From the demonstrations by labor against the killing of students at Ahmedu Bello University Zaria in 1986, the demonstrations against Margaret Thatcher and the persistent resistance to fuel price hikes, organized labor has been one of the most significant channels of opposition to bad governance and the quest for democracy in Nigeria.

113. See Kukah, "Be Still and Know that I am God (Ps 46:10)."
114. Lakemfa, "The Trade Union Movement: Travails and Struggle" 104–106.
115. See the Academic Staff Union of Nigerian Universities www.asuu-ng.org (accessed August 17, 2015). Cf. *The Constitution and Code of Practice of the Academic Staff Union of Universities (ASUU)* as amended 2010; See also Kukah, *Democracy and Civil Society in Nigeria,* 158. The major objective of ASUU is to promote education and learning and serve to regulate relations between academic staff and employers as well as between members. Kukah has noted that even though ASUU has as one of its objectives the protection and advancement of the socio-economic and cultural interests of the nation, it was only a few left-wing academics who took this commitment seriously and all they could do was to support student unions in their struggles. University professors traded off their professional expertise for many perquisites of power like political appointments, contracts, and consultancies during the years of the oil boom. However, failed political and economic experimentations resulting in a distressed economy and poverty forced ASUU to wake up to the reality of the contradictions in society and the role it was originally founded for.
116. *Ibid.*
117. Kukah, *Democracy and Civil Society in Nigeria,* 161.
118. *Ibid.*
119. *Ibid.* 161–162.
120. A. A. Jekayinfa, "The role of Nigerian Women in Culture and National Development," *Journal of Educational Theory and Practice* 5 (1999): 1–2. Jekayinfa notes that in northern Nigeria, the dominant Hausa people culturally belong to a civilization characterized by matrilineal succession and women held high political offices. A case in point was queen Amina of Zaria who succeeded her father's throne and ruled for thirty-four years. Most of these traditional rights were, however lost as western values gained influence in colonial Nigeria. Islamic practices in the north implied less formal education, early teenage marriages, which were often polygamous, especially in rural areas. Women were confined to the household, except for visits to family, ceremonies, and they could enter the workplace only if employment were available and permitted by a girl's family or husband. Fortunately, this trend seems to be changing considerably today, especially for the daughters of the business and professional elites.
121. Kukah, *Democracy and Civil Society in Nigeria,* 162.
122. *Ibid.* The turn of the last century brought into sharp focus the women's movement globally, with the United Nations, for example, organizing several conferences leading to the Beijing Conference in 1995; this placed the interests and rights of women on the national and global development agenda. Since the declaration of 1985 as Women's year by the UN, the affiliation of Nigerian women to such international organizations as the Inter-

national Federation of Female Lawyers, Soroptimist International, Rotary International (where women are called Inner Wheel), as well as their participation in international fora under the auspices of such bodies as International Federation of University Women (IFUN), Young Women Christian Association (YWCA), World Council of Catholic Women (WUCWO), have added a sense of urgency to call for the deserved place of women in national development.

123. Central Intelligence Agency, "The World Fact book," Webpage last updated on June 24, 2014, https://www.cia.gov/library/publications/the-world-factbook/goes/ni.html, accessed on August 14, 2015. The last Nigerian population census that was conducted in 2006 placed the country's population at 140 million.

124. Anne Arabome, "Woman, You are Set Free!" Women and Discipleship in the Church"" in Agbonkhianmeghe E. Orobator, ed. *Reconciliation, Justice, and Peace: The Second African Synod*, 119–130; Cf. Ngozi Frances Uti "Come, Let Us Talk This Over: On the Condition of Women Religious in the Church" in Agbonkhianmeghe E. Orobator, ed. *Reconciliation, Justice, and Peace: The Second African Synod*, 131–142; Iorapuu, *Patriarchal Ideologies and Media Access*.

125. Cf. Iorapuu, Patriarchal *Ideologies and Media Access*, Ngozi Frances Uti "Come, Let Us Talk This Over: On the Condition of Women Religious in the Church" in Agbonkhianmeghe E. Orobator, ed. *Reconciliation, Justice, and Peace: The Second African Synod*, 131–142.

126. Aylward Shorter, "The Synod is over; The Synod Has Just Begun," *The Nigerian Journal of Theology* Vol. 11, No. 1 (June 1997): 72.

127. Gutierrez, A *Theology of Liberation*, as quoted in Enwerem, A *Dangerous Awekening*, 213.

· 5 ·

INVIGORATING THE CALL OF THE AFRICAN SYNODS I AND II IN LIVING OUT OF THE CHRISTIAN FAITH IN NIGERIA

The preceding chapters have indicated that the Christian faith is, in fact, "constituted by justice, expressed, and embodied in our social relations as well as in our personal lives."[1] However, the practice of Christianity in Nigeria has "too often been isolated from its social and cultural context."[2] This disposition has impeded Christianity's witness in the public life of the country and calls for rethinking.

Contemporary public discourse concerning the common good revolves around two opposing variants: those who argue that all of humanity must do something about the right ordering of society and those who contend that it is the sole responsibility of governments to keep society ordered to address the needs of the common good. Many Christians in Nigeria fall on the latter side of the debate, believing that, for the most part, the Christian call is limited to perform simply acts of charity. Popular African religiosity has been shaped particularly in the direction in which spatio-temporal concerns are not the prerogative of good Christians, but, rather, those in civil governments are the only leaders capable of handling "worldly" matters.[3] As Orobator notes, the basic understanding of any African regarding the Kingdom of God is, "God will offer access to the kingdom as a reward to the "saved" in the dramatic event of the "rapture" (*cf.* 1 Thess. 4:16–17). This entrance into God's eschatological domain is understood as 'the kingdom of heaven.'"[4] However, the review in chapter two of this study has revealed that, like Jesus, who "went about doing good works and healing all who were in the grip of the devil" (Acts 10:38), following the same Jesus in the Nigerian context raises the challenge to make the Kingdom that is preached from the pulpit a part of the lived reality. Alongside Jesus who forgave sinners, healed the sick and raised the dead, those who follow Jesus must absolutely work for the temporal well-being of all people and for the transformation of the whole of society. In practical terms, therefore, what might this mean for the followers of Jesus in Nigeria?

Despite the crucial theological endeavor of the Church in Africa at the two African Synods, especially regarding the role of the Church in society, the question remains: "How many of the recommendations of these Synods have, in fact, been implemented?" Several African theologians[5] agree that most of the recommendations of these Synods have remained largely on paper, and many people, including clergy, appear ignorant of their recommendations, especially regarding the role of the Church in public life. In the light of the preceding remarks and some recommendations of the Synods in relation to the role of the Church in Africa that were reviewed in the previous chapter, the following section sieves out some implications of those synods for a more creative and a mutually-transformative engagement of the faith with Nigeria's historical and contextual reality.

Implications for Following Christ in Nigeria Considering African Synods I and II

The Church as Family

The theme of Church as family, as we saw in the last chapter, was very central to the First Synod. This brings out a major implication for following Christ in Nigeria in the light of that synod; relocating the Church, from a hierarchical preoccupation to a Church, which encompasses the whole people of God as equals, whose mission is serve humanity, based on the ideals of the kingdom.[6] This means understanding that the role of the laity is not one that is a mere extension of the Church hierarchy (*Lumen Gentium* 33). The lay faithful members of the Church, who receive a direct mandate of call to discipleship from Jesus Christ, will need to be educated to the fact that all that affects their day to day lives is part of the demand of faith and is part and parcel of their life of discipleship (Mk. 1:17; Mtt. 4:19, 9:9; Mtt. 28:18–20).

Orobator indicates that in Nigeria, "the dominant understanding of the prophetic mission of the Church collapses this mission into the function of 'church leaders' issuing statements on the social condition of Nigeria. How this function becomes the collective and mobilizing self-understanding of the ecclesial community remains unclear."[7] Through an extensive study of statements, press releases, and communiqués the bishops of Nigeria issued between 1993 and1997, Orobator identifies "an appreciable awareness on the part of the bishops regarding the socioeconomic and political issues affecting the mission of the church in Nigeria."[8] However, he continues, "any functions which might relate to the church's social mission seem concentrated at the top of the ecclesiastical structure, while activities at the base appear as residual consequences or the 'trickle-down' effect of this hierarchical configuration."[9]

This understanding of Church, which largely ignores in part the laity who number most among the members of the Church in Nigeria, undermine the ability of the people to appreciate the teachings of these synods for the Church in Nigeria. Whenever these synods occur, the social teachings they announce remain almost entirely unknown to the average lay person. Consequently, the Nigerian laity continues to be ignorant of the social implications of following Christ. The Church ought to embrace the model of a loving family where each member is important and has a role to play.

Education of the Laity

As the review in chapter three indicates, for the laity to realize its role in the ministry of Jesus, the clergy must develop openness and transparency to educate the laity in the rich corpus of the social teachings of the Church as the Second Vatican Council demands and the African Synods I and II affirm.[10] The *Instrumentum Laboris* for the African Synod II encourages Christians to make conscious efforts in "the fight against every sort of human poverty,"[11] and calls for them to take practical steps, so that "Africa emerges from poverty and marginalization in a general movement of globalization."[12] It is the duty of the Church to educate the laity to understand this role as a demand of faith:

> it is important we break with African practices that still maintain a theology of "'pie in the sky when you die'" and excuse baptized Christians from a radical commitment to further just economic, political, and cultural activities in the society. Faithful

Christians must reject any teaching that does not enable the baptized to consider action against every sort of spiritual or historical poverty as a duty.[13]

By keeping the laity ignorant of the social teachings of the Church, which should inform them of legitimate ways of actively working toward a better society, the Church cooperates in their oppression. This point to the great challenge Latin American liberation theologian, Ellacuría offers to Nigerian theologians: to face reality with honesty. He insists that the Church in El Salvador of his day had to "take on history" by naming and denouncing the powers of death that crucified the Salvadoran poor and by remembering God is a God of life who liberates and raises them to new life.[14] The Church in Nigeria can, thus, only begin to provide a sincerer contribution to liberation of the people of God by reorienting its theological formation and praxis as a force of liberation in Nigerian society. In effect, the processes of formation of priests in the seminaries should emphasize this unity between the spiritual and the material, and the laity should be formed in the consciousness that any effort to overcome poverty, injustice, and oppression are a central part of their Christian faith, and not "rebellion" nor "worldly matters"—as they are currently made to believe.

Commitment to Justice in the Church

Clearly, for the Church in Nigeria to become sincerely committed to the education of the laity concerning economic justice and the right ordering of society as constitutive practical means of following Christ, it must first model justice with its own employees. Church workers are among the least paid workers in Nigeria, and in most cases with no benefits. While this researcher worked as pastor at St Joseph's Parish Akpehe in Benue State of Central Nigeria between 2007 and 2011, all the four workers on the payroll of the parish were temporally staff and their salaries were not anything near what government workers in similar positions earned. This was not an isolated case, since in many other parishes, such workers were mostly volunteers.

Emeka Christian Obiezu insists: "the [C]hurch cannot promote good working conditions, just wages and regular payment of worker's salaries, without first treating its own employees with this love and justice. It cannot insist on a government policy that makes adequate provision for the poor without the poor and their concerns occupying a prominent place in the programme of the [C]hurch."[15] Most Church workers in Nigeria have no contractual agreements for their jobs and do not have any benefits upon retirement. Priests can hire and fire people at will and Church workers have no place to seek redress, since their jobs have no binding agreements, neither do mission workers belong to any union.

Besides being poorly paid, Church workers have no form of job security. Obiezu asserts, "by asking [Church workers] to see their work as a 'vocation' or 'ministry' that therefore cannot be compared to correlative positions in the secular business world,"[16] the Church in Nigeria participates in further acts of oppression rather than liberation, since church workers are discouraged from forming unions. How, then, can the Church in Nigeria call the government to accountability when only the bishop knows what income enters the diocesan coffers and nobody dare ask to see his budget? How can the Church support workers' unions in their struggles for a living wage when church workers are not allowed to unionize or form a union for church workers? The Church in Nigeria should educate its own members and workers to understand that all people are entitled to earn a decent wage for their labors, and that is their right, which corresponds to a renewed sense of obligation on the part of the workers to offer their very best work as service to God.

Church Support for Liberation of Women

Following Christ faithfully amid the current circumstances in Nigeria will require the Church likewise to take a lead in recognizing the dignity of women by offering women equal opportunities to participate in Church administration positions. While the Church in Nigeria continues to issue elaborate statements about how it prioritized the equal dignity of women, in the Church, it is rare that women have equal opportunities to contribute their creative abilities in the administrative work of the Church. This is one area the Church in Nigeria and all of Africa should lead by example, by acknowledging the equal dignity of women as children of God, equally endowed with gifts and talents by God.

The clergy in particular will need to demonstrate to a society steeped in the practices of patriarchy that they have truly taken on the words of Jesus who says "You know that the rulers of the Gentiles lord it over them, and the great ones make their authority over them felt. But it shall not be so among you" [Matthew 20:25]. Obiezu shines a compelling light on the plight of "communities of professed religious women who have for decades served the church for slave wages."[17] In Europe and America, many communities of women religious are compelled to close due to several reasons, including the effects of growing secularism, smaller families with fewer births, more work and educational options for women, and an overwhelmingly aging population with diminished income sources when health cost skyrocket. This situation is quickly catching up in Africa, with a need for the Church in Nigeria to brainstorm proactive ways to read these signs of the times and to respond appropriately.

An Exemplary Church: Simplicity of Lifestyle

Another implication for follow Christ faithfully in the current circumstances of Nigeria, is for Church leaders to reflect the simplicity of evangelical poverty through their personal lifestyles, serving to challenge the scandalous affluence typical of Nigerian faith and secular leaders.[18] After all, how can the Church preach salvation and good news to the people when they see the clergy dining and sharing in the privileges of power with politicians whose very ascent to power is questionable and dubious by all standards, with the claim that "all authority comes from God?"[19] How can Church leaders in Nigeria justify ostentatious lifestyle and opulence, living in luxurious mansions at the highest cost of living standards, while their flocks who are living in extreme poverty and ravaged by misery finance their overt wealth? In many communities where priests minister, the priest is the only one who can afford an alternative source of power where there in no public supply, the priest drives the most decent car or has several cars when a greater percentage of their congregation can hardly feed not to talk of owning a car. There is hardly any bishop in Nigeria that has less than two or three cars, mostly SUVs. As it is, the Church in Nigeria can hardly be said to articulate in practice its mission to liberate people from all forms of oppression.

Commitment to Justice and Peace

The African Synod II in particular, encouraged the Church in Africa specifically to promote the practical link between evangelization and human promotion.[20] However, it is impossible to do so if the Church does not break loose from practices that provoke a rupture between the Gospel of Jesus Christ and the fight against poverty, oppression, nepotism, abuse of power and injustice.[21] The Church in Nigeria has been, and continues to be, concerned to excess with wealth and power and caught up in overt service to those elite members of the privileged sectors of Nigerian society. The tuition of *Veritas* University Abuja, owned by the Catholic Bishops Conference of Nigeria, for example, is simply unattainable for the children of the poor. This applies equally to high schools, such as the Loyola Jesuit College in Abuja, as well as to private grade Catholic schools. This cannot help but connote grave consequences for the basic function of the Church as a sign of Christ on earth, and for its evangelical liberty and effectiveness. It is not only the fact that the Nigerian Church runs the risk of turning worldly, becoming salt without savor and leaven that does not lift up the common man but also that, the majority of its leaders view this as the sole means to carry out the task of evangelization.

Commitment to Leadership by Service

The *Lineamenta* for the African Synod II declares, "We must find solutions in order to emerge from the crisis faced by Africa."[22] One of the acute problems facing Africa and Nigeria in particular as we have noted is lack of purposeful leadership, both in Church and society at large. Contemporary society finds absurd the authority of the Gospel upon which the Church stands, which criticizes and denounces constantly every abuse of power, calling for equality of all of God's children, when at the same time, it upholds stratification within its own structures. It has become clear in the present time that the Church must model equitable and healthy structures found in contemporary civil society organizations or movements that are more compatible with the growing sense of our common humanity and that favors a more fraternal community promoting the participation of the greatest number of people (Gal 3: 26–29: you are one in Christ; Matt 23:8: you are all brothers; Jas 2:2–4: there must be no distinction between you).

In the light of the above, the call of the Synods requires the Church in Nigeria to learn from civil society. "Civil society has learned over the last two centuries that good government calls for (1) the elimination of nobility; (2) the separation of powers; (3) the principle of subsidiarity (what can be done at a lower level of society should be done there); and (4) a system of checks and balances."[23] Trusting that everything will be fairly decided by a central government is a model most people recognize as a failed global political strategy. However, if the Church adopts similar principles from civil society, it will lean more toward collegiality in its administrative and leadership structures.

In the light of the African Synods therefore, the Church in Nigeria, is challenged to cultivate an appropriate understanding of the ecclesial practice and of its accompanying implications couched most adequately in the visions set forth from the Synods. Indeed, the concerns of daily life and the pains Nigerians experience are not "worldly" concerns, but impinge directly mission of the Church. The joys and sorrows of the people are to be the joys and sorrows of the Church as Vatican II teaches, and affirmed by the synods.

Following Christ in Nigeria: The Example of Jesus

The present discussion does not indicate an attempt to question or dismiss the spiritual dimension of the Church and its importance in society. No doubt, the Church remains always a divine institution and for that reason serves as a practical metaphor for the mystery of God's action among humanity. What I argue for is a review of the emphasis on the spiritual dimension of the Church that separates transcendence from history and results in an ahistorical theology that views social action as evil and "worldly." Such a theology, even when it does recognize the true nature of the Church's practical role in society, favors reserving such roles exclusively to bishops and clergy. Thus, as the situation in the Nigerian Church indicates, if the Church collapses inevitably into a formal role as a mere social club, issuing official proclamations and exhorting the faithful to look up to God peacefully for deliverance from their earthly plight, this denies the laity their legitimate role as members of the body of Christ to voice their concerns and to roll up their shirt sleeves to serve the most vulnerable within every society. A closer look at Jesus' approach to human suffering and challenges during his ministry might help to underscore the importance of all levels of church leadership having the ability to enact social action in following Christ.

Chapter two of this study indicated a concrete New Testament image of Jesus as spiritual leader preoccupied entirely with proclaiming the kingdom of God in present, to unbind suffering men and women from evil (demons, sin and oppression from the legal casuistry of the scribes) while at the same time working in effect for an eternal kingdom to come. I deduce this from evidence found in the New Testament itself:

> ". . . at the one extreme we have those who maintain that he was guilty (at least as far as the Roman authorities were concerned) because he did claim to be the Messiah and he did want to start a violent revolution to overthrow the Roman imperialists. .

.. At the other extreme we have those who maintain that Jesus was completely innocent of those political charges."[24]

Even though contemporary New Testament research maintains the position
that Jesus neither sought nor encouraged his followers to seek political authority, nevertheless, it is safe to consider that some of the issues of that time were
political, since, for the Jews of that period, they would have considered such
issues in terms of their religion.[25] Thus, Jesus could be said to have been "political in the more comprehensive and important sense of the word: politics as
shaping of a community living in history."[26]

Justin S. Ukpong lays down three presuppositions to understand Jesus'
ministry vis-a-vis the political order of his day:

(a) First, for the Jews of Jesus' time, there was no separation of religion
    from politics and economics, and for that matter any other aspect of
    life. They all were seen integrally from the perspective of religion. The
    life of a Jew was tied around the covenant, which was the Jewish daily
    way of life. To buttress the intricate link of Jewish life to the Cove-
    nant, Ukpong quotes Bernard J Lee, who states:

> The Covenant included God's transformation of history. God and the world are not
> separated metaphysically. The distinction between temporal and non-temporal was
> not instinctively Jewish. . . For the ancient Jew, moving back and forth between
> politics and piety is largely a matter of emphasis, of responsiveness to the needs of the
> Jewish spirit at some particular moment in history.[27]

To say, then, that Jesus' ministry was concerned with only spiritual and moral
aspects of life in exclusion of the social and political cannot possibly be correct.

(b) Second, Jesus lived and preached at a time when Judea was under
    the oppressive regime of the Roman Empire. Of this period, Ukpong,
    quoting Pinchas Lapide writes:

> The much-touted Pax-Romana was the tyrannical rule of a Roman occupational
> force that threatened to break the people down by its arrogant arbitrariness, shame-
> less corruption, and brutal violation of law. . .under the pressure of an acute Jewish
> eschatological expectation and the scourge of this triple oppressive front, the dicta-
> tion came from repeatedly to open insurrection ...[28]

Continuing, he notes that it is possible to identify three groupings in Judea at the time—that had nothing to do with political and religious ties, including:

(i) The mass of the despondent whose primary concern was survival (the peasants);

(ii) Those who aligned with the oppressors (leading classes of the Sadducees as collaborators, and Pharisees as inactive spiritualizers); and

(iii) The freedom fighters (the zealots as nationalists and the Essenes as an extreme intransigent group).[29]

As is common in most situations of oppression, the poor were most affected. Because Jesus' message was meant to be good news to the poor, it is totally inconceivable that he would have remained indifferent to any situation of political oppression in his ministry.

(c) Third, the fact that Jesus was executed as a political criminal with the derisive inscription over his head, "king of the Jews," indicates most certainly that both the Roman and the Jewish authorities, who collaborated in his execution, identified Jesus as a political revolutionary. As Ukpong notes, if Jesus was not in fact, a political revolutionary, "what in his ministry led to such interpretations of him? In what ways, could he have been a political threat in Palestine?"[30] I believe however, that the accusation made that Jesus was a political revolutionary was nothing more than a way for the Sanhedrin/high priest to interest Pontius Pilate in the case.

The political climate surrounding Jesus' birth made him into a Jewish political figure.[31] At the time of Jesus' birth, the unpopular regime of the house of Herod emerged at the time of Roman direct rule of Judea from 6 AD with the heavy taxation of the colonized territories, the domination of the daily life of the Jews by the scribes and Pharisees with their legalistic interpretation and observance of the law, the rise of Zealotism (from 6 BCE) and the generalized mood of messianic expectation. In such a tense environment, it is extremely unlikely that any religious statement could be politically neutral. Thus, it is safe to say that when Jesus and his followers attacked the ideological use of religion by the scribes and the Pharisees to hold Jewish men or women under the bondage of legalism, it would be difficult for the audience not to read their actions as antagonistic to the politics of his world. Through his radical interpretation of the law, Jesus attacked indirectly this official religious authority. He reinterpreted the laws of the Old Testament. For example, Jesus healed people on the Sabbath, which was not unlawful, and told the healed man to pick up his pallet (bedroll), which was against the Sabbath.

Jesus took time to explain the law to the simple, the poor, the uneducated, stressing the truth, that justice and mercy were the essential kernels of wisdom at the core of his message. In this way, Jesus launched an indirect attack on the scribes, who were collaborating with the Romans, and the Pharisees who, while hating Roman domination, did nothing to change the situation, but, rather, enjoyed a privileged position within the oppressive order of things. More importantly, it is evident that, in the desire to be at peace with the state, as the New Testament testifies, the Christian community saw its faith in Jesus as imposing a new social alternative. "There is neither Jew nor Greek, there is neither slave nor free, there is neither male or female, for you are all one in Christ" (Gal 3:28).[32] All sorts of discrimination were abolished in principle overnight, and people whose upward social mobility was due to be halted because of societal circumstances (e.g., wealthy slaves, aliens not eligible for Roman citizenship, women, etc.) found the Christian alternative attractive. "So, what is at issue for most Christians is not whether the message of Jesus has a political dimension."[33]

Furthermore, in Judea, political, social, and economic oppression went hand in hand. The Roman soldiers were engaging in widespread extortion and intimidation of the people, to which John the Baptist drew their attention and which he condemned (Lk 3:13–14). Taxation was, indeed, a heavy burden that contributed to the impoverishment of the people. Hence, the people hated tax collectors who were collaborating with the oppressors. Under such conditions, Galilee, the "kingdom" of Herod and Judea, the "kingdom" of Pontius Pilate fell most certainly under the severe judgment of God's universal rule as Jesus preached. Before Jesus, John the Baptist also preached on the same theme of the imminent coming of the kingdom of God, and challenged Herod's moral life (Mk 6:14–19). Since, for the Jews, there was no way to compartmentalize moral and political life, whereby one would be shielded from the other, this challenge was as much political as it was religio-moral. It would have not only hit the nail on the head of Jewish complacency, but also undermined Herod's political authority. Hence, per Josephus, as Ukpong cites, "John was executed for inciting a revolution."[34] John Howard Yoder summarizes:

> According to Josephus, John's imprisonment was connected with Herod Antipas's fear that he might foment an insurrection. Luke's account of John's offense speaks not only of "Herodias his brother's wife," but also of "all the evil things Herod had

done," which might well involve some substantial political critique. Herod's putting away his first wife and taking Herodias in her place was itself a public political issue, as it brought on a war with the first wife's father, Aretas IV of Nabatea. Even if John's judgment upon the remarriage was motivated first by his rejection of divorce and adultery, his imprisonment had a political symbolic meaning, as did perhaps the choice of Machaerus, the fortress on the Nabatean border, as the place of John's imprisonment and execution.[35]

Thus, at the very beginning of his ministry "In what the Gospel of Luke portrays as the inaugural sermon of Jesus' ministry, Jesus announces that the reason for his anointing by God and the purpose of his mission in the world are one and the same—to proclaim radical economic, social, and political change."[36] In the synagogue at Nazareth, (Luke, drawing on the prophecy of Isaiah 61:1–2), emphasizing both the social dimension and the mission of a prophet, Jesus presents God's vision of a 'better world for all,' exhorting:

> The spirit of the Lord has been given to me, for He has anointed me. He has sent me to bring the good news to the poor, to proclaim liberty to the captives and the blind new sight, to set the downtrodden free, to proclaim the Lord's year of favor (Lk 4:18).

This proclamation would have been viewed as good news by the poor. It would have meant that they would have not needed earthly permission from political or economic authorities to break the bonds of economic exploitation that kept them poor, which, in turn, would have meant that they could call into question and protest the political control that enforced that exploitation. If it were in all actuality emulated, it would have meant liberation for the oppressed and the most marginalized in society. This indicates that Jesus liberates the whole person who is weighed down by many forms of slavery, including but not limited to political and social oppression, brainwashing through propaganda of both secular and religious false prophets/prophetesses, and manipulation by propaganda. This shows that although Jesus was not merely a political messiah, the political sphere was definitely part of his sphere of interest when he set about to do his ministry to proclaim the good news in spirit and in truth.

Sobrino indicates consistently in his writings that one of the most historically certain aspects of Jesus' ministry recent scripture scholarship has credentialed is that the central reality of Jesus' ministry and preaching is the immanent coming of the Kingdom of God.[37] Corroborating the view of the reign of God, which looks to the future, yet is at hand, he notes the record of the start of Jesus' public ministry in Mark and Matthew saying, ". . . Jesus came to Galilee, proclaiming the good news from God, and saying, 'The time is fulfilled and the Kingdom of God has come near; repent and believe in the good news' (Mark 1:14–15; Matt. 4:17)."[38] Continuing, Sobrino reveals, "In Luke the start of his public life takes place in the synagogue at Nazareth with the proclamation of the good news to the poor and the liberation of the oppressed (Luke 4:18), but Jesus himself relates the good news to the Kingdom: 'I must proclaim the good news of the Kingdom of God to the other cities also; for I was sent for this purpose' (4:43, cf. 8:1)."[39] Thus, there is absolutely a crucial correlation between the Kingdom of God and the life and ministry of Jesus, since Jesus came for the exact purpose to announce the Kingdom and to bring it to fruition. "Aware of the hunger faced by the crowd, Jesus, the bread of eternal life (Jn 6:35), halted his preaching to take care of the hungry people (Lk 9:19; Jn 6:1–15). He affirmed through his acts and words that God is not insensitive to the misery that strikes the people of God (Lk 9:13; Jn 6:5–6)."[40] Giving the basis for his Christology, structured intrinsically in the Kingdom of God, Sobrino surmises:

> Jesus proclaimed the Kingdom and did many things related to the Kingdom. This is shown programmatically in the Synoptics where their accounts of the beginning of his public mission describe him not only *proclaiming* the Kingdom, but carrying out related *activities*. 'And he went throughout Galilee, proclaiming the message in their synagogues and casting out demons' (Mark 1:39); 'and he cured many who were sick with various diseases and cast out many demons' (Mark 1:34; Matt. 8:14; Luke 4:40 ff.). And the summary in Acts 10:38 describes how Jesus 'went about doing good, and healing all who were oppressed by the devil.' The Gospels then speak clearly and at the outset of both 'sayings' and 'actions' of Jesus, as Vatican II says. In Kingdom terminology, we can say that Jesus is both *proclaimer* and *initiator* of the Kingdom of God.[41]

In other words, Jesus' ministry focuses on the active reign of God to grant people salvation from and victory over the antireign forces of death: sickness, hunger, corruption, oppression, injustice, greed, and others.[42]

The Church in Nigeria needs to adopt this understanding of salvation that refers not exclusively, but most importantly, to the present assurance of what is hoped for. By doing so, the ministry of the Church will be dedicated consciously to manifest God's will through actions that transform the bad reality into a good reality for all of society. Following Jesus in this way will result in individual Christians and the organized body of the Church committing to enact and achieve salvific actions on behalf of the people.

In summary, Sobrino, presents a portrait of God in Jesus as *savior-liberator*.[43] In his ministry, Jesus, through his words and deeds, presents God's reign specifically as salvation for human existence, mercy for sinners, compassion for victims, and freedom for captives. Following Christ in a country such as Nigeria, the Church will not only have to offer pious exhortations but must play a more direct political role in the struggle for social justice. The Church in Nigeria must move beyond the words of Jesus to emulate his actions in service of the kingdom and must work actively toward addressing basic needs of food, clothing, shelter, education, health, sanitation, clean drinking water, and public transportation, among others. Following Christ, the Church in Nigeria will have to educate Christians to step up their civic responsibility to challenge corrupt and oppressive leadership in governance. This requires the Church to back up its words with actions by forming and supporting self-help community-based associations to design realistic alternatives to the unjust structures they are challenging, and, in fact, begin the process of bringing alternatives into being.

Furthermore, Sobrino makes an important distinction, proposing that these actions of Jesus are simply "signs" of the presence of the Kingdom in history and should not be interpreted as the "reality" of the Kingdom.[44] This avoids the danger of reducing Jesus' entire ministry into a mere one time stint of short-term altruistic social activism, thus, obscuring the eschatological hope of the Christian faith in future growth as more people take on the challenge of reproducing elements of the kingdom through their own actions. Yet, the signs of Jesus in service of the Kingdom, although not the entire reality of the Kingdom, express something of the reality of the Kingdom and "point to the direction this will take in its fullness."[45] By following Christ in Nigeria, specifically through this example of a liberation Jesus, will arouse the hope in Nigerian Christians that living out the Kingdom in reality is possible, and this will serve as good news to the people. The image of following Jesus in his service of the reign of God will, thus, integrate soteriology and spirituality for the Church and individual Christians in Nigeria.

Concluding Observations

Following Christ in the context of present-day Nigeria draws inspiration from the above considerations. The life and mission of Jesus, a life that dedicated to the service of the Kingdom of God, enables us to locate the mission of the

Church in Nigeria as one that guarantees a holistic concept of life, a life in which Jesus came so that we may have it to the fullest (John 10:10). This is the view of life on which Jean-Marc Ela expounds, saying:

> Here the church must see that the demands of faith are largely rooted in the organization of the city of the earth. It cannot refrain from intervening when lives and dignity of women and men are threatened. It must speak to them in a meaningful way and discover the internal bond between faith and the problems of people's everyday lives.[46]

In the present context of Nigeria, therefore, a priest, pastor, or Imam can no longer be satisfied with offering pious exhortations, leading prayers, organizing vigils, and healing sessions alone. An integral part of their duties includes the need to open the eyes of the faithful to the political and the social realities around them. In doing so, religious leaders not only will challenge them to take actions inspired by the spirit to work to bring about alternatives for the better, but also will be part of such initiatives for change themselves. Clearly, the Kingdom of God that Christianity preaches cannot be inaugurated here on earth to be fulfilled in heaven if people do not work toward it.

The mark of the Church as the sacrament of Christ's presence in Nigeria, then, is not how little involved the Church is in the world of Nigerians, because the Church is a spiritual body—how far away the Church manages to remain from the daily "tombs" of human living—but, rather, how the Church enters them fearlessly and joyfully in order to restore people to life. The resurrection of Jesus, for example, has more meaning if the Church witnesses to the Gospel by bringing newness and peace into the lives of people, and if their encounters with Christians as witnesses of the resurrection become life-changing events for them. So many in our society today are sick and cannot access adequate medical care because of poverty; some live in slums because they cannot afford decent housing; others take drugs and alcohol because harsh economic times have driven them to despair; others go to school and graduate without any opportunities for employment; other young people cannot aspire to political leadership because money in politics schemes throw them out. These situations represent forms of death. A life witnessing to the resurrection involves overcoming these deaths.

The fact that Jesus was raised by God not only entails the expectation that one day we, too, will rise to heaven but also calls us to engage in the mission of lifting the victims of this world. Those who follow Christ should be raisers who seek justice for victims and new life for those who experience "deaths" imposed on them by the structures of society. This is an inalienable part of the mission of the Church in Nigeria, to proclaim the good news and restore hope for the whole society.

Notes

1. John F. Kavanaugh, *Following Christ in a Consumer Society*, 25th ed. (Maryknoll: Orbis Books, 2006), xii.
2. *Ibid.*195.
3. See, for example, the excellent explication of a typical African understanding of 'The Kingdom of God' by Orobator, "The Idea of the Kingdom of God in African Theology," *Studia Missionalia* 46 (1997): 227–257.
4. Orobator, "The Idea of the Kingdom of God in African Theology," 331.
5. See Orobator, *The Church as Family*, Ehusani, *A Prophetic Church*, Uzukwu, "The Birth and Development of a Local Church: Difficulties and Signs of Hope."
6. Orobator, *The Church as Family*, 88.
7. *Ibid.* 83.
8. *Ibid.* 82–84.
9. *Ibid.*
10. See Vatican Council II, *Apostolicam Actuositatem*.
11. *Instrumentum Laboris* for the African Synod II, no. 1, as quoted by Soédé, "The Enduring Scourge of Poverty and Evangelization in Africa," 186.
12. *Ibid.*
13. Soédé, "The Enduring Scourge of Poverty and Evangelization in Africa," 186.
14. Kevin Burke, *The Ground Beneath the Cross*, 212.
15. Emeka Christian Obiezu, OSA, *Towards a Politics of Compassion: Socio-Political Dimensions of Christian Responses to Suffering* (Bloomington, IN: Authorhouse, 2008), 115.
16. *Ibid.*
17. *Ibid.*
18. *Ibid.* 116.
19. Many church leaders base this claim on Paul's letter to the Romans 13:1, to cow tow people into blind obedience to corrupt and inept leadership in Nigeria.
20. Benedict XVI, *Africae Munus*, # 81–83. Cf Nathanaél Yaovi Soédé, "The Enduring Scourge of Poverty and Evangelization in Africa," in *Reconciliation, Justice and Peace*, Orobator, ed. 185.
21. *Ibid.* 186.
22. *Lineamenta* for the African Synod II, no. 1, as quoted by Soédé, "The Enduring Scourge of Poverty and Evangelization in Africa," 186.
23. Thomas J. Reese, "Reforming the Vatican: The Tradition of Best Practices," in *Catholics and Politics: The Dynamic Tension Between Faith and Power*, Kristin E. Heyer, Mark J. Rozell, Michael A. Genovese, eds. (Washington DC: Georgetown University Press, 2008), 216.

24. Albert Nolan, *Jesus before Christianity*, (Maryknoll: Orbis, 1989), 92–93. *Cf.* Justin S. Ukpong, "The Political Dimensions of Jesus' Ministry: Implications for Evangelization in Africa." *WAJES* 3.1 (1995): 2, as quoted by Asue, "The Political Involvement of Catholic Bishops in Nigeria." This section follows closely Asue's interpretation of Jesus as a political persona.

25. *Ibid.* 93.

26. Marcus J. Borg, *Jesus a New Vision: Spirit, Culture, and the life of Discipleship* (San Francisco: HarperSanFrancisco, 1991), 125.

27. Bernard J. Lee, *The Galilean Jewishness of Jesus* (New York: Paulist Press, 1988), 105–106.

28. Ukpong, "The Political Dimensions of Jesus' Ministry," 2.

29. *Ibid.* 2–3. *Cf.* Lee, *The Galilean Jewishness of Jesus*, 96–147.

30. *Ibid.* 3. Some scholars dispute such an interpretation of Jesus as a political persona, arguing that Jesus and his followers preached a religious message, even rejecting the path of violent resistance to their Roman overlords. R. T. France, in his collection, *The Gospel of Matthew* The International Commentary on the New Testament (Grand Rapids: William Eerdmans Publishing Company, 2007), for example, holds that Matthew 5:1–7:29 is addressed to the narrow section of Jesus' disciples taken apart to teach them what life in the Kingdom of God is about. "The teaching will frequently describe them as a special group who stand over against, and indeed are persecuted by, people in general. They are those who entered a new relationship with 'your Father in heaven,' and who in consequence are called to a radically new lifestyle, in conscious distinction from the norms of the rest of society. They are to be an alternative society, a 'Christian counter-culture.'" (153). This is quite different from the impression that Jesus was setting out on a definite route to revolution as Ukpong holds. Commenting on Matthew 20:20–22, David A. Hagner, in his *World Biblical Commentary* Volume 33B Matthew 14–28 (Dallas, Texas: Word Books, 1995), 583, says, "The sons of Zebedee make a request that from one point of view seems natural and acceptable. That point of view, however, reflects the distorted perspective of human fallenness . . . There will be eschatological rewards for the disciples, of course, but these are not for the present nor are the disciples to have them uppermost in their minds. Instead the disciples are to be marked by the humility, servant hood, and obedience to death that characterized Jesus, in the knowledge that to suffer with him may mean to drink the cup that he drank before ultimately reigning with him (*Cf.* Rom 8:17)." Cf John P. Meier, *The Mission of Christ and His Church*, Good News Studies 30 (Wilminton, Delaware: Michael Glazier, Inc, 1990). Citing several passages where Jesus speaks of his possible death with no hint of reprieve or reversal, and even affirming his inability to assure seats at his right and left in the kingdom, Meier notes, "What is especially noteworthy in all these passages is that there is no saving significance attributed to Jesus' death, no idea of vicarious sacrifice. The death of Jesus is simply predicted; it has no positive value." (27). See also Meier, *The Vision of Matthew: Christ, Church and Morality in the First Gospel* (New York: Paulist Press, 1979). To attach a solely eschatological meaning to the teachings and actions of Jesus would however inadvertently amount to resignation.

31. Obery M. Hendricks, *The Politics of Jesus: Rediscovering the True Revolutionary Nature of Jesus' Teachings and How They Have Been Corrupted* (New York: Doubleday, 2006), 1–96.

32. Some scholars note however, an underlying eschatological intent in Paul's teaching here, rather than offering a new social alternative. Commenting on Galatians 3:28 for example, Richard N. Longenecker in *World Biblical Commentary* Volume 41 Galatians (Dallas, Texas: Word Books, 1990), 155, says, "In the liturgy, the saying would communicate information to the newly initiated, telling them of their eschatological status before God in anticipation of the Last Judgment. . . Certainly the proclamation of the elimination of divisions in these three areas should be seen first of all in terms of spiritual relations: that before God, whatever their differing situations, all people are accepted on the same basis of faith and together make up the one body of Christ." It is true that baptism was offered to all who embraced the faith, and that early Christianity cut through the various social lines then extant—radical in itself vis-á-vis the Judaism of the time—but that did not in fact imply necessarily for them that there would be a change in the social order itself; slaves and women remained in their places outside the circles of the church. Thus, Jeremy Punt, in his book, Postcolonial Biblical Interpretation: Reframing Paul, Studies in Theology and Religion 20 (Leiden: Brill, 2015), 170, cautions any premature conclusions when it comes to reading Paul. "Scholars oscillate between different understandings of Paul, presenting the apostle as someone who perpetuated first-century social systems which could today be seen as unjust or at least unpalatable, with issues relating to politics, gender, slavery, and sexual orientation probably most often discussed. On the other hand, numerous studies can be cited which claim Paul either fundamentally challenged or at least to some extent attenuated the excesses of oppressive or hegemonic social systems."
33. Hendricks, *The Politics of Jesus*, 7.
34. Ukpong, "The Political Dimensions of Jesus' Ministry," 4.
35. John Howard Yoder, *The Politics of Jesus* (Grand Rapids: William B. Eerdmans Publishing Company, 1994), 23–24.
36. Hendricks, *The Politics of Jesus*, 7.
37. For details, see Sobrino, *Jesus the Liberator*, 67–104. Sobrino dwells extensively on the intrinsic relationship between Jesus Christ and the Kingdom/Reign of God in Chapter four of this book, which he tittles "Jesus and the Kingdom of God," to specifically draw out the social, ethical implications of Jesus' life and mission. This section adopts Sobrino's interpretation of the life of Jesus as one dedicated to the service of the Kingdom. The follower of Jesus will imitate his words and actions in service of the Kingdom also.
38. *Ibid.* 68.
39. *Ibid.*
40. Soédé, "The Enduring Scourge of Poverty and Evangelization in Africa," 187.
41. Sobrino, *Jesus the Liberator*, 87.
42. *Ibid.* 87–100.
43. *Ibid.*
44. *Ibid.* 108–109.
45. *Ibid.*
46. Jean-Marc Ela, *African Cry*, trans. Robert J. Barr (Eugene, Oregon: Wipf and Stock Publishers, 2005), 136.

CONCLUSION

Doing the Will of God on Earth
as It Is in Heaven

This work makes a call on the Catholic Church in Nigeria to rediscover its identity and mission as a sacrament of liberation. The identity and mission necessarily invites the Church to work for liberation from unjust structures and the creation of new structures that foster dignity and freedom as constitutive of the Church's mission of reconciliation, justice, and peace. To be able to do this effectively, this work calls the Church to re-examine its self-understanding regarding active witness in society. From time immemorial, Christian thinkers have struggled with two complementary aspects of the mystery of the Godhead—the transcendence of God and the immanence of God. Beginning with the Jewish roots of Christianity through to this day, humanity has exhibited the general tendency to emphasize one aspect of this mystery to the neglect or the diminution of the other. Indeed, many religious traditions are in a schema, which holds at one extreme the transcendence of God without His immanence, and at the opposite extreme the immanence of God to the neglect of His transcendence.

A swinging motion has occurred between the two ideologies throughout the history of the Catholic Church, in terms of our understanding of Church governance, the magisterium, worship, the understanding of grace, and the nature of the Christian community. At the source of this movement is our understanding of Christ and his redemptive role, his promise of salvation, the nature of his mystical body, and the role of the sacraments, all of which shape ultimately an understanding of the relationship between the Church and the world. Since the self-understanding of the Church originates from its identification with Christ, and more specifically, from the human nature of Christ acting as the earthly instrument of his divine nature, I argued that the approach of Jesus Christ to his earthly ministry, which was dedicated to the inauguration of the reign of God, should become the paradigm for the Catholic Church in Nigeria to carry out the mission received from Christ. In other words, our human acts as instruments of Christ's human acts become carriers of God's grace, incarnating the supernatural in human history.

Ellacuría's method of historicization led me to explore the concrete, historical reality of Nigeria today, arguing consistently in this study that salvation is not exclusively that which happens after this life. As the ministry of Jesus indicates, salvation involves finding answers to question that plague the daily lives of people; how can we escape famine and hunger, how can we live in decent housing, how can we send our children to school to be educated, how can we stay in good health and support ourselves? Thus, to answer the messengers whom John the Baptist sent to verify if Jesus was the Messiah, the promised one who would assist the Jews in realizing their deepest dreams, Jesus responded: "Go and tell John what you hear and see; the blind regains their sight, the lame walk, lepers are cleansed, the deaf hear, the dead are raised, and the poor have good news proclaimed to them" (Matt. 11:2–6, Cf. Luke 7:22–23). Doing the will of God in Nigeria requires an understanding of faith-incarnate, as being lived and professed in the quest for justice in society.

As we saw in this work, the Church in Nigeria needs to move from condemning to confronting evil. Such faith needs necessarily to push theology from merely identifying and even condemning evil and its causes, to pose the question: what is to be done? This is the push that the Church in Latin America received from the wave of liberation theology that swept around the region in the 1970s–80s. Archbishop Romero's witness along with the rich ecclesiological models of theologians, such as Jesuit, Ignacio Ellacuría, sparked a new interpretation of the Christian Gospel that brought the Church's theology face to face with the challenges posed to the faith by issues of injustice and privilege in the society. Ellacuría's liberative praxis of Christian salvation, for example, is a powerful tool to link a critical understanding of salvation to an efficacious understanding and practice of the Church that provokes it to face the problems of the modern world, being attentive especially to the suffering of the most vulnerable.

Orobator has proposed a three-tier hermeneutical grid for interpreting the idea of the kingdom of God that provides a deep meaning to an African living in these circumstances: "annunciation (good news), denunciation (prophetic action), transformation (praxis)."[1] The Synoptic Gospels indicate that Jesus travelled around Galilee announcing the good news of the kingdom of God to the poor, the sick, the outcasts, and hungry of his time. It, therefore, follows that in announcing the message of the kingdom, a task with which the Church in Nigeria clearly identifies, the Church ought to be publicly announcing the good news of food for the hungry, health for the sick, employment for the teeming numbers of young graduates, improved working conditions for workers, defending the cause of the defenseless and vulnerable. In such actions as these, the message of the gospel will echo more clearly and meaningfully to Nigerian Catholics and others.

Relatedly, the Synoptic Gospels portray that the inauguration and functioning of the Kingdom of God is always in conflict with opposing kingdoms.[2] A necessary character of the Kingdom of God, then, is "prophetic denunciation of oppressive socioeconomic and political structures."[3] Clearly, upholding the cause of the Kingdom of God becomes a risky venture for all who are dedicated to that cause as it was to Jesus himself, leading, in fact, to his death. The presupposition of this study is that if the Church in Nigeria is to be an effective sign of God's presence in the world, it ought to conflict with the antikingdoms of oppression, corruption, bad governance, and crude accumulation of wealth by a few privileged Nigerians.

Doing the will of God in Nigeria, as it is done in heaven, will, therefore, require the Church in Nigeria to educate the children of God about their obligation to resist bad governance as an honorable Christian duty; it will require the Church in Nigeria to initiate, nurture and sustain meaningful pressure on the entrenched corrupt practices of government and public servants as a legitimate means to positive change; and it will require the Church to offer appropriate prophetic witness to the state.[4] The implication is that the Church will first of all, take the lead in its witness, upholding transparency, checks and balances and best practices within Church institutions and structures.

To be able to announce the Kingdom of God in Nigeria, in a praxis-oriented fashion as envisioned above, I argued that the Church in Nigeria must first acknowledge the truism that the factors of economic, political, and religious coexistence in Nigeria are related, with implications for an understanding of salvation. The lack of this sensitivity, which has been characteristic of ecclesial practice in Nigeria, as elsewhere, has resulted in an ahistorical theology of church and has limited its witness value. Indeed, as Cynthia D. Moe–Lobeda notes,

> One of the great self-betrayals of Christian faith by the tradition itself is the teaching that God's intended reign (traditionally referred to as heaven) is for life after death only; life on earth does not really matter, for our reward and hope are found after death in heaven. This teaching was used for centuries to subdue peoples into accepting their own oppression and domination. It betrays the promise that God's gift of eternal life begins on earth and that God intends creation to flourish.[5]

Since all religious traditions change over time as they adapt out of necessity to new circumstances, our belief and expectation is that it is time for the Church in Nigeria to adopt a new pastoral strategy for effective witnessing and evangelization: (a) a reform in the training program of agents of evangelization to particularly imbibe the tenets of Catholic social teaching, and (b) a strengthening of ecumenical/interreligious structures of dialogue, formation of community-based self-help associations, and collaboration with civil arms of the society. Indeed, "Where systemic injustice damages well-being and causes suffering, seeking the well-being or good of those who suffer—actively loving—entails challenging that injustice."[6] This study, thus, identifies as a basic challenge posed to faith in the public life of Nigeria now: to identify systemic evil for what it is, and not only to condemn it, but also to resist it and to create more just alternatives.

Recommendations for a Way Forward: Context and Pastoral Response

The call to follow Jesus in every age and circumstance always carries with it certain demands. The responses to the costly discipleship that awaits those who choose to follow Jesus, however, vary according to their unique circumstances. Orobator outlines specific issues of social concern in Africa and the corresponding obligations and implications for the identity and mission of the entire community called church in Sub-Saharan Africa.[7] Moreover, his assessment is quite valid for the Nigerian context. However, in this study, I offer the following insights that inform my belief in the liberating power of the Spirit, that salvation in the current context of Nigeria would be best understood as liberation. As a sacrament of Christ's presence in Nigeria, what would be an adequate pastoral response for the Church in the context of present-day Nigerian reality to serve as an instrument of salvation for all the members of God's family in Nigeria?

An Adequate Education in Catholic Social Teaching

"My people perish for want of knowledge!" (Hosea 4:6). The prophet's cry in ancient Israel is quite apt in describing the situation of many Nigerian Catholics. As I noted earlier, the teaching of the Second Vatican Council has remained obscured, especially regarding the social vocation of Christian, in the teachings of the Church in Nigeria. So, too, have many pastors glossed over the urgent calls of the recent African Synods I and II for the Church in Africa to take the social reality of the continent seriously as a demand of faith. Hence, the laity continue to be unaware of the social obligations of their faith. Despite the solid bases this provides them for social action, and the specific call of these Synods for pastors to commit to educating the laity in the social responsibilities of their faith, many pastors either avoid voicing relevant sections of the teachings that deal with such issues or distort them consciously, presenting an ahistorical understanding of the Christian faith, emphasizing that "our true home is in heaven," not on this earth.

Several Nigerian theologians agree that the Catholic faith in Nigeria has overlooked the dimension of activity in this world, in this place, now.[8] There is greater concern for the organizational institution of the Church, and its internal earthly dealings form, than for the lives of the lay people who count themselves as the faithful and interpersonal community engagements. Since the average Nigerian Christian faithful is typically deferential, perhaps even dependent, on the words of the priests and the bishops, the curious inability of the pastors to teach the social dimension of the faith accounts, in part, for the people's losing sight of the historical visibility of grace and the necessity to configure one's life in accordance with the historical life of Jesus of Nazareth.

This situation has persisted because, from a sociological perspective, the Nigerian Church operates a manner like what Leornardo Boff calls an authoritarian system.[9] A system is authoritarian when those in power exclude their subordinates from the free and spontaneous acknowledgement of that authority.[10] The uncompelled submission of a group of people to an individual or an institution distinguishes authority from power and domination. Without natural conditions in place, which allow for equal relationships to flourish, authority becomes ever more authoritarian. Since exercise of power within the Nigerian Church as is the case in most of the Roman Catholic Church, is effected through inadequate catechesis, theological formation, and deference to traditional transmission accepted from generation to generation, the faithful are compelled to accept whatever the priests tell them is true to faith.

Typically, it is considered in the Catholic Church then that the higher someone appears to be in the hierarchy, the closer to God they are, and so that person must have a greater share in God's divine power. To obey those in power, thus, is to obey God, transforming obedience of the elite into a religious act.[11] According to Leonardo Boff, criticism of Church structures within the Church becomes "only possible from a higher authority," thereby making movements for societal transformation appear to attack God who is the perceived author of both hierarchical order and the institutional structures of sacred power.[12] It would be obviously absurd for the Church to constantly criticize and denounce consciously civil leaders who abuse power, if on the one hand, they are calling for equality of all of God's children, while on the other hand upholding internal institutional hierarchical stratification. Hence, it has become difficult for the Church to proclaim effectively and adequately social aspects of the Gospel that can lead to liberate the children of God.

To dedicate itself genuinely to educate the laity in the rich corpus of the social teachings of the Church that can lead them to liberation from oppression and injustice, this work calls on the Nigerian Church to learn from successful social movements in postmodern civil society, as I have indicated above. This should include a concerted effort by the Church to become more actively involved in shaping and in clarifying the moral vision for a new society. Rather than complain about bad politics and corruption in our country, Nigerian Church leaders are called to equip Catholics with fundamentals of the Church's social teachings and to begin to train youth and the laity as leaders to provide outreach and evangelical roles in public life. When the Church liberates itself from the grip of power and self-preservation through providing a sound education of the faithful, it will be better enabled to proclaim the truth that God does not desire the evil of poverty and want in Nigerian society, but that indeed these and other ills are human-made and should be resisted and reformed. Only then can the Church in Nigeria sensitize honestly and transparently the laity to know that faith obliges them legitimately to oppose injustice. Such knowledge will reveal to the Nigerian laity the power that will lead them inevitably to their own liberation to become the free children of God that they are meant to be.

An Adequate Spirituality of Social Engagement

The Second Vatican Council document, the Dogmatic Constitution on the Church *Lumen Gentium*, "Light of the Nations" describes succinctly the precise vocation of the laity in the specific terms of seeking the Kingdom of God through their engagement in temporal affairs and in ordering them according to the plan of God. The document states emphatically:

> They live in the ordinary circumstances of family and social life, from which the very web of their existence is woven. They are called there by God that by exercising their proper function and led by the spirit of the Gospel, they may work for the sanctification of the world from within as a leaven. . . Since they are tightly bound up in all types of temporal affairs, it is their special task to order and to throw light upon these affairs, in such a way that they may come into being and then continually increase, according to Christ, to the praise of the Creator and the Redeemer (*Lumen Gentium*, no. 31)

Essentially, since Catholicism is central to the lives of many individuals and groups in Nigeria, it becomes an unavoidable element in the socio-political and economic life of the nation. Thus, the basic challenge to Nigerian Catholics is to bring the principles of faith to bear on their lives in such a way that they can serve the nation as exemplary Catholics and as good citizens. In the context of contemporary Nigeria, an adequate spirituality of social engagement is one that includes both political and economic implications for the faith of Nigerian Catholics.

Politically, Christian responsibility of active participation in public life is of prime importance. Politics, as Vatican II describes it, should be considered an eminent field of the Christian apostolate, indeed, it should be regarded as "a noble art" that serves as a means of rendering service for the community of God's children on earth. Pursued for the right motives, politics can be a legitimate way to render service and to do the maximum amount of good for the greatest number of people possible. An adequate spirituality of social engagement is one that is built on a concept of politics, which understands political power as a role, which belongs to God and is held in trust by human beings for service. This work thus, calls individual Catholic Christians to seek political office with the justified intent of rendering service and of working for the right ordering of society for the good of all. Same call is equally made on

the Church in Nigeria to educate and to support the faithful to be more politically active, and through their political participation, play a part in bringing
about a just and a peaceful society for all. This will require further education
as well as concrete structures that will lead to such a goal, such as forming
associations that seek promotion of the common good, which can also serve
as a base threshold for Christians who seek political office to serve the wider
community.

Economically, an adequate spirituality of social engagement in Nigeria
is one that does not simply offer statements condemning the bad state of the
economy, poverty, and hunger and stops at that. Apart from identifying the
root causes of poverty and hunger, and educating the people to resist actively
those causes and structures, whenever the Church proclaims the Gospel, it
needs to address specific conditions of poverty and hunger by working practically on ways to help people support themselves and by moving them out of
poverty and hunger. This calls the Church to form and nurture pastoral, social, and economic programs, such as vocational centers, counseling centers,
cooperatives, farmers and worker's unions and community-based self-help
associations in parishes and villages. Through popular participation in self-
help associations that Church communities at the grass roots nurture for the
economic advancement of the people, the Church will serve its most key role
as an agent of social transformation.

As a sacrament of the continuing presence of the Risen Lord, the Church
in Nigeria is called to continue to proclaim the good news of Christ, which
renews the culture of fallen humanity and removes the evil of the sad news of
hunger, poverty, and disease to transform their lives. An adequate spirituality
of social engagement in Nigeria, therefore, must aim to transform the lives
and conditions of people from within and them new, able to walk in the foot-
steps of Jesus, who says, "I am making the whole creation new" (Rev. 21:5, cf.
2 Cor. 5:17, Gal. 6:15). Such spirituality should be guided by the truth that
material poverty, hunger, disease, and other limiting conditions to the human
situation "make the gospel difficult to speak and painful to hear."[13]

An Adequate Focus Level of Efforts for Social Change

In this study, I have maintained that in Nigeria, a nation characterized by religious and ethnic pluralism, it is imperative to seek and to promote common
grounds for nation building in a spirit of mutual respect. Sadly, the failure to
translate their intellectual weight into establishing linkages with other progressive forces in the nation remains a major drawback to the social witness of

all religions in Nigeria, including that of Christianity. Consequently, religion has been largely politicized into a facade, masking the real causes of violence in Nigeria as having religious origins, when the real causes are corruption and bad governance. Indeed, if corruption and bad politics persist, violence will continue to haunt people in Nigeria and most of Africa.

Furthermore, specific policy decisions and actions on the part of superpowers and multinational corporations in their quest for control over resources in Africa, such as oil and diamonds are often the source of the current troubles. In Nigeria, for example, the violence unleashed by Boko Haram is more likely a symptom of frustrations that have spread across the Arab world in reaction to superpowers playing politics to benefit economically from resources in the Middle East. At the personal, local, organized, and international levels, this study calls for bonds of dialogue and collaboration to be deepened to end the violence of the mobs that threaten the foundation of our survival. In this way, we will be better able to create an environment conducive to collective liberative action.

The Church in Nigeria cannot, therefore, be a true sacrament of Christ when it separates itself from other religious bodies by building walls of distrust, prejudice, antagonism, and disrespect, which promote more rhetoric of religious violence. Such apparent contradictions between faith and practice weaken the credibility of the Gospel message and limit its value to be able to witness the good news of liberation in a broken society. Therefore, the Church ought to recognize in the first place, that all religious bodies have potential to imagine emancipatory ideas beyond what the Church alone can achieve on its own. This study thus, calls the Church in Nigeria to engage in strategic alliance with the progressive forces in the other church denominations and other religions at the local, regional, or national levels to forge and to articulate a common cause of action for the right ordering of Nigerian society.

In the light of the above discussion, I urge more interchurch/interreligious cooperation on projects that aim to oversee more efficient administration of public affairs in the areas of politics and the economy, which are, in fact, the root cause of most social problems of Nigeria. The Church should partner with other faith communities to form stronger groups that can advocate for transparency and accountability in government. Such inter-faith bodies will be much more effective serving to check and balance on the government. Similar bodies should be established to work toward empowering the most vulnerable members of the society, women, and youth to access more opportunities in public life.

The negative impacts of the economy on the youth, for example, minimize their ability to participate in social life, which frustrates and renders them vulnerable to bad choices. Many universities turn out graduates every year, when there are no business and job opportunities available for them. Political leadership requires party membership, money, and connection, none of which is within the reach of even our most well educated youth. The Church in Nigeria ought to partner with other faith communities to initiate and to sustain youth programs to identify the talents, the abilities and the achievements through which even these young people could even rise to leadership and actualization in community. Such collaboration should have several social functions integrated uniquely with the religious one, due to adversity in the social environment, especially for youth.

Specific programs geared to skills acquisition and entrepreneurial training, and leadership development will be able to address more practically the structures of oppression that consign many Nigerians to mediocrity and non-achievement by encouraging young people that they can run public office and influence the agenda of the state in other ways Most importantly, a more adequate level of focus on efforts for social change by the Church in Nigeria cannot be complete without its making more conscious efforts to harness the potentials of women in the religious community and one society at large, to enhance social transformation and integral development. The significant roles women play in the education of children and the formation of their consciences should be recognized in the religious community by opening opportunities for women in higher levels of leadership. Religious bodies are called, therefore, to encourage and support programs that aim to advance the cause of women and that work for their well-being.

In a summary, bearing in mind the central thesis of my study, that economic, political, and religious factors of coexistence are interrelated, with deeper implications for understanding salvation, I call for an approach in the Nigerian Church that connects salvation theory and ecclesial practice. To do this effectively, the Church ought to cultivate an appropriate understanding of this ecclesial practice and of its accompanying implications to follow Christ authentically and contextually. This has been the essential call of the African Synods I and II.

Notes

1. Orobator, "The Idea of the Kingdom of God in African Theology," 333.
2. *Ibid*. 337.
3. *Ibid*. 338.
4. *Ibid*. 352.
5. Cynthia D. Moe–Lobeda, *Resisting Structural Evil: Love as Ecological-Economic Vocation* (Minneapolis: Fortress Press, 2013), 153.
6. *Ibid*. 176.
7. Orobator, *Church as the Family of God*, 149–166.
8. See Orobator, *Church as the Family of God*; Ukpong, "The Political Dimensions of Jesus' Ministry," Ehusani, *A Prophetic Church*; Obiezu, OSA, *Towards a Politics of Compassion*.
9. Leonardo Boff, *Church, Charism and Power: Liberation Theology and the Institutional Church* (London: SCM Press Ltd. 1985) 40.
10. *Ibid*.
11. *Ibid*.
12. *Ibid*.
13. Kavanaugh, *Following Christ in a Consumer Society*, 136.

APPENDIX I

Table AI.1: GOOD SHEPHERD MAJOR SEMINARY KADUNA, KADUNA STATE, NIGERIA—THEOLOGY COURSES

CODE	COURSE TITLE	STATUS	CREDIT
BST 111	Introduction to the New Testament		3
BST 112	Historical Books of the Old Testament		3
BST 113	Introduction to Christian Ethics		3
BST 114	Introduction to the Gospels		3
BST 115	Origin, Nature & Structure of the Church		3
BST 116	Trinity		3
BST 117	Rise and Spread of Islam		2
BST 118	Problems of Philosophy		3
BST 119	Spiritual Theology		2
SEM 101	Use of English		2
SEM 102	Interpersonal Communication		2
SEM 103	Cultural Anthropology		2
SEM 104	Basic Concept in African Religion		2
SEM 105	Political and Cultural Systems in Africa		2

CODE	COURSE TITLE	STATUS	CREDIT
BST 121	Principles of Biblical Hermeneutics		3
BST 122	Intro to New Testament Greek		3
BST 123	Introduction to Canon Law		3
BST 124	Introduction to Theology		2
BST 125	Fundamental Theology		2
BST 126	The Church in the Roman Empire		2
BST 127	Introduction to Liturgy		2
BST 211	Prophetic Writings		3
BST 212	Acts of Apostles		3
BST 213	Catholic Epistles		2
BST 214	Social Morality I		3
BST 215	Pauline Epistles		3
SEM 202	Documents of the Church		2
SEM 203	Traditional African Society		2
SEM 204	Use of English		2
SEM 205	Speech and Diction		2
SEM 206	Theory & Practice of Administration		2
SEM 207	Development Administration		2
BST 217	Theological Anthropology		2
BST 219	Theory and Practice of Liturgy		2
BST 220	African Church History		2
BST 221	Ecumenism		2
BST 222	Canon Law (Org. God's People)		3
BST 223	Ecclesial History of the Medieval Period		3
BST 224	Patrology		2
BST 225	New Testament Greek Translation		3
BST 228	Pastoral Theology		2
BST 230	Dialogue with People of Living Faith		3
BST 231	Letter to the Hebrews		2
SEM 301	Homiletics		2
SEM 302	African Christian Theology		2
BST 311	Pentateuch		3
BST 312	Lit & Theology of Gospel of John		3

CODE	COURSE TITLE	STATUS	CREDIT
BST 313	Baptism and Christian Initiation		3
BST 315	Social Morality II		3
BST 317	History of Early Christian Doctrine		3
BST 318	Intro to Psychology & Counseling		3
BST 319	Mariology		3
BST 320	Introduction to Biblical Hebrew		3
BST 321	Christology and Soteriology		3
BST 322	Canon Law: Church and Sacraments		2
BST 323	Research Methodology		2
BST 323	Research Methodology		2
BST 324	Ecclesial History of Reformation Era		3
BST 325	The Church & Inculturation		2
BST 226	Eschatology		3
BST 229	Theory and Practice of Catechesis		2
BST 323	Research Methodology		2
SEM 401	Practical Liturgy		6
SEM 402	Parish Finance Administration		2
SEM 403	Special Questions in Theology		3
SEM 404	Parish Administration		2
BST 411	Wisdom Literature		3
BST 412	Apocalyptic Literature		3
BST 413	Johannine Writings		3
BST 414	Ethical Problems in African Context		2
BST 415	The Church's Healing Ministry		3
BST 416	Eucharist and Ministry		3
BST 417	Theology of Marriage		3
BST 418	Theology of the Priesthood		2
BST 419	Contemporary Ecclesial history		3
BST 420	Missiology		3
BST 421	Christianity & Other Religions		3
BST 422	Canon Law (Church & Marriage) II		2
BST 423	Research Project		6

Source: Fr. Victor Jamahh Usman Ag. Dean of Studies.

Table AI.2: ALL SAINTS MAJOR SEMINARY, UHIELE, EKPOMA, EDO STATE, NIGERIA—CORE CURRICILUM

PHILOSOPHY			
CODE	COURSE TITLE	STATUS	CREDIT
PHL 101	Introduction to Philosophy	C	3
PHL 102	Introduction to Logical Reasoning	C	3
PHL 103	Traditional Logic	C	3
PHL 104	Introduction to Metaphysics	C	3
PHL 105	Introduction to Epistemology	C	3
PHL106	Introduction to Ethics	C	3
PHL 107	Ancient Philosophy	C	3
PHL 108	Introduction to African Philosophy	C	3
PHL 109	Philosophical Problems	C	3
PHL 201	Critical Thinking	C	3
PHL 202	Introduction to Symbolic Logic	E	3
PHL 203	History & Theories of Metaphysics	C	3
PHL 204	History & Theories of Knowledge	C	3
PHL 205	History & Theories of Ethics	E	3
PHL 206	Introduction to Socio-Political Philosophy	C	3
PHL 207	Philosophy of Nature	C	3
PHL 208	Philosophical Anthropology	C	3
PHL 209	Philosophy of Value	E	3
PHL 210	Medieval Philosophy	C	3
PHL 211	African Traditional Philosophy	C	3
PHL 212	Islamic Philosophy	C	3
PHL 301	Symbolic Logic	E	3
PHL 302	The Being of God	C	3
PHL 303	Advanced Epistemology	C	3
PHL 304	Professional Ethics	C	3
PHL 305	Philosophy of the Social Sciences	E	3
PHL 306	Socio-Political Philosophy	C	3
PHL 307	Philosophy of Language	C	3
PHL 308	Philosophy of Mind	E	3

PHILOSOPHY

CODE	COURSE TITLE	STATUS	CREDIT
PHL 309	Philosophy of History	C	3
PHL 310	Philosophy of Education	E	3
PHL 311	Modern Western Philosophy	C	3
PHL 312	Modern African Philosophy	C	3
PHL 313	Oriental Philosophies	E	3
PHL 314	British Philosophy	E	3
PHL 315	North American Philosophy	E	3
PHL 316	South American Philosophy	E	3
PHL 317	Comparative Philosophy	E	3
PHL 318	Marxism	E	3
PHL 401	Advanced Logic	E	3
PHL 402	Certitude and Skepticism	C	3
PHL 403	Contemporary Issues in Ethics	C	3
PHL 404	Thomistic Tradition in Philosophy	C	3
PHL 405	Philosophy of Law	C	3
PHL 406	Philosophy of Art	E	3
PHL 407	Philosophy of Literature	E	3
PHL 408	Existentialism and Phenomenology	E	3
PHL 409	Contemporary African Philosophy	C	3
PHL 410	Philosophy of Religion	C	3
PHL 411	Analytic Philosophy	C	3
PHL 412	Ideology and Philosophy	E	3
PHL 413	Philosophy of the Physical Sciences	E	3
PHL 414	Special Topics	E	3
PHL 415	Long Essay	C	6

Source: Handbook of the Seminary of All Saints, Uhiele, Ekpoma, C2014.

Table AI.3: ALL SAINTS MAJOR SEMINARY, UHIELE, EKPOMA, EDO STATE, NIGERIA—ELECTIVES

SOCIAL SCIENCES			
CODE	COURSE TITLE	STATUS	CREDIT
SOC 101	Introduction to Sociology	E	2
SOC 102	Introduction Psychology	E	2
SOC 103	Introduction to Economics	E	2
SOC 104	Introduction to Political Science	E	2
SOC 105	Introduction to Mathematics	E	2
SOC 201	Sociology of Knowledge	E	2
SOC 202	Experimental Psychology	E	2
SOC 203	Psychology of Human Personality	E	2
SOC 204	Community Development	E	2
SOC 205	Principles of Administration & Management	E	2
SOC 301	History of Social Thought	E	2
SOC 302	Sociology of Religion	E	2
SOC 303	Current Issues in Sociological Studies	E	2
SOC 304	Social Psychology	E	2
SOC 305	Psychology of Religion	E	2
SOC 306	Psychology of Deviant Behavior	E	2
SOC 307	History of Political Economy	E	2
EDUCATION			
EDU 101	History of Nigerian Education	E	2
EDU 201	Theories of Learning and Instruction	E	2
EDU 202	Guidance and Counseling	E	2
EDU 301	Curriculum Development	E	2
EDU 302	Sociology of Education	E	2
AFRICAN STUDIES			
AFR 101	African History and Civilization	E	2
AFR 201	Issues in African Literature	E	2
AFR 202	African Art	E	2
AFR 203	Nigerian Art	E	2
AFR 204	Religious Art in Nigeria	E	2

SOCIAL SCIENCES

CODE	COURSE TITLE	STATUS	CREDIT
AFR 205	History of Nigerian Music	E	2
AFR 301	Religion in Africa	E	2
AFR 302	African Socio-Political Thought	E	2
AFR 303	Theories and Issues of Economic Development in Africa	E	2
AFR 304	African Law and Jurisprudence	E	2

LANGUAGE STUDIES

LANG 101	Introductory Yoruba	E	2
LANG 102	Introductory Igbo	E	2
LANG 103	Introductory Hausa	E	2
LANG 104	Introductory Edo/Esan	E	2
LANG 105	Introductory Latin	E	2
LANG 106	Introductory French	E	2
LANG 107	Introductory German	E	2
LANG 201	Advanced Latin	E	2
LANG 202	Advanced French	E	2
LANG 203	Advanced German	E	2
LANG 204	Advanced English	E	2

RELIGIOUS STUDIES

RCS 101	Introduction to the Bible	E	2
RCS 102	Theology of Prayer	E	2
RCS 103	Principles of Liturgy	E	2
RCS 104	Introduction to Church History	E	2
RCS 105	Sacred Music	E	2
RCS 106	Introduction to Spirituality	E	2
RCS 107	Church Documents	E	2
RCS 217	Phenomenology and History of Religion	E	2
RCS 218	History of Israel	E	2
RCS 219	Pentateuch	E	2
RCS 220	History of Spirituality	E	2
RCS 221	The Church in the Roman Empire	E	2

SOCIAL SCIENCES

CODE	COURSE TITLE	STATUS	CREDIT
RCS 222	History of the Catholic Church in Nigeria	E	2
RCS 318	Christian Maturity	E	2
RCS 319	African Church Fathers	E	2
RCS 320	Medieval Christendom	E	2
RCS 321	Liturgy of the Hours	E	2
RCS 322	Biblical Inspiration	E	2
RCS 323	Old Testament Psalms	E	2
RCS 415	Basic Elements of Christian Theology	E	2
RCS 416	Christian Religious Education	E	2
RCS 417	Catholic Social Doctrines	E	2
RCS 418	Theology of Liturgy	E	2
RCS 419	Theology of Orders	E	2
RCS 420	Missiology	E	2
RCS 421	Issues in Contemporary Nigerian Church	E	2
RCS 422	Seminar: Biblical Apostolate	E	2
RCS 423	Seminar: Catechism of the Catholic Church	E	2
RCS 424	Seminar: Pastoral Year	E	2

GENERAL STUDIES

CODE	COURSE TITLE	STATUS	CREDIT
GES 101	Research Methodology	E	2
GES 102	Theory of Music	E	2
GES 103	Practical Music	E	2
GES 104	Use of English	C	3
GES 105	Effective English	C	3
GES 106	Communication Skills (Speech)	E	2
GES 201	Introduction to Audio-Visual Aids	C	3
GES 202	History of Science and technology	C	3
GES 203	Nigerian Peoples and Cultures	C	3
GES 204	Introduction to Computer Science	C	3
GES 205	Advanced Computer Science	C	3

SOCIAL SCIENCES			
CODE	COURSE TITLE	STATUS	CREDIT
THEOLOGY			
SSC 601	The World of the Old Testament	C	2
SSC 602	Introduction to the New Testament	C	2
SSC 603	Literature and Theology of Mark	C	2
DTH 601	The God of the Christian Faith	C	2
DTH 602A	Christology I	C	3
DTH 602B	Christology II	C	3
DTH 603	Pneumatology	C	2
MTH 601	Fundamental Principles of Moral Theology I	C	3
MTH 602	Fundamental Principles of Moral Theology II	C	3
LIT 601	Liturgy	C	2
CCL 601	Introduction to Canon Law	C	2
CCL 602	Canon Law – People of God	C	2
PST 601	Christian Initiation	C	2
CCH 601	Patrology II	C	2
CCH 602	The Church of the Reformation	C	2
CCH 603	Modern and Contemporary Church	C	2
LNG 601	Introduction to Classical Greek	C	2
LNG 602	New Testament Greek Translation	C	2
CCO 601	Biblical Methodology	C	2
CCO 602	African Theology	C	2
CCO 603	Introduction to the Study of Religion	C	2
CCO 604	Introduction to Islam	C	2
CCO 605	Homiletics	E	1
CCO 606	Seminar: Mission/Ministry/Apostolate	E	1
CCO 607	Speech	E	1
CCO 608	Vernacular	E	1
SSC 701	Theology of the Old Testament	C	2
SSC 702	Prophecy in Israel	C	2
SSC 703	Literature and Theology of John	C	2
SSC 704	Pauline Epistles	C	2

SOCIAL SCIENCES

CODE	COURSE TITLE	STATUS	CREDIT
DTH 701	The Christian Eucharist	C	2
DTH 702	Theology of Orders	C	2
DTH 703	An Evolutionary Creation	C	3
DTH 704	Soteriology/Grace	C	3
DTH 705	Theistic Problems	C	2
MTH 701	Theological Virtues	C	3
MTH 702	Cardinal Virtues	C	3
LIT 701	Theology of Liturgy	C	2
CCL 701	Canon Law: Govt. & Structure of the Church	C	2
CCL 702	Canon Law and Marriage	C	2
PST 701	Pastoral Theology	C	2
SPT 701	Counseling Skills and Journals	C	2
CCH 701	Christian Missionary Enterprise in Africa	C	2
LNG 701	Introduction to Biblical Hebrew	C	2
LNG 702	Advanced Biblical Hebrew	C	2
CCO 701	Islam in Nigeria and West Africa	E	2
CCO 702	The Structure of West African Traditional Religion	E	2
CCO 703	Contemporary Protestant Theology	E	2
CCO 704	Ecumenism	C	2
CCO 705	Inter-Religious Dialogue	E	2
CCO 706	Homiletics	E	1
CCO 707	Speech	E	1
CCO 708	Vernacular	E	1
SSC 801	Literature and Theology of Luke	C	2
SSC 802	Hebrews and Catholic Epistles	C	2
SSC 803	Prophecy in Israel II	C	2
SSC 804	Wisdom Literature	C	2
DTH 801	Theology of the Church	C	2
DTH 802	Eschatology	C	2

SOCIAL SCIENCES

CODE	COURSE TITLE	STATUS	CREDIT
DTH 803	Mariology	C	2
MTH 801	Moral Theology on Marriage	C	2
MTH 802	Applied Ethics	C	2
MTH 803	Moral Theology: Virtue of Religion	C	2
LIT 801	Pastoral Liturgy & Practical Liturgy	C	2
SPT 801	Spiritual Mentoring & Spiritual Direction	C	2
PST 801	Sacrament of Reconciliation	C	2
PST 802	Sacrament of Anointing of the Sick	C	3
CCH 801	Issues in Contemporary Nigerian Church	C	2
CCH 802	Christian Movement in West Africa	E	2
CCO 801	Islamic Theology and Ethics	E	2
CCO 802	The Church and the Mass Media	E	2
CCO 803	Homiletics	E	1
CCO 804	Vernacular	E	1
CCO 805	Long Essay	C	4
CCO 806	Celibacy, Human Sexuality and Development	E	1
CCO 807	Principles of Financial and pastoral Administration	E	1

Source: Handbook of the Seminary of All Saints, Uhiele, Ekpoma, C2014.

Table AI.4: THE NATIONAL MISSIONARY SEMINARY OF ST PAUL, GWAGWALADA, FCT. ABUJA

PHILOSOPHY

CODE	COURSE TITLE	STATUS	CREDIT
	African Philosophy	C	3
	African Traditional Religion	RE	3
	Analytic Philosophy	C	3
	Ancient Philosophy	C	3
	Biblical Greek I	R	4
	Biblical Greek II	E	4
	Biblical Greek III	E	4
	Biblical Hebrew I	E	4
	Biblical Hebrew II	E	4
	Communications Skills in English	C	4
	Community Service	C	1
	Contemporary Issues in Ethics	C	3
	Contemporary Philosophy	C	3
	Cosmology	C	3
	Descartes and Kant	C	3
	Empiricism and Pragmatism	C	3
	English	R	2
	Epistemology	C	6
	Ethics (Moral Philosophy I)	C	3
	French I	R	4
	French II	E	4
	Hausa I	R	4
	Hegel and Marx	C	3
	History and Philosophy of Science	C	2
	Introduction to Computer	C	3
	Introduction to Language	C	3
	Introduction to Logic and Philosophy	C	2
	Introduction to Philosophy	C	2
	Introduction to Research Methods	C	3
	Introduction to Social and Political Philosophy	C	3

PHILOSOPHY

CODE	COURSE TITLE	STATUS	CREDIT
	Introduction to the Bible	R	4
	Introduction to the Study of Literature	C	3
	Latin I	R	4
	Logic	C	3
	Major World Civilizations	RE	3
	Marxist Philosophy	C	3
	Medieval Philosophy	C	3
	Metaphysics (Ontology)	C	6
	Modern Philosophy	C	3
	Nigerian Peoples and Cultures	C	2
	Phenomenology and Existentialism	C	3
	Philosophical Anthropology	AE	4
	Philosophy and Theories of Development	C	3
	Philosophy of Arts and Aesthetics	C	3
	Philosophy of Language	C	3
	Philosophy of Law	C	3
	Philosophy of Religion	C	3
	Philosophy of Science	C	3
	Philosophy of Social Sciences	C	3
	Philosophy Project	C	3
	Professional Ethics	C	3
	Psychology	AE	4
	Research Methodology II	C	3
	Sexuality and Celibacy	R	2
	Social and Political Philosophy	C	3
	Sociology	AE	4
	Symbolic Logic	C	3
	Theodicy (Natural Theology)	AE	4
THEOLOGY			
T 305	African Theology	R	4
T 104	Background to the Old Testament	R	2
T 107	Background to the New Testament	R	2

PHILOSOPHY

CODE	COURSE TITLE	STATUS	CREDIT
T 310	Bioethics	R	3
T 204	Canon Law	R	8
T 313	Canon Law Seminar	R	2
T 208	Church History	R	9
T 215	Church History Seminar	R	2
S 201	Community Life Seminar	R	2
T 216	Comparative Study of World Religions	R	2
T 202	Dogmatic Theology	C	12
T 103	Fundamental Liturgy	R	2
T 102	Fundamental Moral Theology	R	3
T 106	Fundamental Theology	R	3
T 217	Homiletics	R	2
T 108	Introduction to Biblical Exegesis	R	2
T 101	Introduction to Theology	R	2
T 110	Islam	R	2
S 202	Leadership Seminar	R	2
T 205	Liturgy	R	6
T 412	Liturgy Seminar	R	2
T 403	Mission Theology	C	6
S 404	Mission Theology Seminar	R	2
T 203	Moral Theology	C	12
T 409	Moral Theology Seminar	R	2
T 307	MSP History	R	2
T 316	MSP Constitution and Policies	R	2
T 209	New Testament Exegesis	C	9
	New Testament Seminar	R	2
T 201	Old Testament Exegesis	C	9
S 302	Old Testament Seminar	R	2
S 301	Pastoral Administration and Management	R	2
	Pastoral Catechetics	R	2
T 402	Pastoral Counseling	R	2

PHILOSOPHY

CODE	COURSE TITLE	STATUS	CREDIT
	Pastoral Theology	R	4
S 403	Pastoral Theology Seminar	R	2
T 105	Patristics	R	4
	Sacramental Theology	R	6
	Social Teachings of the Church	R	4
	Spiritual Theology	R	4
S 204	Spiritual Theology Seminar	R	2
T 415	Theology Project	R	6
	The Teachings of Vatican II	R	3

Source: Handbook of the National Missionary Seminary of St. Paul, Gwagwalada, Abuja. C2010.

Table AI.5: ST. AUGUSTINE'S MAJOR SEMINARY, JOS, PLATEAU STATE, NIGERIA

CODE	COURSE TITLE	STATUS	CREDIT
BTH 111	Introduction to the New Testament	C	3
BTH 112	Historical Books of the Old Testament	C	3
BTH 113	Introduction to Christian Ethics	C	3
BTH 114	Introduction to the Gospels	C	3
BTH 115	The Origin, Nature, & Structure of the Church	C	3
BTH 116	God in Jewish and Christian Tradition	C	3
SEM 100	Introduction to Canon Law	C	3
SEM 016	The Church in the Roman Empire	C	3
SEM 309	Liturgy	C	3
GSS 005	Interpersonal Communication	C	--
GSS 001	The Use of English	C	--
BTH 117	The Rise and Spread of Islam	E	2
BTH 118	Basic Concepts of African Religion	E	2
BTH 119	Problems of Philosophy	E	3
BTH 121	Principles of Hermeneutics	E	3
BTH 122	Introduction to New Testament Greek	E	3
BTH 211	Prophetic Writings	C	3
BTH 212	Pauline Writings	C	3
BTH 213	Family Morality	C	3
BTH 214	Theological Anthropology	C	3
BTH 215	The Structure of Christian Existence	C	3
BTH 216	Theory and Practice of Liturgy	C	3
SEM 045	Dialogue with People of Living Faith	C	3
SEM 200	Canon Law (Organization of the People of God)	C	3
GSS 005	Research Methodology	C	--
GSS 006	Cultural Anthropology	C	--
BTH 217	African Church History	E	2
BTH 218	Ecumenism	E	2
BTH 219	Traditional African Society	E	3
BTH 221	Philosophy of Religion	E	3
BTH 222	New Testament Greek Translation	E	3

CODE	COURSE TITLE	STATUS	CREDIT
BTH 311	The Pentateuch	C	3
BTH 312	The Literature & Theology of St John	C	3
BTH 313	The Church's Healing Ministry	C	3
BTH 314	Ethics of Human Life	C	3
BTH 315	Social Morality	C	3
BTH 316	History of Early Christian Doctrine	C	3
SEM 301	Canon Law (Church & Sacraments)	C	3
SEM 311	Mariology	C	3
SEM 315	Christology	C	3
SEM 310	Introduction to Pastoral Theology	C	2
SEM 410	Johannine Writings II	C	2
GSS 007	Homiletics	C	2
SSM 003	Seminar: Counseling	C	2
SSM 031	Seminar: Inculturation	C	2
BTH 317	Psychology and Counseling	E	3
BTH 318	Introduction to the Study of Law	E	3
BTH 319	Political & Cultural Systems in Africa	E	2
BTH 321	Introduction to Biblical Hebrew	E	2
BTH 322	The Church and Inculturation	E	2
BTH 323	Eschatology	E	2
BTH 411	Wisdom Literature	C	3
BTH 412	Apocalyptic Literature	C	3
BTH 413	Selected Ethical Problems in an African Context	C	3
BTH 414	Baptism & Christian Initiation	C	3
BTH 415	Eucharist and Ministry	C	3
BTH 416	Theology of Christian Marriage	C	3
BTH 417	Christianity and Other Religions	C	3
BTH 418	Long Essay	C	6
SEM 401	Canon Law I	C	3
SEM 406	Missiology	C	3
SEM 401	Canon Law (Church & Marriage)	C	4
SEM 004	Seminar: Parish Administration	C	2
SEM 041	Practical Liturgy	C	2

Source: Curriculum Studiorum, St Augustine's Major Seminary Jos, Plateau State, Nigeria, C2000.

Table AI.6: ST. THOMAS AQUINAS' MAJOR SEMINARY, MAKURDI, BENUE STATE, NIGERIA

PHILOSOPHY			
CODE	COURSE TITLE	STATUS	CREDIT
BPH 101	Introduction to philosophy	C	3
BPH 103	Traditional Logic	C	3
BPH 105	Ancient Philosophy	C	3
BPH 107	Fundamental Ethics	C	2
REL 101	Early Foundations of the Christian Religion	C	2
BPH 109	Introduction to Epistemology	C	2
REL 103	Introduction to Scripture	C	2
GST 101	English and Communication Skills	C	2
GST 103	Latin	C	2
REL 105	Mystery of Christ	E	2
BPH 102	Introduction to Metaphysics	C	3
BPH 104	Greco – Roman Philosophy	C	3
REL 102	Introduction to Sociology of Religion	C	2
BPH 100	Introduction to African Philosophy	C	2
REL 104	Early Church History	C	2
REL 106	Introduction to Islam	C	2
BPH 112	Research Methodology	C	2
GST 104	Introduction to Psychology	C	2
GST 106	Use of Library	C	1
REL 108	Introduction to African Traditional Religion	E	2
BPH 201	Epistemology	C	2
BPH 203	Cosmology 1	C	2
BPH 205	Philosophical Anthropology	C	2
BPH 207	Medieval Philosophy	C	2
REL 207	Phenomenology of Religion	C	2
BPH 209	Social Ethics	C	2
BPH 211	Social and Political Philosophy	C	2
BPH 213	Philosophy of Science	C	2
BPH 215	Logical Thinking	C	2

PHILOSOPHY

CODE	COURSE TITLE	STATUS	CREDIT
GST 201	Introduction to Spirituality	C	2
GST 203	English for Academic Use	C	2
GST 205	Introduction to Vatican II	C	1
BPH 202	Metaphysics II	C	2
BPH 204	Philosophical Anthropology II	C	2
BPH 206	Modern Philosophy 1	C	3
REL 202	History of Israel	C	2
REL 204	Philosophy of Religion	C	2
REL 206	Comparative Religions	C	3
BPH 208	Cosmology II	C	2
GST 202	Psychology and Human Development	C	2
BPH 210	Aesthetics	E	2
BPH 301	Modern Philosophy II	C	3
BPH 303	African Philosophy	C	3
BPH 305	Philosophy of Education	C	2
REL 301	History of the Reformation	C	2
REL 303	New Testament Introduction	C	2
BPH 307	Symbolic Logic	C	2
BPH 309	Philosophy of Social Sciences	C	2
REL 305	Natural Theology	C	2
BPH 311	Synthesis of Thomistic Philosophy	E	2
BPH 313	Philosophy and Theology	E	2
BPH 302	Contemporary African Philosophy	C	2
REL 302	Islam in West Africa	C	2
REL 304	Pauline Epistles	C	2
BPH 304	Comparative Philosophy	C	2
REL 306	Prophetic Literature	C	2
BPH 310	Applied Ethics	C	3
BPH 306	Advanced Epistemology	C	2
BPH 308	Advanced Metaphysics	C	2
BPH 310	Contemporary Philosophy 1	C	3

PHILOSOPHY

CODE	COURSE TITLE	STATUS	CREDIT
BPH 312	Research Methodology	C	2
BPH 314	Socio-Cultural Anthropology	E	2
BPH 401	Philosophy of Law	C	2
BPH 403	Philosophy of Language	C	2
BPH 405	Contemporary Philosophy II	C	2
REL 401	Gospels	C	2
REL 403	Christianity in West Africa (18–20c)	C	2
REL 405	Church History	C	2
REL 407	Fundamental Theology	C	2
REL 409	Pentateuch	C	2
REL 411	Old Testament Greek Morphology	C	2
REL413	Spiritual Theology	C	2
REL 415	Theological Method	C	2
BPH 402	Long Essay	C	6
BPH 404	Philosophy of Mind	C	2
REL 402	Contemporary Islamic Groups in Nigeria	C	2
REL 404	Indigenous Christian Movements in West Africa	C	2
REL 406	Fundamental Moral Theology	C	2
REL 408	Ecclesiology	C	2
REL 410	Patrology	C	2
REL 412	Canon Law	C	2
REL 414	Liturgy	C	2

THEOLOGY

BTH 101	Fundamental Theology	C	4
BTH 102	Dogma: God in Judeao-Christian Trads.	C	4
BTH 103	Dogma: Ecclesiology	C	4
BTH 104	Sacred Scripture: Pentateuch	C	4
BTH 105	Sacred Scripture: Introduction to the NT	C	4
BTH 106	Sacred Scripture: The Gospels	C	2
BTH 107	New Testament Greek Morphology	C	4

PHILOSOPHY

CODE	COURSE TITLE	STATUS	CREDIT
BTH 108	Fundamental Moral Theology	C	4
BTH 109	Canon Law	C	4
BTH 110	Church History	C	3
BTH 111	Patristic	C	4
BTH 112	Liturgy: Introduction	C	4
BTH 113	Spiritual Theology	C	4
BTH 114	Islam	C	2
BTH 115	African Traditional Religion	C	2
BTH 116	Theological Method	C	2
BTH 201	Dogma: Christology	C	4
BTH 202	Dogmatic Sacramental Theology	C	4
BTH 203	Sacred Scripture: The Prophetic Writings	C	4
BTH 204	Sacred Scripture: Pauline Corpus	C	2
BTH 205	The Gospel of St. Mark	C	2
BTH 206	Sacred Scripture: The Book of Daniel	C	2
BTH 207	Moral Theology	C	4
BTH 208	Canon Law	C	4
BTH 209	Church History	C	3
BTH 210	Pastoral Theology	C	2
BTH 211	Missiology	C	2
BTH 212	Mariology	C	2
BTH 213	Catholic Social Teachings	C	2
SEM 214	Independent African Churches	E	1
L 200	Hebrew	C	4
L 201	The Use of English	C	4
BTH 301	Dogma: The Eucharist	C	2
BTH 302	Dogma: Eschatology	C	2
BTH 303	Dogma: Pneumatology	C	2
BTH 304	Literature and Theology of John	C	2
BTH 305	Acts of the Apostles	C	2
BTH 306	Psalms	C	2

PHILOSOPHY

CODE	COURSE TITLE	STATUS	CREDIT
BTH 307	Samuel and Kings	C	2
BTH 308	Moral Theology	C	4
BTH 309	Canon Law	C	4
BTH 310	Litu Liturgy		2
BTH 311	Rite of Christian Initiation of Adults	C	2
BTH 312	Ecumenism	C	2
BTH 313	Church History	C	3
SEM 314	Dialogue	C	2
SEM 315	Homiletics	C	4
SEM 316	Pastoral Counselling	C	2
L 300	Use of English	C	4
BTH 401	Dogma: God-Creation-Original Sin-Justification-Grace	C	4
BTH 402	Dogma: The Sacraments Of Healing	C	2
BTH 403	The Apocalyptic Literature	C	2
BTH 404	1 Corinthians	C	2
BTH 405	Catholic Epistles	C	2
BTH 406	Letter To The Hebrews	C	2
BTH 407	Wisdom Literature (Job)	C	2
BTH 408	Moral Theology	C	4
409	Canon Law Book Vi: Sanctions In The Church	C	4
SEM 401	Liturgy	C	2
SEM 411	Vatican11 And Inculturation	E	2
SEM 413	Accounting	E	
SEM 414	Church Leadership	E	2
SEM 415	Communications	E	2

Source: Fr. Samuel Akagwu, Dean of Studies.

Table AI.7: SS. PETER AND PAUL MAJOR SEMINARY, BODIJA, IBADAN, NIGERIA

PHILOSOPHY			
CODE	COURSE TITLE	STATUS	CREDIT
SS/PHL/101	Introd. to Philosophy	C	3
SS/PHL/102	Introd. to Logical Reasoning	C	3
SS/PHL/105	Ancient Philosophy	R	3
SS/GES/101	Use of English	C	3
SS/GES/102	Research Methodology	C	2
SS/GES/104	Communication Skills	C	2
SS/SOC/101	Sociology	E	2
SS/RCS/101	Introduction to Scripture	E	2
SS/RCS/102	Introduction to Prayer	E	2
SS/MUS/101	Introduction to Music	E	2
SEM/RCS/103	Vatican II	E	1
SEM/LANG/101	Nigerian Languages	E	1
SS/PHL/202	Symbolic Logic	C	3
SS/PHL/203	Hist. & Theory of Metaphysics	C	3
SS/PHL/204	Introd. to Epistemology	C	3
SS/PHL/206	Social Political Philosophy	R	3
SS/PHL/211	Medieval Philosophy	E	3
SS/PHL/212	African Trad. Philosophy	R	3
SS/GES/202	Science and Mankind	3	R
SS/GES/203	Nigerian Peoples & Cultures	R	2
SS/GES/204	Advanced English	R	2
SS/RCS/209	Old Testament Psalms	E	2
SS/RCS/220	Hist. of Christian Spirituality	E	1
SS/LANG/201	Nigerian Languages	E	1
SS/PHL/303	Professional Ethics	R	3
SS/PHL/306	Philosophy of Science	E	3
SS/PHL/312	Contemporary Philosophy	E	3
SS/PHL/311	Philosophy of Social Science	E	3
SS/EDU/302	Guidance and Counseling	E	2
SS/SOC/305	Psychology of Religion	E	2
SS/RCS/318	Christian Maturity	E	2

PHILOSOPHY

CODE	COURSE TITLE	STATUS	CREDIT
SS/RCS/319	Patrology I	E	2
SEM/LANG/301	Nigerian Languages	E	1
SS/PHL/401	Certitude and Skepticism	C	3
SS/PHL/403	Applied Ethics	E	3
SS/PHL/405	Philosophy of Law	E	3
SS/PHL/407	Philosophy of African Literature	R	3
SS/LAW/401	Civil Law & Human Rights	E	2
SS/RCS/409	Theology of Orders	E	2
SS/RCS/416	Basic Elements of Christian Theology	E	2
SS/RCS/418	Principles of Liturgy	E	2
SS/RCS/420	Social Teachings of the Church	E	2
SS/LANG/401	Nigerian Languages	E	1
THEOLOGY			
SS/RCS/401	Lit. & Theology of Luke		2
SS/RCS/412	Applied Ethics		2
SS/RCS/405	Theology of the Church		2
SS/RCS/410	Islamic Theology & Ethics		2
SS/RCS/411	Church of the Reformation		2
SS/RCS/413	Inspiration		2
SS/RCS/414	Pastoral Theology & Liturgy		2
SS/SEM/375	Canon Law: Marriage		2
SS/RCS/402	Prophecy II		2
	Social Moral Theology		2
SS/RCS/302	Lit. & Theology of John		2
SS/RCS/309	An Evolutionary Creation		2
SS/RCS/318	Ecumenism		2
SS/RCS/312	Canon Law: Hierarchical Constitution of the Church		2
SS/RCS/311	Missionary Enterprise in Africa		2
SS/RCS/301	Introd. to Biblical Hebrew		2
SS/RCS/310	Theological Virtues		2
SS/SEM/288	Practical Homiletics		1

PHILOSOPHY			
CODE	COURSE TITLE	STATUS	CREDIT
SS/RCS/306	Theology of the Old Testament		2
	Fundamental Liturgy		2
SS/RCS/202	Introd. to the New Testament		2
SS/RCS/201	Introd. to New Testament Greek		2
SS/RCS/211	Introd. to Canon Law		2
SS/RCS/212	Philosophy of Religion		2
SS/RCS/207	The God of Christian Faith		2
SS/RCS/209	Christian Ethics		2
SS/RCS/215	Introduction to Islam		2
SS/RCS/203	Pentateuch		2
SS/RCS/413	Patrology II		2
SS/SEM/287	Homiletics		1
SS/SEM/543	Mission, Ministry & Apostolate		2
	Consecrated Life in the Church		2
	Research Methodology		1

Source: Fr. Anselm Jimoh, Dean of Studies

Table AI.8: BIGARD MEMORIAL SEMINARY, ENUGU, NIGERIA

PHILOSOPHY

CODE	COURSE TITLE	STATUS	CREDIT
BLH 101	Latin 1	C	3
BMF 101	French 1	E	2
BRC 101	Introduction to Liturgy	E	2
BRC 102	Introduction to Religion	E	2
BLG 101	German	E	2
BTH 103	Music: Singing	E	2
BSG 105	Culture and Civilization and Research Method	C	3
BAF 101	African Thought and Culture I	E	2
BST 107	Spiritual Theology	C	3
BLI 101	General Introduction to Igbo Language	E	3
BLI 201	Igbo Grammar	E	3
BCG 101	Introduction to New Testament Greek	E	3
GES 101	English 1	C	3
GES 102	Introduction to Computer Science	R	3
GES 103	English 2	C	3
GES 104	Speech Techniques	E	2
PHI 101	Introduction to Philosophy	C	3
PHI 102	Arguments and Critical Thinking	C	3
PHI 103	Philosophy of Value	E	3
PHI 104	Methodology of Rational Inquiry	E	3
PHI 105	Ancient Philosophy	R	3
BCH 201	Introduction to Biblical Hebrew	E	2
BUS 201	Business Administration	E	2
BAF 201	African Thought and Culture II	E	2
BPY 201	Introduction to Psychology	E	3
BSO 201	Sociology I	E	2
BCS 201	Introduction to Scripture	E	2
BRS 201	Religions of Nigerian Peoples	E	2
ECO 202	Introduction to Accounting	E	2

PHILOSOPHY

CODE	COURSE TITLE	STATUS	CREDIT
BPH 203	Arab and Jewish Philosophy	E	3
BPH 206	Ethical Values	E	3
PHI 201	Introduction to Epistemology	R	3
PHI 202	Introduction to Logic	C	3
PHI 203	Ethics	R	3
PHI 204	Medieval Philosophy	E	3
PHI 205	Introduction to Political Philosophy	E	3
PHI 206	Introduction to Metaphysics	R	3
PHI 207	Introduction to African Philosophy	C	3
PHI 208	Philosophy, Language and Communication	E	3
BPY 301	Clinical Psychology	E	3
BPY 302	Psychology of Religion	E	3
BPH 301	Traditionalist movements in African Philosophy	R	3
BSO 301	Sociology of Religion	E	3
BAF 301	African Traditional Religion	E	3
BPH 302	Philosophy and the African Predicament	R	3
BPH 303	The Hermeneutical Current in Contemporary African Philosophy	R	3
BPH 311	Political Philosophy	E	3
BPH 312	Philosophy of Education	E	3
BPH 313	African Political Theories	E	3
BST 315	Apostolic Vocations	E	2
PHI 301	Metaphysics	R	3
PHI 302	Symbolic Logic	R	4
PHI 303	Ethical Theories	R	3
PHI 304	Philosophy of Science	E	3
PHI 305	Social and Political Philosophy	E	3
PHI 306	Early Modern Philosophy	C	3
PHI 307	African Philosophy	R	3
PHI 308	Philosophy of the Social Science	E	3

PHILOSOPHY

CODE	COURSE TITLE	STATUS	CREDIT
PHI 309	Philosophy and Literature	E	3
PHI 311	Philosophy of Religion	E	3
PHI 312	Aesthetics	E	3
PHI 313	Social and Political Thought in Africa	E	3
PHI 314	Philosophy of Culture	E	3
PHI 315	Asian Philosophy	E	3
BPH 401	The Nationalist Ideology Movements in African Philosophy	E	3
BPH 402	Texts in Contemporary African Philosophy	E	3
BPH 406	Topics in Metaphysics	E	3
BPH 407	Analytic Philosophy	E	3
BPH 411	Metaphysical Study of Man	E	3
BST 413	Development of Spiritual Life	E	2
BST 414	Means of Spiritual Growth	E	2
PHI 401	Epistemology	C	3
PHI 402	Topics in Logic	E	3
PHI 403	Applied Ethics	E	3
PHI 404	Marxist Philosophy	E	3
PHI 405	Comparative Philosophy	E	3
PHI 406	Recent Modern Philosophy	R	3
PHI 407	Issues in African Philosophy	R	3
PHI 408	Phenomenology, Existentialism and Hermeneutics	E	3
PHI 409	Philosophy of Mathematics	E	3
PHI 411	Philosophy of Law	E	3
PHI 412	Philosophy of History	E	3
PHI 413	Philosophy of Mind	E	3
PHI 414	Philosophy of Language	E	3
PHI 416	Long Essay	C	6
PHI 417	Twentieth Century Analytic Philosophy	E	3

PHILOSOPHY

CODE	COURSE TITLE	STATUS	CREDIT
PHI 418	Post-Analytic Philosophy	E	3
PHI 419	Special Subject	E	3
THEOLOGY			
THEO 101	Fundamental Theology I	C	2
THEO 102	Fundamental Theology II	C	2
THEO 103	Fundamental Moral Theology I	C	2
THEO 104	Fundamental Moral Theology II	C	2
THEO 105	Fundamental Scripture OT	C	2
THEO 106	Fundamental Scripture NT	C	2
THEO 107	Introduction to Sacraments	R	1
THEO 108	Ecclesiology- Introduction to Ecumenism	R	2
THEO 109	Fundamental Liturgy	R	2
THEO 101	Patrology	R	1
RSI 101	Islam	E	1
BLH 101	Biblical Hebrew	R	2
BLG 101	Biblical Greek	R	1
PSY 101/102	Themes in Human Formation	E	1
CL 101	Fundamental Canon Law	R	1
MIS 101	Missiology	C	1
CCH 101	Church History	C	1
SPTH 101	Spiritual Theology	C	1
THEO 201	De Deo Uno et Trino	C	2
THEO 202	Creation	C	2
THEO 203	De Gracia	C	2
THEO 204	De Deo Creante et Elevante	C	2
THEO 205	Sacramental Theology: Initiation	C	2
THEO 206	Ecclesiology: Catholicism and Ecumenism	C	2
THEO 207	Moral Theology: Eucharist	C	2
THEO 208	Moral Theology: Love of Neighbor and Justice	C	2

PHILOSOPHY

CODE	COURSE TITLE	STATUS	CREDIT
THEO 209	Moral Theology: Baptism and Confirmation	C	2
THEO 210	Moral Theology: The Christian and Earthly Goods	C	2
THEO 211	The OT: Pentateuch	C	2
THEO 212	The NT: The Basileia of God in the Life and Ministry of Jesus	C	2
THEO 213	The Synoptic Gospels and the Acts of the Apostles	C	2
THEO 214	History of Liturgy	C	1
BLH 201	Biblical Hebrew	R	2
BLG 201	Biblical Greek	R	1
CL 201	Canon Law: Ministries/Hierarchy	R	2
MIS 201	Missiology	C	2
CCH 201	Church History: Church in the Reformation Era	C	1
PSY 201	Psychology and Human Development I	E	1
PSY 202	Personal Development I	E	2
PAT 201	The Golden Age of the Fathers	R	2
SPTH 201	Spiritual Theology of the Middle Ages	C	1
CCH 202	Church History: History of the Church in Africa	C	2
SPTH 202	Spiritual Theology: Modern Spirituality	C	1
THEO 301	De Peccato Original	C	2
THEO 302	The Incarnate Word	C	2
THEO 303	De Maria Virgine	C	1
THEO 304	Sacramental Theology: Sacraments of Orders and Matrimony	C	1
THEO 305	Ecclesiology: The Mystery of the Church	C	2
THEO 306	Moral Theology: Honour, Truth and Fidelity	C	2
THEO 307	Moral Theology: Holy Orders	C	2

PHILOSOPHY

CODE	COURSE TITLE	STATUS	CREDIT
THEO 308	Moral Theology: Virtue of Religion and Theological Virtues	C	2
THEO 309	Catholic Social Teaching	C	2
THEO 310	Gospel of John and the Book of Revelation	C	2
THEO 311	Biblical Exegesis: Pentateuch	C	2
THEO 312	Biblical Exegesis II	C	2
THEO 313	NT Exegesis: Synoptic Gospels and the Acts of the Apostles	C	2
THEO 314	NT Exegesis: John and Revelation	C	2
THEO 315	OT Biblical Theology	C	2
THEO 316	The Exodus Event	C	2
THEO 317	Liturgy: Sacraments of Initiation	C	2
THEO 318	Liturgy of the Hours	R	1
PSY 301	Pastoral Theology: Pastoral Counseling	R	1
PSY 302	Pastoral Psychology	E	2
CL 301	Canon Law: Marriage	R	1
SPTH 302	Spiritual Theology: Liturgical and Priestly Spirituality	C	1
ACT 301	African Christian Theology	C	2
CAT 301	Catechesis	R	1
THEO 401	De Resurrectio	C	2
THEO 403	Sacramental Theology: Healing	C	2
THEO 404	Ecclesiology	C	2
THEO 405	Moral Theology: Penance and Reconciliation	C	2
THEO 406	Moral Theology: Ethical Problems of Life and Death	C	2
THEO 407	Moral Theology: Human Sexuality and Marriage	C	2
THEO 408	Theology and the Spirituality of the Psalms	C	2
THEO 409	Theology of the OT Prophets	C	2
THEO 410	Biblical Theology	C	2

PHILOSOPHY

CODE	COURSE TITLE	STATUS	CREDIT
THEO 411	Pauline Theology	C	2
THEO 412	NT: Revelation Theology	C	2
THEO 413	Prophetic Books: Exegesis	C	2
THEO 414	Wisdom Literature and Psalms	C	2
THEO 415	Pauline Corpus	C	2
THEO 416	Catholic Epistles and Letter to the Hebrews	C	2
THEO 417	Liturgy: Liturgical Praxis	C	2
THEO 418	Liturgy: Sanctification of Time	C	2
PSY 401	Pastoral Psychology	E	1
PTH 401	Pastoral Theology	R	2
SPTH 401	Spiritual Theology: Spiritual Leadership	R	1

Sources: Student Handbook: Philosophy Department, Bigard Memorial Seminary Enugu, Enugu State, Nigeria, C2014; Curriculum of Studies: Department of Theology, Bigard Memorial Seminary Enugu, Enugu State, Nigeria, C2015.

APPENDIX II

Figure AII.1: WE DE VEREN SHIMA SHA UKPE WUNDU MBA TAR GA (Do not fix your mind on the passing glories of this world.)

Refrain: We de veren shima sha ukpewundu mba tar ga, de veren ashe ough sha asaren a tar (2x).	*Refrain*: Do not fix your mind on the passing glories of this world, do not fix your eyes on worldly desires (2x)
1. Sha yange I ku wough u yem a kwaghga, tere pine ikyondu ga, tere pine nyaregh ga ka uma wough tsegher.	On the day of your death you shall leave the world alone, the Lord will not ask for cloth, the Lord will not ask for money but only your life.
2. Se venda nen tar de se ya ikyar a tar ga, paregh nen tar ne ka tar wase ga.	Reject the world and do not befriend it, distance yourself from the world because it is not ours.
3. A va saan ne iyol, ne mba ilu tuhan ne ken iti iYesu, taver nen shima ne va zua a injar I tsorun.	Your happiness is coming, you who have been persecuted for Christ sake, be strong in faith for you will have the reward of everlasting life.

Source: Composer: Francis C. Agba, Gboko Diocese.

Figure AII.2: HUNGUR NEN KWAGH U A SAREN A TAR NE (Forget about the desires of the world.)

Refrain: Hungur nen kwagh u asaren a tar ne, ter Yesu ngu yilan se shia u ian I lu ne, alu se timber yo se va tser a ian ga, nongu nen er se va vaa afainyo ga yo.

Refrain: Forget about the desires of the world, the Lord Jesus is calling us now that there is still time, if we delay we may not have a chance, try not to live in regrets.

1. A lu se nenge yo shie u tar ne ka u tsan ga, ter Yesu ngu yilan se shie u ian I lu ne alu se timber yo se vat ser a ian ga, nongu nen er se va vaa afainyo ga yo.

If we see the time of this world is brief, the Lord Jesus is calling us now that there is still time, if we delay we may not have a chance, try not to live in regrets when the time comes.

2. Ne a lu a inyaregh kpa van nen hen ter, ichan a lu ne eren, kpa va nen hen ter, Yesu ngu yilan ior chii de vendan ga.

Even if you have money come to the Lord, even if you are suffering come to the Lord, Jesus is calling everyone don't refuse the call.

3. Or ngu er ka humbe yo, ayange a nan nga er mure u a Karen fese nahan, yo de nen timber ashe sha mlu u tar ne, shie u tar ne yo ngu Karen sha er ka mure nahan.

A human being is like breath, the days of living are like a fast moving shadow, so do no waste your time of the glories of the world, the time of the world is passing like a shadow.

4. Yange Aondu va pase se loho na, kpa se ungwa ga, Yesu va pase kpa mbagen ungwa ga, jijingi va ngu pasen, or u nan a ungwa jijingi ga yo shie kar, yange la ter a kende u ke gyam usu.

God has proclaimed the divine word, yet we pay no heed, Jesus has proclaimed but still many pay no heed, the Spirit is proclaiming, whoever pays no heed to the Spirit the time will pass, the Lord will throw you into hell fire.

5. Yo va nen hen shie u jijingi a lu her ne, ga yo or gen u shi va pasen ngu je ga, nongu nen er se va vaa afainyo gay o.

Come now that the Spirit is present, else there is no any other person to come with the message again, try not to live in regrets when the time comes.

Source: Composer: Philip Ucha, Makurdi Diocese

BIBLIOGRAPHY

Achebe, Chinua. *The Trouble with Nigeria*. Enugu: Fourth Dimension Press, 1983.

Akinade, Akintunde E. ed. *Fractured Spectrum: Perspectives on Christian—Muslim Encounters in Nigeria*. New York: Peter Lang, 2013.

Appleby, Scott, R. *The Ambivalence of the sacred: Religion, Violence, and Reconciliation*. Lanham: Rowman and Littlefeld, 2000.

Arnold, Patrick. "The Reemergence of Fundamentalism in the Catholic Church," *The Fundamentalist Phenomenon*, ed. N.J. Cohen. Grand Rapids, Michigan: W. B. Eerdmans, 1990.

Augustine (Saint). *De Trinitate*, XIV. Ch. 8: Philip Schaff, ed., *A Selected Library of the Nicene and Post—Nicene Fathers of the Christian Church*. Grand Rapids, Michigan: Eerdmans, 1955.

Barber, B. *Strong Democracy: Participating Politics for a New Age*. Berkeley: University of California Press, 1984.

Barth, K. *Church Dogmatics* (IV/1). Edinburgh: T & T Clark, 1978.

Baum, G. and Wells, H. eds. *The Reconciliation of Peoples: Challenge to the Churches* (WCC Publications). Maryknoll: Orbis Books, 1997.

Baur, J. *2000 Years of Christianity in Africa*. Nairobi: Paulines Publications Africa, 1994.

Benedict XVI. Apostolic Exhortation *AfricaeMunus* (19 November 2011), available from http://www.vatican.va accessed October 5, 2014.

—. Encyclical Letter *Spe Salvi* (November 30, 2007), 31: AAS 99 (2007).

—. *Light of the World: The Pope, the Church and the Signs of the Times*. Translated by Michael J. Miller and Adrian J. Walker. San Francisco: Ignatius Press, 2010.

Boff, L. *Church, Charism and Power: Liberation Theology and the Institutional Church*. London: SCM Press Ltd., 1985.

Brackley, D. *Divine Revolution: Salvation and Liberation in Catholic Thought*. Maryknoll, NY: Orbis Books, 1996.

Brueggemann, W. *Reality, Grief, Hope: Three Urgent Prophetic Tasks*. Grand Rapids, Michigan: William B. Eerdmans Publishing Company, 2014.

—. *The Practice of Prophetic Imagination: Preaching an Emancipating Word*. Minneapolis: Fortress Press, 2012.

—. *Journey to the Common Good*. Louisville, Kentucky: Westminster John Knox Press, 2010.

Bujo, B. *Foundations of an African Ethic: beyond the Universal Claims of Western Morality*. New York. Crossroads, 2001.

—. *African Theology in its Social Context*. Trans John O'Donahue. Eugene, Oregon: Wipf & Stock Publishers, 1992.

Burke, Kevin F. *The Ground Beneath the Cross: The Theology of Ignacio Ellacuría*. Washington, D.C.: Georgetown University Press, 2000.

— and Robert Lassalle-Klein, eds. *Love that Produces Hope: The Thought of Ignacio Ellacuría*. Collegeville, MN: Liturgical Press, 2006.

Campbell, J. *Nigeria: Dancing on the Brink*. A Council on Foreign Relations Book. New York: Rwman & Littlefield, 2011.

Carola, J. *Augustine of Hippo: The Role of the Laity in Ecclesial Reconciliation*. Roma: Editrice Pontificia Università Gregoriana, 2005.

Castillo, José M. *El Reino de Dios: Por la vida y la dignidad de los seres humanos*. 6th ed. Bilbao: Desclée de Brouwer, c2010.

Cavanaugh, William T. *et al*. eds. *An Eerdmans Reader in Contemporary Political Theology*. Grand Rapids, Michigan: William B. Eerdmans Publishing Company, 2012.

Cavanaugh, William T. *God, State, and the Political Meaning of the Church*. Grand Rapids, Michigan: William B. Eerdmans Publishing Company, 2011.

Charles, R. *Christian Social Witness and Teaching: The Catholic Tradition from Genesis to Centesimus Annus. Volume 2*. Leominster, Herefordshire: Gracewing Fowler Wright Books, 1998.

Chelimo, R. K. *African Palaver as a Reconciliation Model: A Missiological Study in the Social Context of Kenya* (Doctoral thesis). Rome: Pontifical Urban University, 2012.

Cone, James H. *Black Theology and Black Power*. Maryknoll: Orbis Books, 1997.

Congregation for the Doctrine of Faith. Instructions on Certain Aspects of the "Theology of Liberation." St Paul Editions, 1984.

—. "Instructions on Christian Freedom and Liberation" (March 22, 1986). In *Liberation Theology: A Documentary History*, ed. Alfred T. Henelly, 461–497. Maryknoll, NY: Orbis Books, 1990.

Costadoat, J. *Trazos de Cristo en América Latina: Ensayos Teológicos*. 2nd ed. Teología de los tiempos, 4. Santiago de Chile: Ediciones Universidad Alberto Hurtado, 2012.

Daye, R. *Political Forgiveness: Lessons from South Africa*. Maryknoll: Orbis, 2004.

De Gruchy, John W. *Reconciliation: Restoring Justice*. London: SCM Press, 2002.

Donovan, Vincent J. *Christianity Rediscovered*. 25th ed. Maryknoll: Orbis, 2003.

Duke, F. E. *Resolving Public Conflicts: Transforming Community and Governance*. Manchester: University Press, 1996.

Dulles, A. *Models of the Church*. Expanded edition. New York: Image Books, 1991.

Dych, William V. *Thy Kingdom Come: Jesus and the Reign of God*. New York: Crossroad, 1999.

Edwards, D. *What are they sayin about Salvation?* New York: Paulist Press, 1986.

Ehusani, George O. *A Prophetic Church*. Ede, Nigeria: Provincial Pastoral Institute Publications, 1996.

Ela, J-M. *African Cry*. trans. Robert J. Barr. Eugene, Oregon: Wipf & Stock Publishers, 2005

—. *My Faith as an African*. trans. John Pairman and Susan Perry. Eugene, Oregon: Wipf & Stock Publishers, 2009.

Ellacuria, I. *Freedom Made Flesh: The Mission of Christ and his Church*. Translated by John Drury. NY: Orbis Books, 1976.

—. "Iglesia y realidad historia." *ECA*, no. 331 (1976): 213–220.

—. "? Por que muere Jesus y por que lo matan?" *Mission Abierta*, no. 2(1977): 17–26.

—. *Essays on History, Liberation and Salvation*. Edited by Michael Lee, commentaries by Kevin F. Burke. NY: Orbis Books, 2013.

—. *Filosofia de la realidad historia*. San Salvador: UCA Editores, 1990.

Ellacuria, Ignacio y Jon S., eds. *Mysterium Liberationis: Conceptos Fundamentales de la teologia de la Liberacion*. San Salvador: UCA Editores, 1991.

Enwerem, Iheanyi M. *Crossing the Rubicon: A Socio-Political Analysis of Political Catholicism in Nigeria*. Ibadan: BookBuilder, 2010.

—. *A Dangerous Awakening: The Politicization of Religion in Nigeria*. Ibadan: IFRA, 1995.

Flannery, A., ed. *Vatican Council II: Constitutions, Decrees, Declarations*. Northport, New York & Dublin, Ireland: Costello Publishing Company & Dominican Publications, 1996.

Freud, S. *Civilization and Its Discontents*. London: Hogarth, 1963.

—. *The Future of an Illusion*. New York: Norton, 1990.

Fuellenbach, J. *The Kingdom of God: The Message of Jesus Today*. Maryknoll, NY: Orbis Books, 1995.

—. *Church: Community for the Kingdom*. American Society of Missiology Series 33. Maryknoll, NY: Orbis Books, 2002.

Gaillardetz, Richard R. *The Church in the Making*. New York: Paulist Press, 2006.

—. *Ecclesiology for a Global Church: A People Called and Sent*. Maryknoll, NY: Orbis Books, 2008.

Gerard C. and Michael J. Eds. *Development, Civil Society and Faith-Based Organizations: Bridging the Sacred and the Secular*. (International Political Economy Series), England: Palgrave Macmillan, 2008.

Gifford, P. *Christianity, Development and Modernity in Africa*. London: Hurst & Company, 2015.

—. *African Christianity: Its Public Role*. London: Hurst, 1998.

—. *Christianity, Politics and Public Life in Kenya*. London: Hurst, 2009.

González, A. *La Novedad Teológica de la Filosofía de Zubiri*. Madrid: Fundación Xavier Zubiri, 1993.

Gutiérrez, G. *Teología de la Liberación: Perspectivas*. 14th ed., revised and enlarged. Salamanca: Ediciones Sigueme, 1990.

Haight, R. *Christian Community in History*. 3 Vols. New York: Continuum, 2004.

—. *Dynamics of Theology*. Mahwah, N.J.: Paulist Press, 1990.

—. *Jesus Symbol of God*. Maryknoll: Orbis Books, 1991.

Haughey, John C. ed. *The Faith that does Justice: Examining the Christian Sources for Social Change*. (Woodstock Studies 2), New York: Paulist Press, 1977.

Hennelly, Alfred T. *Liberation Theologies: The Global Pursuit of Justice*. Mystic, CT: Twenty-Third Publications, 1995.

Herbert, D. *Religion and Civil Society: Rethinking Public Religion in the Contemporar World*. England: Ashgate, 2003.

Himes, Kenneth R. ed. *Modern Catholic Social Teaching: Commentaries & Interpretations*. Washington D. C.: Georgetown University Press, 2005.

Holland, J. *Modern Catholic Social Teaching*. New York: Paulist Press, 2003.

Hunter, James D. *To Change the World: The Irony, Tragedy, and Possibility of Christianity in the Late Modern World*. New York: Oxford University Press, 2010.

Iber, Simeon T. *The Principle of Subsidiarity in Catholic Social Thought: Implications for Social Justice and Civil Society in Nigeria* (American University Studies, Series VII, Theology and Religion Vol. 308) New York: Peter Lang, 2011.

International Theological Commission. *Memory and Reconciliation: The Church and the Faults of the Past*. Nairobi: Paulines Publication Africa, 2000.

Iorapuu, Moses A. *Patriarchal Ideologies and Media Access: How to Overcome Discrimination Against Tiv Women for Sustainable Rural Development Promoting People Controlled and Participatory Communities*. Doctoral Thesis No. 819 Salesian Pontifical University, Rome, 2012.

John, P., II. Encyclical Letter, *LaboremExercens*.September 14, 1981 AAS 73, 1981: 577–647.

—. *Centesimus annus*. In *Catholic International* 2:2 (June 15–30), 1991.

—. *Redemptoris missio*. In *Catholic International* 2:6 (March 16–31), 1991.

—. *Sollicitudo rei socialis*. *Origens* 17:38 (March 3, 1988), 641–60.

—. *Tertio Millennio Adveniente*, apostolic letter. Vatican City: Libreria Editrice Vaticana, 1995.

—. *Ecclesia in Africa*, apostolic exhortation. Vatican City: Libreria Editrice Vaticana, 1995.

Ka, M. *Christians and Churches of Africa; Salvation in Christ and Building a New African Society*. Maryknoll: Orbis Books, 2004.

Kavanaugh, John F. *Following Christ in a Consumer Society: The Spirituality of Cultural Resistance*, 25th ed. Maryknoll: Orbis, 2006.

Kaitholil, G. *Church: The Sacrament of Christ. Patristic Vision and Modern Theology*. Alba House, 1998.

Katongole, E. *The Sacrifice of Africa: a Political Theology for Africa*. Grand Rapids: Eerdmans, 2011.

Knitter, Paul F. *Introducing Theologies of Religions*. Maryknoll, NY: Orbis Books, 2003

Kukah, Matthew H. *Witness to Justice: An Insider's Account of Nigeria's Truth Commission*. Ibadan: Bookcraft, 2011.

—. *Democracy and Civil Society in Nigeria*. Ibadan: Spectrum Books Limited, 1999.

—. *The Church and the Politics of Social Responsibility*. Lagos: Sovereign Prints Nig Ltd., 2007.

Küng, H. *The Church*. New York: Burns and Oates, 2001.

—. *Infallible?—An unanswered enquiry*. New York: Continuum 1995.

Lee, Michael E. *Bearing the Weight of Salvation: The Soteriology of Ignacio Ellacuría*. New York: Crossroad, 2009.

Lohfink, Norbert F. *Option for the Poor: The Basic Principle of Liberation Theology in the Light of the Bible*. Berkeley, CA: Bibal Press, 1986.

Magesa, L. *African Religion: The Moral Traditions of Abundant Life*. Maryknoll: Orbis1997.

—. *Anatomy of Inculturation: Transforming the Church in Africa*. Maryknoll: Orbis, 2004.

—. *The Church and Liberation in Africa*. Eldoret, Kenya: Gaba Publications, 1976.

Massaro, T. *Living Justice: Catholic Social Teaching in Action*. Third Classroom Edition. New York: Rowman & Litlefield, 2016.

Mendieta, E. and Jonathan V., eds. *The Power of Religion in the Public Sphere*. New York: Columbia University Press, 2011.

Metz, Johann B. *A Passion for God: The Mystical-Political Dimension of Christianity*. Edited and translated, with an introduction by J. Matthew Ashley. New York: Paulist Press, 1998.

—. *Faith in History and Society: Toward a Practical Fundamental Theology*. New translation by J. Matthew Ashley, with study guide. New York: Crossroad, 2007.

Moe-Lobeda, Cynthia D. *Resisting Structural Evil: Love as Ecologica-Economic Vocation*. Minneapolis: Fortress Press, 2013.

Moltmann, J. *The Church in the Power of the Spirit: A Contribution to Messianic Ecclesiology*. New York: Harper and Row, 1977.

—. *The Crucified God: the Cross of Christ as the Foundation and Criticism of Christian Theology*. Translated by R. A. Wilson and John Bowden. Minneapolis: Fortress, 1993.

Ndagoso, Matthew M. *Christian Unity in the Quest for a Relevant and Credible Evangelization in Nigeria*. Rome: N. Domenici-Pecheux, 1998.

O'Brien, David J. and Thomas A. S., eds. *Catholic Social Thought: The Documentary Heritage*. Expanded Edition. Maryknoll: Orbis Books, 2010.

O'Keefe, M. *What are they saying about Social Sin?* New York: Paulist Press, 1990.

Ogbonnaya, J. *African Catholicism and Hermeneuitics of Culture: Essays in the Light of African Synod II*. Oregon: Wipf & Stock Publishers, 2014.

Okoye, John C. "The Special Assembly for Africa and Evangelization." *Studia Missionalia* 44 (1995): 275–285.

Onaiyekan, John O. *The Church and the State: The Imperative of Collaborating Towards Political Stability in Nigeria*. Abuja: Gaudium et Spes Institute, 2008.

—. *Thy Kingdom Come: Democracy and Politics in Nigeria Today*. Faith and Life Series, Vol 13. Abuja: Gaudium et Spes Institute, 2003.

Ormond, R. *Still Interpreting Vatican II: Some Hermeneutical Principles*. New York: Paulist Press, 2004

Orobator, Agbonkhianmeghe E. ed. *Reconcilitaion, Justice, and Peace: The Second African Synod*. Maryknoll, New York: Orbis Books, 2011.

—. *From Crisis to Kairos: The Mission of the Church in the Time of HIV/AIDS, Refugees and Poverty*. Nairobi: Paulines Publications Africa, 2005.

—. *Theology Brewed in an African Pot*. Maryknoll: Orbis Books, 2009.

—. ed. *Practising Reconciliation, Doing Justice, Building Peace: Conversations on Catholic Theological Ethics in Africa*. Nairobi: Paulines, 2013.

Otto, R. *The Idea of the Holy: An Inquiry into the Non-Rational Factor in the Idea of the Divine and Its Relation to the Rational*. 2nd ed. London: Oxford University Press, 1950.

Phan, Peter C. ed. *The Gift of the Church: A Textbook on Ecclesiology in Honor of Patrick Granfield, O. S. B*. Collegeville, Mn: The Liturgical Press, 2000.

Pope, Stephen J., ed. *Hope and Solidarity: Jon Sobrino's Challenge to Christian Theology*. Maryknoll, NY: Orbis Books, 2008.

Ratzinger, J. *Called to Communion: Understanding the Church Today*. San Francisco: Ignatius Press, 1996.

—. *Eschatology: Death and Eternal Life*. Second Edition. Translated by Michael Waldstein. Washington D. C.: The Catholic University of America Press, 1988.

—. *Church, Ecumenism & Politics: New Endeavors in Ecclesiology*. Translated by Michael J. Miller et al. San Francisco: Ignatius Press, 2008.

—. *What It Means to be a Christian*. Translated by Henry Taylor. San Francisco: Ignatius Press, 2006.

Romero, O. *Voice of the Voiceless: The Four Pastoral Letters and Other Statements*. Introductory essays by Ignacio Martín-Baró and Jon Sobrino. Translated by Michael J. Walsh. Maryknoll: Orbis Books, 1985.

Sanks, T. H. *Salt, Leaven and Light: The Community Called Church*. New York: The Crossroad Publishing Company, 2003.

—. "The Social Mission of the Church: Its Changing Contexts." *Louvain Studies* 25, (2000): 23–48.

—. "Globalization, Postmodernity and Governance in the Church." *Louvain Studies* 28, (2003): 194–216

—. "Reading the Signs of the Times: Purpose and Method," In *Reading the Signs of the Times: Resources for Social and Cultural Analysis*. edited by T. Howland Sanks and John A. Coleman. New York: Paulist Press, 1993.

Schillebeeckx, E. *Ministry: Leadership in the Community of Jesus Christ*. New York: Crossroad, 1981.

—. *The Church with a Human Face*. New York: Crossroad, 1985.

Schreiter, Robert J. *Constructing Local Theologies*. Maryknoll: Orbis Books, 1985.

—., ed. *Faces of Jesus in Africa*. Maryknoll, NY: Orbis Books, 1991.

Sobrino, J. *Jesus the Liberator: A Historical-Theological View*. Translated from the Spanish by Paul Burns and Francis McDonagh. Maryknoll, NY: Orbis Books, 1991.

—. *Christ The Liberator: A View from the Victims*. Translated from the Spanish by Paul Burns. NY: Orbis Books, 2001.

—. *The Principle of Mercy: Taking the Crucified People from the Cross*. Maryknoll, NY: Orbis Books, 2004.

—. "The Kingdom of God and the Theologal Dimension of the Poor: The Jesuanic Principle." In *Who do you say that I am? Confessing the Mystery of Christ*. Edited by John C. Cavadini John C. and Laura Holts, Notre Dame, IN: University of Notre Dame Press, 2004.

Stålsett, Sturla J. *The crucified and the Crucified: A Study in the Liberation Christology of Jon Sobrino*. Studies in the Intercultural History of Christianity, 127. Bern: Peter Lang, 2003.

Stinton, Diane B. ed. *African Theology on the Way: Current Conversations*. London: SPCK, 2010.

—. *Jesus of Africa: Voices of Contemporary African Christology*. Maryknoll, NY: Orbis Books, 2004.

Tanner, N. *The Church and the World*. New York: Paulist Press, 2005.

Usman, Yusufu B. *The Manipulation of Religion in Nigeria, 1977–1987*. Kaduna: Vanguard Printers and Publishers, 1987.

Uzukwu, Elochukwu E. *A Listening Church: Autonomy and Communion in African Churches*. Maryknoll, NY: Orbis Books, 1996.

Viviano, B. *The Kingdom of God in History*. The Good News Studies, Vol. 27. Wilmington, DE: Michael Glazier, 1988.

Wankar, Gabriel T. *Towards the New Evangelization: Lessons fron Pentecostal / Charismatic Christianity to the Catholic Church in Africa*. (Unpublished STL Thesis, JST Berkeley, 2013).

Whitfield, T. *Paying the Price: Ignacio Ellacuría and the Murdered Jesuits of El Salvador*. Philadelphia: Temple University Press, 1995.

Yoder, P. *Shalom: The Bible's Word for Salvation, Justice and Peace*. London: Spire, 1989.

Journals and Articles

Donahue, Bernard F. "Political Ecclesiology." *Theological Studies* 33 (1972): 294–306.

Downey, J. "The Creeping Curriculum." *AFER* 24, no. 6 (December 1882): 324–336.

Hasenhutl, G. "Church and Institution." *Concilium* 10, no. 1 1974: 11–21.

Komonchak, Joseph A. "Ecclesiology and Social Theory: A Methodologcal Essay." *The Thomist* 45 (1981): 262–283.

Orobator, E. "Perspectives and Trends in Contemporary African Ecclesiology." *Studia Misionalia* 45 (1996): 267–281.

Orobator, A. E. "The Idea of Kingdom in African Theology." *Studia Missionalia* 46 (1997): 327–357.

—. "Challenges Confronting the Church in the 21ˢᵗ Century." *Hekima Review* 26 (2001): 71–76.

Phan, Peter C. "Method in Liberation Theologies." *Theological Studies* 61 (2000): 40–63.

Tracy, D. "The Uneasy Alliance Reconsidered: Catholic Theologivcal Method, Modernity and Postmodernity." *Theological Studies* 50 (1989): 548–570.

Elizondo, V. and Friar Leonardo B., eds. Option for the Poor: Challenge to the Rich Countries. *Concilium* 187 (2010) London: SCM.

Geffre, C. and Gustavo G. The Mystical and Political Dimension of the Christian Faith. *Concilium* (1974), Herder and Herder.

Schillebeeckx, E. and Bas Van I. Jesus Christ and Human Freedom. *Comcilium* 3, no. 10 (1974), Seabury Press.

Susin, Luiz C., Jon S., and Felix W., eds. A Different World is Possible. *Concilium* 2004/5 (2011) London: SCM.

Susin, Luiz C. and Eric B. The Economy and Religion. *Concilium* 2011/5 (2012) London: SCM.